JEP - European Journal of Psychoanalysis
Humanities, Philosophy, Psychotherapies
A Semiannual Publication

Editors: **Sergio Benvenuto, Cristiana Cimino, Antonello Correale**
Editorial Board: **Adalinda Gasparini** (Florence, Italy), **Luca Iacovino** (Rome, Italy), **Victor Mazin** (St.Petersburg, Russia), **Antonello Sciacchitano** (Milan, Italy), **Janet Thormann** (San Francisco, USA)

European Journal of Psychoanalysis is edited by the **Italian Institute for Advanced Studies in Psychoanalysis** (ISAP)

Contributors to the JEP - European Journal of Psychoanalysis: **Alan Bass** (New York), **Lorenzo Chiesa** (Canterbury, UK), **Márta Csabai** (Budapest), **Catherine Dolto-Tolich** (Paris), **Bruce Fink** (Pittsburgh, USA), **Per Magnus Johansson** (Göteborg, Sweden), **Christian Klaui** (Basel, Switzerland), **Richard Klein** (New York), **Federico Leoni** (Milan, Italy), **Zvi Lothane** (New York), **Danuza Machado** (Rio de Janeiro), **Romano Màdera** (Milan, Italy), **Benjamin Mayer Foulkes** (Mexico City), **Calum Neill** (Edinburgh, UK), **Roberto Neuburger** (Buenos Aires), **Dany Nobus** (London), **Ian Parker** (Manchester, UK), **Mario Perniola** (Rome, Italy), **Robert Pfaller** (Vienna), **Michel Plon** (Paris), **Claus-Dieter Rath** (Berlin), **Karl Stockreiter** (Vienna), **August Ruhs** (Vienna), **Andrea Tagliapietra** (Milan, Italy), **Davide Tarizzo** (Salerno, Italy), **Rodion Trofimchenko** (Tokyo), **Svetlana Uvarova** (Kiev).

Editor of the journal (Direttore responsabile): **Pierfrancesco Sammartino**
Publisher: **IPOC Italian paths of culture www.ipocpress.com**

Please, address all editorial correspondence to **Cristiana Cimino**
e-mail address: cristianacimino.jep@gmail.com

JEP is member of the Council of Editors of Psychoanalytic Journals (Peter L. Rudnytsky, plr@english.ufl.edu). Rome Court Registration Number: 581/98. ISSN 1125-8217. IPOC R.O.C. Reg. N. 18427

IPOC – 159, Viale Martesana I – 20090 Vimodrone MI Italy
Phone: +39-0236569954 Fax: +39-0236569954 ipoc@ipocpress.com
www.ipocpress.com

Printed in the United States and the United Kingdom on acid-free paper

ISBN: 978-88-96732-01-4 ISSN 1125-8217

All issues are available:
> in paperback format (**Journal**);
> in electronic format as a printer-ready document (**e-Journal**);
> each article is available for purchase in PDF/X-1a:2001 format;
> each article may be combined with others (or book chapters) and printed in a **Custom-made Book**.

Browse our web site, Keywords and Loci sections

ANNUAL SUBSCRIPTION RATES					
Paperback Journal	US$	GBP	EURO	CND$	AUS$
Two issues Institutional	77.00	49.50	55.00	88.00	93.50
Two issues Individual	42.00	27.00	30.00	48.00	51.00
e-Journal	US$	GBP	EURO	CND$	AUS$
Two issues Institutional	63.00	40.50	45.00	72.00	76.50
Two issues Individual	28.00	18.00	20.00	32.00	34.00
Delivery costs for paperback journal only (two issues)					
	US$	GBP	EURO	CND$	AUS$
Italy Parcel Post			0		
EEC Europe and U.S.A.	8.40	5.40	6.00	9.60	10.20
Rest of the world	11.20	7.20	8.00	12.80	13.60
Please note: Double journal numbers are considered two issues.					

JEP - European Journal of Psychoanalysis
Humanities, Philosophy, Psychotherapies
Number 26/27 – 2008 I-II

HISTORY OF PSYCHOANALYSIS

REVIEWS

Introduction to the New Edition

Since its invention, psychoanalysis has been characterised by indefinite boundaries. Psychoanalysis opens onto the biological, nature, and the traces that mental activity impresses on the body and the body impresses on the mind. From this stems the dialogue that, since its very beginning, it maintained with medicine, psychiatry, psychology, biology and the neurosciences. Psychoanalysis intersects with philosophical research with regard to the great problems of the human condition in their universal and shared dimension. From this derives the dialogue that it maintains not only with philosophy, but also with epistemology and the methodologies of research.

Yet, psychoanalysis has also always shaped a specific gaze on society. Suffice it to recall Freud's own renowned statement, in *Group Psychology and the Analysis of the Ego*, according to which "from the very first individual psychology [...] is at the same time social psychology as well". This is the horizon of psychoanalysis's opening towards sociology, political philosophy, and the indissoluble interweaving between society and the individual.

For what concerns textual and linguistic matters, psychoanalysis intersects with hermeneutics, literary criticism, art history, semiotics, and linguistics. It also questions its differences and similarities with these research practices.

The *Journal of European Psychoanalysis*, which was born thanks to the efforts of Sergio Benvenuto and developed in all these years under his guidance, has always preserved, as its inspiration, the following extensive principle: psychoanalysis dialogues with what surrounds it, but also reaffirms the originality of its listening and proposals.

Since 1995, JEP has not been the Journal of a school. It has not represented a single perspective, nor been the spokesman of a specific scientific or cultural identity. It has never been a journal of the psychoanalytical establishment, that is to say, it has never been the organ of a particular association, current or trend of thought. On the contrary, it has been a journal inspired by a strong interdisciplinarity. The latter was never understood as an eclectic synthesis but as a non-conclusive comparison of positions and methods, which involves exploring borderline areas, different languages that speak about common phenomena, and those zones of intersection that seem to be different only because we investigate them with distinct languages and methods. A crucial aspect of this dimension – which unfolds on several fronts – is internationality. The international opening – sustained and stressed by the use of the English language – aims at establishing contact with worlds and traditions that are not European. This need of dialogue between different orientations and histories calls into question any rigid affiliation to an inner circle.

The time has come for JEP to move forward, to strengthen itself. If at all possible, JEP intends to tackle with even more determination those topics that have been its main concern all along, that is to say, the themes that characterise contemporaneity the most: the coexistence of different ethnical and cultural worlds, the impact of religion on social life, the influence of technology on conscious and unconscious mental life, the different orientations of sexual life, the new pathologies linked to the transformation of the forms of life.

On the scientific front, the *European Journal of Psychoanalysis* purposes to give voice to the difficulties that psychoanalysis experiences with regard to a possible revision of Freud's meta-psychology. During the last forty years, and possibly longer, no heresy emerged in psychoanalysis, maybe because it has been busy with the difficult task of welcoming proposals from neighbouring research fields in order to establish a new theory on the mind – first and foremost from the neurosciences, Darwinian biology, quantum physics, and even mathematics.

This being the case, JEP changes publisher and editorial format, aiming at a wider diffusion and increased incisiveness. The editorial board has expanded, co-opting collaborators inspired by the afore-mentioned purposes. While retaining the well-known acronym JEP, the Journal also changes its name: JEP now becomes *European*

Journal of Psychoanalysis. The reasons of this word shift are self-evident: JEP is edited above all in Europe, but it never limited itself to expressing specifically European currents and topics.

What does not change are JEP's editorial line and its underlying inspiration. These will rather be reinforced and further challenged by such changes.

Italian paths of culture

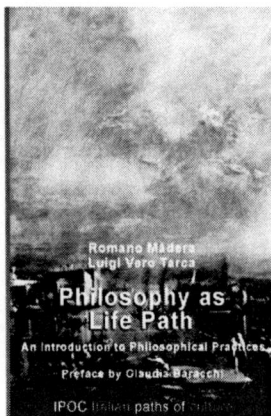

Romano Màdera, Luigi Vero Tarca
Philosophy as Life Path
An Introduction to Philosophical Practices

Book: ISBN 9788895145198 – pp. 200
e-Book: ISBN 9788895145662 – pp. 100
Custom-made Book: chapter(s) – Keywords
and/or Loci Sections

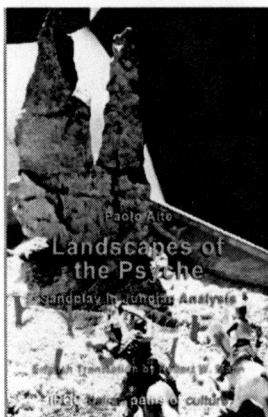

Paolo Aite
Landscapes of the Psyche
Sandplay in Jungian Analysis

Book: ISBN 9788895145211 – pp. 348
e-Book: ISBN 9788895145679 – pp. 174
Book (IMAGES): ISBN 9788895145129 – pp. 24
e-Book (IMAGES): ISBN 9788895145891 – pp. 12
Custom-made Book: chapter(s) – Keywords
and/or Loci Sections

IPOC Italian paths of culture
159, V.le Martesana – I - 20090 Vimodrone MI Italy
Ph. +39-0236569954 – Fax. +39-0236569954
e-mail: ipoc@ipocpress.com
www.ipocpress.com

Freud – So To Speak

Jean-Luc Nancy

I

Because of the times we are living in, we have been asked to consider again what are the issues behind the Freudian invention. We know more or less clearly that it was not conceived so that it could mingle with pre-established knowledge, nor add a complete new chapter of ideas to it [un nouveau continent]. Freud did not invent a mere knowledge – be it understood as a theoretical discipline or as a practical know-how. As it happens, the very idea that the practice of psychoanalysis (the "clinic", as we say in analyst circles) never ceases to strengthen the foundations of the theory, shows in fact – albeit under the threat of a pragmatist confusion – that thought here proceeds by opening itself up to a surge [une poussée] emanating from depths that are always more enigmatic and concealed in the "analysis" itself, whatever meaning we give to that word. This is because – if a layman such as myself is permitted to say it – the "clinic" amounts to nothing else than opening up an access – each time in a unique way – to that which is inaccessible to any unveiling or primordial sense. It is in this sense that the Freudian invention is the most clearly and resolutely unreligious of modern inventions. It is also for this reason that it cannot even believe in itself. As an institution (including not only its "schools" but also the analysts' practices, and even the institutional name of "psychoanalysis") it cannot avoid it, but as a system of thought its guiding principle can only be to defer its own identity.

What we call "Freudian psychoanalysis" is the fact that the analysis – and particularly the analysis of the "cure" – is only ever an *interminable* analysis, even when we can say it is *terminated*. It never stops interpreting itself or inviting us to interpret it, all the while getting further away from what it can suppose itself to be, as a body of "knowledge" and a "know-how". Beyond all analysis, it never ceases to invite us to what Derrida calls a lysis [lyse] without measure and *from which you can never return.*[1]

In the final analysis – if I am permitted to express myself in such a way – Freud does not want to develop a body of knowledge. The evolution of his thought demonstrates it thus: he never ceased moving towards hypotheses or conjectures always more expressly adventurous ("metapsychological", that is to say metaphysical or speculative), towards models that could be less well modelled or constructed (the "second topology", is rather a-topological), towards what Freud himself called "speculation", "representation", or "myth" ("murder of the father", "death drive"), and towards objects that were always less clinical – and in fact always less "objects" at all – such as religion, art, civilisation, war.

This is well known, but it nonetheless still deserves to be considered. What we have to do now is to assess more precisely the gap in Freud between, on the one hand, the positivism found in scientific and instrument-based models (of which the "cure" provides the specific vector), and on the other hand the narrative and imaginative drive which creates a world. For this is what Freud tried to do: to tell a story, to retrace the emergence of being, and the action of the forces involved in it.

That is not to say that we must try to measure this gap in a more precise way than we have done up to now (Lacan, on his part, knew how to measure it by inventing his own fiction of knowledge, although it was subordinated to the instrumental imperative of the institution, and to its function or to the profession itself).

II

What is at stake here cannot be measured easily. Without any doubt, the distance of which we speak grew during Freud's lifetime and with the evolution of his thought, without managing to reach its full potential. But his essential motif or guiding thread runs through the entire length of his oeuvre: the "unconscious" does not

---

[1] *Résistances de la psychanalyse*, Galilée, 1996, p.49.

designate a folding of the soul: it is the soul itself, or if you prefer, it is man. Freud did not discover that man had an unconscious in the way Descartes thought he could discover a pineal gland in man, one which we still have yet to find. It is man in his entirety that Freud puts into question. Man now has a new narrative.

It is the most resolutely unreligious narrative – in other words it is the narrative least likely to rely on any form of belief whatsoever, even on a belief in science. For Freud, science is a shield against the illusion of religion. But he cannot rely on it as if he was constructing a solid object. Science is, at best, a measure of solidity. Let us not fall into the traps which endeavour to transfigure us. All in all, Freud knows too well that the desire to know derives from the desire for power and mastery in general. It is impossible to find a "scholar" or a "scientist", who is not only more modest than him, but, moreover, more sincere when it comes to acknowledging what is uncertain and incomplete, and to admitting the limitations of one's knowledge.

His oeuvre is strewn with the confession that it is insufficient, obscure, or unsatisfactory. Whether it is dealing with "identification", "sublimation", "art", or "civilisation", among many other themes, Freud asks that we accept to be disappointed by his results, and asks us to wait for a later date or to look for a different source of knowledge. What he said about femininity, upon concluding his conference on this theme, can be applied to his work as a whole. After having admitted that his presentation remained incomplete and fragmentary, he declared to his audience:

> if you would like to know more about it, reflect on your own experiences, turn to the poets, or indeed wait for science to bring you more deep and coherent information.[2]

It is clear that the last hypothesis leads to a very uncertain future, if indeed it is not to be taken ironically, while the first two – which must be linked together – clearly indicate, and this is often

---

[2] *New introductory lectures on psychoanalysis* [1932], *Lecture XXXIII, Femininity; GW,* 15; *SE,* 22, p. 135.

repeated in Freud's oeuvre, that it is less a matter of knowing objects than giving a new expression to our existence as subjects.

III

Once this point is understood, one can say that there is no Freudian discovery and that the unconscious is not an organ. But Freud did make an invention, that of a narrative. Another origin and destination are introduced at the very place where man was thought to originate from a creator or a nature, the place where he was promised a celestial afterlife or the survival of his species. Man comes from a momentum [élan] or a surge [poussée] which surpasses him, which far surpasses in any case what Freud designates as the "ego" [moi].

He calls this momentum or surge the *Trieb*. In English this is translated as *drive*. In French, which is the language which I write in, we use the word *pulsion*. What is at stake in the translation is of paramount importance, all the more so because I write this paper to accompany the Japanese translation of the works of Freud! *Drive* and *pulsion* both imply a mechanical and strained surge, each in a different manner. It is a traction which one is subjected to more than it is an attraction which is searched for. In French the term *compulsion* stresses the passive and nearly automatic movement experienced, as if it is ordered from outside. Yet Freud calls this compulsion *Zwang*, which comes from another family of words and which implies coercion, the impossibility to resist (particularly in the context of obsession and repetition). Both registers are quite distinct even though they converge at certain points.

In German *Trieb* designates a surge considered in its activity: the growth of a plant or the care surrounding the growth of an animal. It is about momentum and desire. It moves forward, it activates itself. In the semantics of the verb *treiben* there is a considerable and polymorphic activity. Freud did not choose this defining word by chance. He wants to put in this word both something more than an "instinct" already programmed, and something less than a programming "intention" or "aim". In truth he means a surge which one is subjected to – if you see it from the little "ego" [moi], which is conscious and deliberate – but which at the same time originates from the birth and the growth of this singular "one" which we call the "subject" – a term to which Freud does not attach too much importance – and which far exceeds what is represented by our models of the "person" or the "individual".

The notion of *Trieb* – or of the system of *Triebe* – signifies a movement that has come from elsewhere, from the non-individuated, from what is the hidden archaic state of our origins, proliferating and confused – and that is: nature; the world; the whole of humanity behind us, and behind it what makes it possible; the emergence of the sign and the gesture; the call of each one to the other, and of them all to the elements, to forces, to the possible and the impossible; the sense of infinity lying ahead, behind and amongst us; the desire to answer to this sense of infinity, and to expose oneself to it. We originate from this movement, from this momentum, from this surge. In the final analysis, it is within this movement and as such a movement that we can *grow* – as we say in French when talking about plants: it is thanks to this movement that we rise, and become what we are capable of being.

This surge comes from elsewhere than us. It makes of us a grown individual, a being which has not been "produced" by a set of causes, but led, launched, projected, or even "thrown" (to reuse a word of Heidegger's). This "elsewhere" is not a "beyond", it is neither a theological transcendence, nor a simple immanence as some theologies reversed into atheism have understood it to be. This "elsewhere" is inside us: it forms within us the most creative and the most powerful engine driving this momentum, which is what we are. This is because it is nothing less than our being, or it is being in itself once it has detached itself from its ontological moorings. It is "being" considered in the meaning of the verb "to be": it is a motion, a movement, an emotion, the shock and rise of desire and fear, waiting and attempting, trying, accessing, even crisis and exaltation, exasperation or exhaustion, the forming of forms, the invention of signs, the incoercible tension moving to an unbearable point where it fragments or lays itself down.

IV

What I call here Freud's "narrative" is this attempt to retrace man, considered as the origin and the renewed coming of such a surge: the growth of nothing else than a sign traced on the obscure and infinitely opened background of a being which could not be explained neither by any god, nor by any nature, nor by any history. It is the most powerful attempt to define man since the end of metaphysics. It has not fallen into the double trap: the auto-production of man, from which Marx cannot escape, and the resurrection of some sort of divinity, which is the case for Heidegger.

This is why the greatness of this attempt keeps it suspended between its two fragile edges: on the one hand we have the positivism of a supposed science or of a technique (and it is out of the question to refute the fact that it can work, although it is always more visibly limited by the deep mutation of civilization and with it of the "psyche"), and on the other hand we have the belief in all sorts of depths or fantasmatical powers, the whole imaginary of "primitivism", which psychoanalysis attempts precisely to refute.

But what is refuted, either as a supposed object or as an invented origin, has nonetheless its own consistency: it acts as a support for what we are calling here the Freudian *narrative*. This narrative tells of and explains how men tell themselves where they come from and where they are going, in relation to an infinite surpassing of themselves, in relation to an excessive surge which precedes and follows them, which gives birth to them [qui les met au monde] and makes them die, all the while demanding that in this world they give form to this force which is out of this world.

In *Group Psychology and the Analysis of the Ego* Freud put on stage the first narrator, the first mythologist, who tells his horde that he has killed the father: it is an impossible narrative since the father only exists because of his murder, and consequently the murderer will only have killed the pre-paternal animal. According to Freud, myth is the means by which individuals detach themselves from group psychology. In other words, it is through myth that we have the structure needed for the "ego" [moi] to detach itself from the "id" [ça] – and this detachment is brought about by the mythical creation of a "hero", in other words an "ego" [moi]. Everything that Freud invented starts here: the subject tells his own story, he comes into existence through his narrative. It is not a tale because it is not the "speaking subject" who operates here, it is rather the one to whom speech gives birth [celui que la parole met au monde] – speech, or rather signification, the opening up of the possibility of meaning [sens].

Freud knew that we must not ask for the meaning (of life); according to him, this question is already pathological. But he knew that signification forces us to ask this question. To be obliged by meaning to do so, means that we are carried away by what we are supposed to carry. This is the answer given by speech when considered as myth: it does not tell tales, it does not write fictions, it tries to allow that which precedes speech itself to speak – signification in its nascent stage. The *Trieb* – surge, momentum, pulsation, enthusiasm, ardour – is the name found by Freud (particularly to be opposed to "instinct") to express this effort, even this forcing of meaning that occurs before and after any signification: the force of a desire which carries man beyond himself.

Freud has been able to reopen mythical speech at the precise point where science stops and where religion is of no avail. He gave a name, albeit as provisional as any mythical name (and perhaps as any name), to what propels us into our being. Did he not write "The doctrine of drives is, so to speak, our mythology. Drives are mythical beings, spectacular in their indetermination"?[3]

So to speak ("sozusagen"): but we always say "so", approximately, nearly, as close as possible and always infinitely far away from what will have driven us to speak.

Translated from the French by Guillaume Collett

---

[3] *New introductory lectures on psychoanalysis [1932], Lecture XXXII: Anxiety and instinctual life; GW*, 15; *SE*, 22, p. 95.

ON SLAVOJ ŽIŽEK

Slavoj Žižek,
The Perverse Subject of Politics:
Lacan as a Reader of Mohammad Bouyeri

Fabio Vighi, Heiko Feldner,
The Challenge of Power in Žižek and Foucault

Sergio Benvenuto,
Introduction to the Italian Edition
of Daly & Žižek *A Conversation with Žižek*

The Perverse Subject of Politics:
Lacan as a Reader of Mohammad Bouyeri

Slavoj Žižek

Keywords: Perverse position – Regime of Truth – Mimicry – Positive Knowledge

Summary: *The perverse subject acts as an instrument of the Other's Will, thereby escaping ethical responsibility; the religious fundamentalist takes the position of the pervert by displacing division unto the Other. The fundamentalist knows the Truth and reduces belief to knowledge, taking no account of the truth of lying or deception and admitting no mediation. Like the cynic, the fundamentalist threatens belief, since the fundamentalist does not make an ethical decision to believe.*

Recall a Stalinist politician who loves mankind, but nonetheless performs horrible purges and executions – his heart is breaking while he is doing it, but he cannot help it, it's his Duty towards the Progress of Humanity. This is the perverse attitude of adopting the position of the pure instrument of the big Other's Will: it's not my responsibility, it's not me who is effectively doing it, I am merely an instrument of the higher Historical Necessity.[1] The obscene enjoyment of this

---

[1] It would be profoundly revealing to write a detailed history of how the entire Bolshevik movement related to medicine, to doctors taking care of the Leaders; three documents are crucial here: (1) Lenin's letter to Gorky from before the revolution, where, perturbed by Gorky's notions about the humanist ideology of "construction of God," Lenin proposes that Gorky fell into this deviation because of his bad nerves, and advises him to go to Switzerland and get there the best medical treatment – ideological difference is reduced to a medical problem of over-excited nerves...; (2) Stalin's speech at Lenin's funerals ("On the Death of Lenin") delivered on January 26, 1924, which begins with: "Comrades, we Communists are people of a special mould. We are made of a special stuff. We are those who form the army of the great proletarian strategist, the army of Comrade Lenin. There is nothing higher than the honour of belonging to this army. There is nothing higher than the title of member of the Party whose founder and leader was Comrade Lenin. It is not given to everyone to be a member of such a party. It is not given to everyone to withstand the stresses and storms that accompany membership in such a party."; 3) the fact that Stalin's last paranoiac obsession concerned the so-called "doctor's

situation is generated by the fact that I conceive of myself as *exculpated for what I am doing*: I am able to inflict pain on others with the full awareness that I'm not responsible for it, that I merely fulfill the Other's Will. The sadist pervert answers the question "How can the subject be guilty when he merely realizes an objective, externally imposed, necessity?" by subjectively assuming this objective necessity, by finding enjoyment in what is imposed on him.

This was already Heinrich Himmler's dilemma. When confronted with the task of liquidating the Jews of Europe, Himmler, the chief of SS, adopted the heroic attitude of "Somebody has to do the dirty job, so let's do it!": it is easy to do a noble thing for one's country, up to sacrificing one's life for it – it is much more difficult to commit a *crime* for one's country... In her *Eichmann in Jerusalem*, Hannah Arendt provided a precise description of this twist the Nazi executioners accomplished in order to be able to endure the horrible acts they performed. Most of them were not simply evil, they were well aware that they are doing things which bring humiliation, suffering and death to their victims. The way out of this predicament was that, "instead of saying: What horrible things I did to people!, the murderers would be able to say: What horrible things I had to watch in the pursuance of my duties, how heavily the task weighed upon my shoulders!"[2] In this way, they were able to turn around the logic of resisting temptation: the temptation to be resisted was the very temptation to succumb to the elementary pity and sympathy in the presence of human suffering, and their "ethical" effort was directed towards the task of resisting this temptation NOT to murder, torture and humiliate. My very violation of spontaneous ethical instincts of pity and compassion is thus turned into the proof of my ethical grandeur: to do my duty, I am ready to assume the heavy burden of inflicting pain on others.

plot" (all doctors who treated him and the top Soviet leadership were arrested and tortured to confess that they were part of an international US-Jewish conspiracy to kill the Soviet leadership – see Jonathan Brent and Vladimir P. Naumov, *Stalin's Last Crime*, New York: HarperCollins, 2003). The continuity is clear: a Bolshevik "cadre" is perceived as the one who possesses a special body, not a body like others (which is why special care should be taken of it, and the body deserves to be preserved in a mausoleum...).

[2] Hannah Arendt, 1963, p. 98.

The same perverse logic operates in today's religious fundamentalism. When, on November 2, 2004, the Dutch documentary film-maker Theo van Gogh was murdered in Amsterdam by an Islamist extremist (Mohammad Bouyeri), a letter was found stuck into a knife hole in his belly, addressed to his friend Hirshi Ali, a female Somalian member of the Dutch parliament known as a bitter fighter for the rights of Muslim women (*Letter which was found on the body of Theo van Gogh*). If there ever was a "fundamentalist" document, this is one. It begins with the standard rhetorical strategy of imputing terror to the opponent:

> Since your appearance in the Dutch political arena you have been constantly busy criticizing Muslims and terrorizing Islam with your statements.

In Bouyeri's view, she is the "unbelieving fundamentalist," and in fighting her, one fights fundamentalist terror. This letter demonstrates how the sadistic stance, generating suffering and terror in its addressee, is only possible after the subject (writer-sender) makes himself the object of another's will. Let us look in more detail at the key passage of the letter which focuses on death as the culmination of human life:

> There is but one certainty in our entire existence, and that is that everything comes to an end. A child who comes into this world and fills the universe with his first cries of life, will finally leave this world with a death rattle. A blade of grass which can stick out of the dark earth and is touched by the sunlight and fed by falling rain, will finally rot into dust and disappear. Death, Mrs. Hirshi Ali, is a shared theme of everything in creation. You, I, and the rest of creation cannot get loose from this truth.
> There will come a Day when one soul will not be able to help another soul. A Day of horrible tortures and painful tribulations which will go together with the terrible cries being pressed out of the lungs of the unjust. Cries. Mrs. Hirshi Ali, which will cause chills to run up someone's spine, and cause the hair on their head to stand straight up. People will appear to be drunk with (with fear) even though they arent drunk. On that Great Day the atmosphere will be filled with *fear*.

The passage from the first to the second part is crucial here, of course; from the general platitude on how everything passes and disintegrates, how all living ends in death, to the much more constrained, properly *apocalyptic*, notion of this moment of death as the moment of truth, the moment at which every creature confronts its truth and is isolated from all its links, deprived of all solidary support, absolutely alone facing the merciless judgment of its Creator – this is why the letter goes on quoting the description of the Judgment Day from *Kuran*:

> On that day man will flee from his brother. And the mother from the father. And the woman from her children. And everyone of them on that Day shall have an occupation which is enough for them. Faces (of the unbelievers) will be covered with dust on that Day. And they will be ringed in darkness. These are the sinful unbelievers. (*Kuran* 80:34-42)

Then comes the key passage, the staging of the central confrontation:

> Of course you as an unbelieving extremist don't believe in the scene which is described above. For you this is just a fictitious dramatic piece out of a Book like many. And yet, Mrs. Hirshi Ali, I would bet on my life that you will break into a *sweat of fear* when you read this.
> You, as unbelieving fundamentalist, of course don't believe that there is a Higher Power who runs the universe. You don't believe in your heart, with which you repudiate the truth, that you must knock and ask this Higher Power for permission. You don't believe that your tongue with which you repudiate the Direction of this Higher Power is subservient to His laws. You don't believe that this Higher Power grants life and Death.
> If you really believed in all of this, then you will not find the following challenge a problem. I challenge you with this letter to prove that you are right. You don't have to do much for that, Mrs. Hirshi Ali: wish death if you are really convinced that you are right. If you do not accept this challenge, you will know that my Master, the Most high, has exposed you as a bearer of lies. "If you wish death, then you are being truthful". But the wicked ones "never wish to die, because of what their hands (and sins) have brought forth. And Allah is the all-knowing over the purveyors of lies." (2:94-95). *To prevent myself of having the same wish coming to me as I wish for you, I shall wish this wish for you*: Master give us death to give us happiness with martyrdom. (Italics added.)

Each of these three paragraphs is a rhetorical pearl in its own. In the first one, it is the direct jump from the fear we humans will experience when, at the moment of death, we will face God's final judgment, to the fear the addressee of this very letter (Hirshi Ali) will experience while reading it. This direct short-circuit between the fear instigated by the direct confrontation with god in the moment of truth, and the fear engendered here and now by reading this letter, is a trademark of perversion: Hirshi Ali's concrete fear of being killed, aroused by Bouyeri's letter, is elevated into a direct embodiment of the fear a mortal human being is expected to feel when directly confronted with the divine gaze. The pearl in the second paragraph is the precise example used to evoke the omnipotence of god: it is not only that Hirshi Ali doesn't believe in god – what she should believe is that even her very slander of god (the tongue with which she is doing it) is also determined by god's will. However, the true pearl is hidden in the last paragraph, in how the challenge addressed at Hirshi Ali is formulated: in its brutal imposition of (not only the readiness to die, but) the *wish* to die as the proof of one's truthfulness. We get here an almost imperceptible shift which signals the presence of the perverse logic: from Bouyeri's readiness to die *for* the truth to his readiness to die as direct *proof* of his truthfulness. This is why he not only does not fear death, but actively *wishes* to die: from "If you are truthful, you should not fear death," a pervert passes to "if you wish death, you are truthful." This section ends in an unbelievable *taking-over of another's wish*: "I shall wish this wish for you." Bouyeri's underlying reasoning is here complex and yet very precise: he will do what he has to do "to *prevent myself of having the same wish coming to me as I wish for you*" – what can this mean? Is it not that, by wishing death, he is doing precisely what he wanted to prevent? Doesn't he accept the same wish (that of death) that he wishes for her (he wishes her dead)?

The letter does not challenge Hirshi Ali on her false beliefs; the accusation is rather that she does not really believe what she claims to believe (her secular slanders), that she doesn't have what is called "the courage of her own convictions": "If you really believe what you claim to believe, then accept my challenge, wish to die!" This brings us to the subjective position of the pervert as defined by Lacan: the pervert subject displaces division onto the Other. Hirshi

Ali is a divided subject, inconsistent with herself, lacking the courage of her own beliefs; to avoid getting caught in such a division, the letter's author will embrace the death wish, thereby taking upon himself what she should have believed. The letter's final proclamation should then not surprise us:

> This struggle which has burst forth is different then those of the past. The unbelieving fundamentalists have started it and the true believers will end it. There will be no mercy shown to the purveyors of injustice, only the sword will be lifted against them. No discussions, no demonstrations, no petitions: only DEATH will separate the Truth from the Lies.

The situation is brought to extreme here: there is no space left for symbolic mediation, for argumentation, reasoning, proclamations, preaching even – the only thing that separates Truth from Lie is death, the truthful subject's readiness and wish to die. No wonder Michel Foucault was fascinated by the Islamic political martyrdom. In it, he discerned the contours of a "regime of truth" different from the West's, a regime in which the ultimate indicators of truth are not factual adequacy, the consistency of reasoning, or the sincerity of one's confessions, but the readiness to die.[3] The late Pope John Paul II propagated the Catholic "culture of Life" as our only hope against today's nihilist "culture of death," whose manifestations are unbridled hedonism, abortions, drug addiction, blind reliance of scientific and technological development, etc. Religious fundamentalism (not only Muslim, but also Christian) confronts us with another morbid "culture of death" which is much closer to the very heart of the religious experience than believers are ready to admit.

The question we should confront here is what, then, does the pervert miss, in his endeavor to absolutely separate the Truth from Lies? The answer is, of course: *the Truth of the Lie itself,* the truth that is delivered in and through the very act of lying. Paradoxically, the pervert's falsity (lie) resides in his very unconditional attachment to truth, in his refusal to hear the truth resonating in a

---

[3] See Janet Avery and Kevin B. Anderson, *Foucault and the Iranian Revolution.*

lie. It was Shakespeare whose plays, long ago, provided a breath-takingly refined insight into the entanglement of truth and lies. In his *All's Well That Ends Well*, Count Bertram, who on the King's orders was forced to marry Helen, a common doctor's daughter, refuses to live with her and consummate the marriage, telling her that he will agree to be her husband only if she removes the ancestral ring from his finger and bears his child; at the same time, Bertram tries to seduce the young and beautiful Diana. Helen and Diana concoct together a plan to bring Bertram back to his lawful wife. Diana agrees to spend the night with Bertram, telling him to visit her chamber at midnight; there, in full darkness, the couple exchange their rings and make love. However, unknown to Bertram, the woman with whom he spent the night was not Diana but Helen, his wife – when they are later confronted, he has to admit that both of his conditions for recognizing the marriage are met. Helen removed his ancestral ring and bears his child. What, then, is the status of this bed-trick? At the very end of Act III, Helen herself provides a wonderful definition:

> Why then to-night
> Let us assay our plot; which, if it speed,
> Is wicked meaning in the lawful deed
> And lawful meaning is a wicked act,
> Where bot not sin, and yet a sinful fact:
> But let's about it.

We are effectively dealing both with a "wicked meaning in a lawful deed" (what can be more lawful than a consummated marriage, a husband sleeping with his wife? And yet the meaning is wicked: Bertram thought he is sleeping with Diana…) and a "lawful meaning in a wicked act" (the meaning – Helen's intention – is lawful, to sleep with her husband, but the act is wicked: she deceives her husband, who does it thinking he is cheating on her) – their affair is thus "not sin, and yet a sinful fact": not sin, because what happened is merely a consummation of marriage, but a sinful fact, something that involved intentional cheating from both partners. The true question here is not merely if "all's well that ends well," if the final outcome (nothing wrong effectively happened, and the married couple is reunited, the marriage bond fully asserted) cancels the sinful tricks and intentions, but a more radical one: what if the rule of law can *only* be asserted through wicked (sinful) meanings and acts? What if, in order to rule, the law *has* to rely on the subterranean interplay of cheatings and deceptions? This, also, is what Lacan aims at with his paradoxical proposition *il n'y a pas de rapport sexuel* (there is no sexual relationship): was not Bertram's situation during the night of love effectively the fate of most married couples? You make love to your lawful partner while "cheating in your mind," fantasizing that you are doing it with another partner? The actual sex-relationship has to be sustained by this fantasmatic supplement.

As You Like It proposes a different version of this logic of double deception. Orlando is passionately in love with Rosalind who, in order to test his love, disguises herself as Ganymede and, as a male companion, interrogates Orlando about his love. She even takes on the personality of Rosalind (in a redoubled masking, she pretends to be herself, i.e., to be Ganymede who plays to be Rosalind) and persuades her friend Celia (disguised as Aliena) to marry them in a mock ceremony. In this ceremony, Rosalind literally feigns to feign to be what she is: truth itself, in order to win, has to be *staged* in a redoubled deception – in a homologous way to *All's Well* in which marriage, in order to be asserted, has to be consummated in the guise of an extramarital affair.

The same overlapping of appearance with truth is often at work in one's ideological self-perception. Recall Marx's brilliant analysis of how, in the French revolution of 1848, the conservative-republican Party of Order functioned as the coalition of the two branches of royalism (orleanists and legitimists) in the "anonymous kingdom of the Republic."[4] The parliamentary deputees of the Party of Order perceived their republicanism as a mockery: in parliamentary debates, they all the time generated royalist slips of tongue and ridiculed the Republic to let it be known that their true

[4] See Karl Marx, "Class Struggles in France", p. 95.

aim was to restore the kingdom. What they were not aware of is that they themselves were duped as to the true social impact of their rule. What they were effectively doing was to establish the conditions of bourgeois republican order that they despised so much (by for instance guaranteeing the safety of private property). So it is not that they were royalists who were just wearing a republican mask: although they experienced themselves as such, it was their very "inner" royalist conviction which was the deceptive front masking their true social role. In short, far from being the hidden truth of their public republicanism, their sincere royalism was the fantasmatic support of their actual republicanism – it was what provided the passion to their activity. Is it not, then, that the deputees of the Party of Order were also *feigning to feign* to be republicans, be what they really were?

What, then, is, from the Lacanian perspective, *appearance* at its most radical? Imagine a man having an affair about which his wife doesn't know, so when he is meeting his lover, he pretends to be on a business trip or something similar; after some time, he gathers the courage and tells the wife the truth that, when he is away, he is staying with his lover. However, at this point, when the front of happy marriage falls apart, the mistress breaks down and, out of sympathy with the abandoned wife, starts to avoid meeting her lover. What should the husband now do in order not to give his wife the wrong signal? How not to let her think that the fact that he is no longer so often on business trips means that he is returning to her? He has to *fake* the affair and leave home for a couple of days, thus generating the wrong impression that the affair is continuing, while, in reality, he is just staying with some friend. This is appearance at its purest: it occurs not when we put up a deceiving screen to conceal the transgression, but when we fake that there is a transgression to be concealed. In this precise sense, fantasy itself is for Lacan a semblance: it is not primarily the mask which conceals the Real beneath, but, rather, *the fantasy of what is hidden behind the mask*. Say, the fundamental male fantasy of the woman is not her seductive appearance, but the idea that this dazzling appearance conceals some imponderable mystery.

In order to exemplify the structure of such redoubled deception, Lacan evoked the anecdote about the competition between Zeuxis and Parrhasios, two painters from the ancient Greece, about who will paint a more convincing illusion (see 1977a, p. 103). First, Zeuxis produced such a realistic picture of grapes that birds were lured into picking at it to eat the grape. Next, Parrhasios won by painting on the wall of his room a curtain, so that Zeuxis, when Parrhasios showed him his painting, asked him: "OK, now please pull aside the veil and show me what you painted!" In Zeuxis's painting, the illusion was so convincing that image was taken for the real thing; in Parrhasios' painting, the illusion resided in the very notion that what we see in front of us is just a veil covering up the hidden truth. This is also how, for Lacan, feminine masquerade works: she wears a mask to make us react like Zeuxis in front of Parrhasios' painting – *OK, put down the mask and show us what you really are!* In a homologous way, we can imagine Orlando, after the mock wedding ceremony, turning to Rosalind-Ganymede and telling her: "OK, you played Rosalind so well that you almost made me believe to be her; you can now return to what you are and be Ganymede again..." And it is not an accident that the agents of such double masquerade are always women: a man can only pretend to be a woman; only a woman can pretend to be a man who pretends to be a woman, as only a woman can *pretend to be what she is* (a woman). This is why Lacan refers to a woman who wears a concealed fake penis in order to evoke that she IS phallus:

> Such is woman concealed behind her veil: it is the absence of the penis that makes her the phallus, the object of desire. Evoke this absence in a more precise way by having her wear a cute fake one under a fancy dress, and you, or rather she, will have plenty to tell us about.[5]

The logic is here much more complex than it may appear: it is not merely that the obviously fake penis evokes the absence of the "real" penis; in a strict parallel with Parrhasios' painting, the man's first reaction upon seeing the contours of the fake penis is "OK,

[5] 1977b, p. 310.

put this ridiculous fake off and show me what you've got beneath!" The man thereby misses how the fake penis IS the real thing: the "phallus" that the woman is, is the shadow generated by the fake penis, i.e., the spectre of the non-existent "real" phallus beneath the cover of the fake one. In this precise sense, the feminine masquerade has the structure of mimicry, since, for Lacan, in mimicry, I do not imitate the image I want to fit into, but those features of the image which seem to indicate that there is some hidden reality behind – as with Parrhasios, I do not imitate the grapes, but the veil: "Mimicry reveals something in so far as it is distinct from what might be called an *itself* that is behind." (1977a, p. 99). The status of phallus itself is that of a mimicry: phallus is ultimately a kind of stain of the human body, an excessive feature which does not fit the body and thereby generates the illusion of another hidden reality behind the image.

This brings us back to perversion: for Lacan, a pervert is not defined by the content of what he is doing (his weird sexual practices, etc.). Perversion, at its most fundamental, resides in the formal structure of how the subject relates to truth and speech. The pervert claims direct access to some figure of the big Other (from God or history to the desire of his partnert), so that, dispelling all the ambiguity of language, he is able to act directly as the instrument of the big Other's will. In this sense, both Osama bin Laden and President Bush, although politically opponents, share a pervert structure: they both act upon the presupposition that their acts are directly ordered and guided by the divine will.

It is against this background that one should judge the rise of religious fundamentalism in the US: around half of the US adults have beliefs than can be considered "fundamentalist." A fundamentalist does not believe, he KNOWS it directly. Both liberal-sceptical cynics and fundamentalists share a basic underlying feature: the loss of the ability to believe in the proper sense of the term. What is unthinkable for them is the groundless *decision* which installs every authentic belief, a decision which cannot be grounded in the chain of reasons, in positive knowledge. Think of Anna Frank who, in the face of the terrifying depravity of the Nazis, in a true act of *credo qua absurdum* asserted her belief that there is a divine spark of goodness in every human being, no matter how depraved he or she is – this statement does not concern facts, it is posited as a pure ethical axiom. In the same way, the status of universal human rights is that of a pure belief: they cannot be grounded in our knowledge of human nature, they are *an axiom posited by our decision.* (The moment one tries to ground universal human rights in our knowledge of humanity, the inevitable conclusion will be that men are fundamentally different, that some have more dignity and wisdom than others...). At its most fundamental, authentic belief does not concern facts, but gives expression to an un-conditional ethical commitment.

For both liberal cynics and religious fundamentalists, religious statements are quasi-empirical statements of direct knowledge: fundamentalists accept them as such, while skeptical cynics mock them. No wonder religious fundamentalists are among the most passionate digital hackers, and always prone to combine their religion with the latest results of sciences: for them, religious statements and scientific statements belong to the same modality of positive knowledge. The occurrence of the term "science" in the very name of some of the fundamentalist sects (Christian Science, Scientology) is not just an obscene joke, but signals this reduction of belief to positive knowledge. The case of the Turin shroud (a piece of cloth that was allegedly used to cover the body of the dead Christ and has stains of his blood) is indicative here: its authenticity would be a horror for every true believer (the first thing to do then would be to analyze the DNA of the blood stains and thus resolve empirically the question of who Jesus's father was), while a true fundamentalist would rejoice in this opportunity. We find the same reduction of belief to knowledge in today's Islam where hundreds of books by scientists abound which "demonstrate" how the latest scientific advances confirm the insights and injunctions of Koran: the divine prohibition of incest is confirmed by recent genetic knowledge about the defective children born of incestuous copulation, etc. (Some even go so far as to claim that what Koran offers as an article of faith to be accepted because of its divine origin is not finally demonstrated as scientific truth, thereby reducing Koran itself to an inferior mythic version of what acquired its appropriate formulation in today's science.) The same goes also for Buddhism, where many scientists vary the motif of the "Tao of modern physics," i.e., of how the contemporary scientific vision of reality as a substanceless flux of oscillating events finally confirmed the ancient Buddhist ontology.[6] One is compelled to draw the paradoxical conclusion: in the opposition between traditional secular humanists and religious fundamentalists, it is the humanists who stand for belief, while fundamentalists stand for knowledge. This is what we can learn from Lacan with regard to the ongoing rise of religious fundamentalism: its true danger does not reside in the fact that it poses a threat to secular scientific knowledge, but in the fact that it poses a threat to authentic belief itself.

Bibliography

Arendt, A., *Eichmann in Jerusalem: a report on the banality of evil*, Harmondsworth: Penguin Books, 1963

Avery, J., Anderson, K. B., *Foucault and the Iranian Revolution*, Chicago: The University of Chicago Press, 2005

Bouyeri, M., *Letter to Hirshi Ali which was found on the body of Theo van Gogh*, 2004, http://www.militantislammonitor.org/article/id/320 (accessed 10 March, 2005)

Brent, J., Naumov, V. P., *Stalin's Last Crime*, New York: HarperCollins, 2003

Capra, F., *The Tao of Physics: An Exploration of the Parallels Between Modern Physics and Eastern Mysticism*, Berkeley: Shambhala Publications, 1975

---

[6] One of the ridiculous excesses of this joint venture of religious fundamentalism and scientific approach is taking place today in Israel where a religious group convinced in the literal truth of the Old Testament prophecy that the Messiah will come when a calf with totally red is born, is spending enormous amounts of energy to produce, through genetic manipulations, such a calf.

Lacan, J.:
- *The Seminar XI, The Four Fundamental Concepts of Psychoanalysis*, edited by Jacques-Alain Miller, transl. by Alan Sheridan, New York: W.W. Norton & Co., 1977
- *Écrits: A Selection*, trans. by Alan Sheridan, New York: W.W. Norton, and revised version, 2002, transl. by Bruce Fink, 1977

Marx, K., "Class Struggles in France", *Collected Works*, Vol. 10, London: Lawrence and Wishart, 1978

The Challenge of Power in Žižek and Foucault

Fabio Vighi, Heiko Feldner

Keywords: Žižek – Foucault – Agency – Power – Capitalism

Summary: *The article maps Žižek's notion of agency against the background of Foucault's theory of power, especially as it emerged from* Discipline and Punish *and* The History of Sexuality. *It argues that the awareness of the state of subjection is a necessary but not sufficient cause to effect social change, since any given subjection is inevitably eroticised, sustained by the disavowed pleasure we derive from being caught in a power mechanism. By considering the Foucauldian insight that knowledge is by definition drawn in the workings of power, we maintain that critical theory needs to reflect on the difference between resistance to power and the political act, thus marking the limits of epistemic practices as such. Rooted in the notion of the psychoanalytic act as radically shifting the symbolic coordinates of a given subject, Žižek's theorizations of social transformation go a long way in achieving this. Whether they amount to a model for social change based on collective political practice, however, remains questionable.*

> *If to do were as easy as to know what were good to do,*
> *chapels had been churches,*
> *and poor men's cottagesprinces' palaces.*
> Shakespeare, *The Merchant of Venice*, I.2

From his shadowy existence as provocateur to mainstream thought and bogeyman of Marxist orthodoxy, Foucault has emerged as the ultimate philosopher of the Western left and darling of post-1990 academia. Today no academic conference in the humanities and social sciences can do without a touch of Foucault, as his writings seem to satisfy the widespread demand for a cogent theory for the now unipolar world at history's deplorable, yet inevitable end. The

Foucault-euphoria is symptomatic of a political constellation and intellectual outlook which have been the primary target of Žižek's critique since *The Sublime Object of Ideology* (first published in 1989). Among the key Foucauldian ideas he has subjected to criticism, none have been more thoroughly queried than Foucault's notions of power and resistance.

The following article traces Žižek's notion of agency against the background of Foucault's theory of power as it emerged from *Discipline and Punish* and *The History of Sexuality* (volume I). In a nutshell, the argument is this: in order to effect social change it is not enough to be aware of the existing state of subjection, as the latter is itself part of a power mechanism that is inescapably eroticised, and ultimately sustained by the disavowed pleasure we derive from being caught in it. By taking into serious account the Foucauldian insight that knowledge is always-already implicated in the workings of power, critical theory needs to conceptualise the gap and correlation between resistance to power and the political act, thus marking the limits of epistemic practices as such. Rooted in the notion of the psychoanalytic act as radically shifting the symbolic coordinates of a given subject, Žižek's theorizations of social transformation go a long way in achieving this. Whether they amount to a model for social change based on collective political practice is, however, questionable.

We shall develop the argument in four steps. Part one takes a brief look at Foucault's concept of power as a productive and immanent phenomenon. We then turn to Žižek's critique of Foucault (II) in order to establish how exactly *he* conceives of the relationship between power and agency (III-V). We conclude with some observations on how Žižek and Foucault have or might have an impact on the way social reality is experienced today (VI).

I **"Where there is power, there is resistance…"**

Foucault's concept of discourse is arguably his best received contribution to the humanities and social sciences. The compelling force of his brand of discourse analysis, however, cannot be accounted for without due attention to the concept of power he developed in his later works, the period customarily referred to as his "genealogical phase". Throughout his genealogical works, he repeatedly stressed the vital link between discourse and power analyses, as (Foucault, 1990, p. 100)

it is in discourse that power and knowledge are joined together.

In *Discipline and Punish* and volume one of *The History of Sexuality*, Foucault developed a distinctive concept of power which was set against what he termed the "juridico-discursive" models (ibid., p. 82) represented most prominently by Marxism and psycho-analysis.[1] In these models, Foucault argued, power is centered and operates by repression. Construed as a negative and limiting relationship – it "can 'do' nothing but say no" (ibid., p. 83) – power is guaranteed by institutions (such as the state) that uphold a central law (for example the law of the phallus). Simultaneously, however, the liberationist appeal of these models derives from their promise that, in principle, it is be possible to step outside of the grip of power.

Against the juridico-discursive concepts of power, Foucault proposed a theory which decentred power and rejected the notion that it could ever be monopolized by one focal point. In other words, he no longer conceived of power as an external force exerting itself on society, but as immanent within society; not as a detached institution that intervenes in (directs, distorts, represses) social processes, but as an effective network that inheres in and, ultimately, constitutes the social as such.

The analysis, made in terms of power, must not assume that sovereignty of the state, the form of the law, or the overall unity of a domination are given at the outset, rather, these are only the terminal forms power takes. It seems to me that power must be understood in the first instance as the multiplicity of force relations

---

[1] For a meticulous account of the development of Foucault's concept of power – from his earlier disciplinary models and the concept of "bio-power" through to his attempts to find a formula for the then emerging neoliberalist power technologies ("government of conduct") in his late articles and lecturers – see Thomas Lemke (1997) and Graham Burchell et al. (1991).

immanent in the sphere in which they operate and which constitute their own organization as the process which, through ceaseless struggles and confrontations, transforms, strengthens, or even reverse them; as the support which these force relations find in one another; and lastly, as the strategies in which they take effect, whose general design or institutional crystallization is embodied in the state apparatus, in the formulation of the law, in the various social hegemonies (Foucault, 1990, pp. 92-93).

The key aspects of Foucault's "strategic model" of power as developed in *Discipline and Punish* and the introductory volume of *The History of Sexuality* could be summarized as follows:

1. Power is not an object that can be "acquired, seized, or shared, something that one holds on to or allows to slip away" (Foucault, 1990, p. 94) – power is a relationship.
2. Rather than radiating downwards from a single source, power circulates, "comes from below" and a multiplicity of different sources – we must conceive of power "without the king". (ibid., pp. 94 and 91)
3. Power relations do not reside "in superstructural positions" or any other "position of exteriority with respect to other types of relationships [...] but are immanent in the latter" (ibid., p. 94.) – like a "network which runs through the whole social body." (Foucault, 1980, p. 119)
4. Micro-power does "not merely reproduce, at the [local] level of individuals, bodies, gestures and behaviour, the general form of the law or government; [...] there is neither analogy nor homology, but a specificity of mechanism and modality." (Foucault, 1991, p. 27)
5. On the other hand, the "micro-physics of power" could not function if, "through a series of sequences, it did not eventually enter into an over-all strategy" (Foucault, 1990, p. 99) embodied in state apparatuses and other institutions.
6. "Power relations are both intentional and non-subjective"; the fact that "there is no power that is exercised without a series of aims and objectives [...] does not mean, that it

results from the choice or decision of an individual subject"; there is no "headquarters that presides over its rationality." (ibid., pp. 94f.)

7. Far from being merely negative, repressing what they want to control, power relations "have a directly productive role, wherever they come into play." (ibid., p. 94) Power "traverses and produces things [...] induces pleasures, forms of knowledge, produces discourse." (Foucault, 1980, p. 119)

8. "[D]eployments of power are directly connected to the [human] body" as the privileged objective of modern technologies of power (Foucault, 1990, 51); they "can materially penetrate the body in depth without depending on the mediation of the subject's own representations." (Foucault, 1980, p. 186) Put another way, "human beings are made subjects" not only by "structur[ing] the[ir] possible field[s] of action", i.e. by governing their conduct (Foucault, 1982, pp. 208 and 221), but also by shaping their very "fabric" (bodily attributes and capacities) through the repeated performance of discursive norms. Neither way requires their interpellation through mechanisms of identification.

9. The notion "that knowledge can exist only where the power relations are suspended" should be relinquished (Foucault, 1991, 27). Power does not "distort" knowledge – knowledge is a form of power. "There is no power relation without the correlative constitution of a field of knowledge, nor any knowledge that does not presuppose at the same time power relations." (ibid.)

10. "Where there is power," Foucault avers, "there is resistance, and yet, or rather consequently, this resistance is never in a position of exteriority in relation to power"; it is "inscribed in the latter as an irreducible opposite." (Foucault, 1990, pp. 95f.; see Weedon, 1999, p. 119).

The final point, which is of crucial importance here, has been elaborated by Chris Weedon, who has extensively utilized Foucauldian frameworks for feminist theory:

In Foucault's work, discourses produce subjects within relations of power that potentially or actually involve resistance. The subject positions and modes of embodied subjectivity constituted for the individual within particular discourses allow for different degrees and types of agency both compliant and resistant.... While there is no place beyond discourses and the power relations that govern them, resistance and change are possible from within. (Weedon, 1999, pp. 119f)[2]

It is precisely in "this notion of immanence", that Joan Copjec, one of Foucault's fiercest critics, locates the problem. If "[s]ociety now neatly concide[s] with a regime of power relations", as it does in Foucault, and if, consequently, there is nothing to be found outside power, how is *effective* resistance to power possible? (Copjec, 1994, pp. 6 and 10). Already in 1982, Hubert Dreyfus and Paul Rabinow had concluded their seminal analysis *Michel Foucault: Beyond Hermeneutics and Structuralism* with a similar question:

Is there any way to resist the disciplinary society other than to understand how it works and to thwart it whenever possible? Is there a way to make resistance positive, that is, to move toward a "new economy of bodies and pleasure"? (Dreyfus and Rabinow, 1982, p. 207)

The urgency of this question is undiminished today, which leads us to the second part of the argument, that is to Žižek's critique of Foucault.

III Radicalising Foucault – Žižek's critique of *power* and *agency*

In his numerous interventions on the question of agency, Žižek generally refers to Foucault as a kind of "missed opportunity", a thinker who fails to develop his theoretical position to its full political potential. Focusing mainly on Foucault's central notion of power, Žižek is often caught between general appreciation and a firm critical stance. Interestingly, he calls Foucault "the perverse philosopher", on the grounds that for the French philosopher

---

[2] Foucault's prime example is here the formation of "reverse discourses" by which hegemonic discourses can be turned back on themselves (see Foucault, 1990, p. 101f), which in an important strategy of identity politics.

power and resistance (counter-power) presuppose and generate each other – that is, the very prohibitive measures that categorize and regulate illicit desires effectively generate them. (Žižek, 2000, p. 251)

Foucault is thus seen by Žižek, in fairly canonical terms, as denying the existence of subjective forms of resistance/transgression that escape the reach of power. In fact, the subject who tries to subvert the disciplinary measures is inevitably branded by them:

Power and Resistance are effectively caught in a deadly mutual embrace: there is no power without Resistance (in order to function, Power needs an X which eludes its grasp); there is no Resistance without Power (Power is already formative of that very kernel on behalf of which the oppressed subject resists the hold of Power). (Žižek, 2000, p. 253)

While this is the central argumentative force of Foucault's theoretical edifice, it is also, according to Žižek, its fundamental weakness, as it eventually precludes the development of any meaningful notion of agency.[3]

The way in which the Foucauldian notion of agency is usually deployed in contemporary theory is that one should politicise those spaces for resistance produced by power itself. In Žižek's view, however, the problem with such a strategy is that it falls short of exploring the subversive potential implicit in the very concept of power. To expand on this point, Žižek draws on psychoanalysis as a means to fully "sexualize" the question of power *qua* disciplinatory control. He claims that power does not only repress libido but is also, in itself, libidinally invested:

The repressive law is not external to the libido it represses, but the repressive law represses to the extent that repression becomes a libidinal activity.

---

[3] Žižek adds that if there are exceptions to this "perverse" impasse, in Foucault's work, they are to be found in the idea of Antiquity as articulated in the third volume of the unfinished *History of Sexuality*, alongside the notions of "care of the self" and "use of pleasures". However, Žižek dismisses these notions as "the necessary Romantic-naive supplement to his [Foucault's] cynical description of power relations after the Fall" (Žižek, 2000, p. 252), thus denying them any real cognitive and operative value.

This means that

> the power mechanism itself becomes eroticized, that is, contaminated by what it endeavours to repress (Žižek, 2000, pp. 253-54).

What Foucault's account misses, then, is the properly self-reflexive gesture that reveals how power is "stained" by an excessive amount of libido; the key point is that, in Žižek's view, this excess might well escape power's control and function as a vehicle for subversive action:

> the system itself, on account of its inherent inconsistency, may give birth to a force whose effect it is no longer able to master and which thus detonates its unity [...]. In short, Foucault does not consider the possibility of an effect escaping, outgrowing its cause, so that although it emerges as a form of resistance to power and is as such absolutely inherent to it, it can outgrow and explode it. [...] One is thus tempted to reverse the Foucauldian notion of an all-encompassing power edifice which always-already contains its transgression, that which allegedly eludes it: what if the price to be paid is that the power mechanism cannot even *control* itself, but has to rely on an obscene protuberance at its very heart? In other words: what effectively eludes the controlling grasp of Power is not so much the external In-itself it tries to dominate but, rather, the obscene supplement which sustains its own operation. (Žižek, 2000, pp. 256-7)

Žižek's psychoanalytic critique of Foucault is thus centred on the persuasion that the discursive field produces its own potentially destabilizing excess – just as, in Lacanian terms,

> the Symbolic produces the wound it professes to heal. (Žižek, 1993, p. 180)

This realization is crucial, as it implies that power is split, antagonized by its own excess. More precisely, it means that power is always-already inconsistent, concealing a dark underside which accompanies the stabilization and "policing" of the socio-symbolic sphere. From this critical perspective, Žižek can claim that the task of today's theory is to conceive of a political intervention that breaks free of the vicious circle whereby power reproduces itself by destroying its own surplus.

We are heading, here, towards the Žižekian notion of the act. In order to grasp the significance of this notion, so often criticised as a potentially catastrophic courting with violence or totalitarianism, we need to clarify one preliminary point: to Žižek, who draws on Lacan, the subject exists only insofar as it accepts its fundamental alienation in the symbolic network, or else the fact that its existence is fully defined by the "big Other", which is equivalent to the "discursive context" in Foucault. However, in contrast to Foucault, Žižek claims that the subject can radically subvert and thus attempt to resignify the domain of discourse, subsequently filling it with a thoroughly different content. More specifically, he suggests that this objective can be achieved by drawing on the very inconsistency of the power edifice itself. An act proper, an ethical act in the Lacanian sense, implies precisely that the (revolutionary) subject assumes *as his own* the radical inconsistency of the discursive field, over-identifying with the abyss of negativity that the latter has to conceal if it is to attain symbolic efficiency. This is why Žižek subscribes to the Hegelian motto "subject is substance": he maintains that, structurally, there is no difference between subject and power *qua* social substance, as they both hinge on an abyss – which, ultimately, is nothing but the Lacanian Real, the non-symbolisable dimension that "shines through" the gaps of the Symbolic.[4]

To expand on this question, one should keep in mind that Žižek's dialectical method is founded on a philosophical category that today is widely regarded as illegitimate, if not altogether unacceptable: the category of universality. The key point is that Žižek uses universality as a reflexive category in the Hegelian sense of the word, i.e. a positive determination which emerges through a self-related contradiction, through a relationship with its own excluded/ negative part (*omnis determinatio est negatio*). Thus, in politics, universality does not

---

[4] The Symbolic (*symbolique*), the Imaginary (*imaginaire*) and the Real (*réel*) constitute Lacan's triadic model for the analysis of the human mind and psychoanalytic phenomena. While the Symbolic order is the all-encompassing, autonomous universe of language *qua* symbolic structure which determines the role and function of subjectivity, the Real designates a dimension which, if on the one hand appears "glued" to the Symbolic, on the other it remains totally alien to it, "that which resists symbolisation absolutely." (Lacan, 1988, p. 66)

imply that a given ideological content should impose itself as a universal measure, but rather that what is universally valid is the radical negativity/antagonism (class struggle) which cuts across the social field, and which is repressed/disavowed by the positive socio-symbolic order. The universalization of politics, then, is the reflexive gesture that links a given socio-symbolic order to its structuring "hole", to the non-symbolizable excess whose (dis)avowal determines the (in)consistency of that very order.

This brings us back to the key point of Žižek's critique of Foucault:

> Power is thus not a unique/flat domain of visibility, the self-transparent machine to which the "people" opposes its demand to reveal, to accept into the public discursive space, its demands. [...] What Power "refuses to see" is not so much the (non-)part of the "people" excluded from the police space but, rather, the invisible support of its own public police apparatus. [...] The order of police is never simply a positive order: to function at all, it has to cheat, to misname, and so on – *in short, to engage in politics*, to do what its subversive opponents are supposed to do (Žižek, 2000, p. 235).

Although Žižek confines scope and validity of his critique explicitly to the first volume of *The History of Sexuality* and *Discipline and Punish* (see Žižek, 2000, p. 306, note 3), it is valid for Foucault's genealogical work as a whole.[5] The moral-political implications of Foucault's theorisation of power and resistance are reflected in his philosophical ethos which he described in his essay *What is Enlightenment* as "historical ontology of ourselves".

> (C)riticism is no longer going to be practised in the search for formal structures with universal value but, rather, as a historical investigation into the events that have led us to constitute ourselves, and to recognize ourselves as subjects of what we are doing, thinking, saying. ... this

---

[5] Although in his late writings published shortly before his death, Foucault addressed one of the cardinal problems of his theory or power and resistance, i.e. that subjectivity amounted to little more than a mirror-image of the subject-positions produced within a given discursive regime, the concept of "technologies of the self" which he proposed did not really solve the problem. While he now stressed the importance of a more dynamic notion of agency in the process of subjectivation, it remained unequivocal that conscious or unconscious self-representations were not necessarily required for this. (Foucault, 1988; see Nixon, 1997, pp. 322f)

criticism is not transcendental, ... it is genealogical in its design and archaeological in its method. ... [It] will be genealogical in the sense that... it will separate out, from the contingency that has made us what we are, the possibility of no longer being, doing, or thinking what we are, do, or think (Foucault, 2003, pp. 53f.).

Foucault then goes on to clarify the practical-political implications of this philosophical ethos:

Yet if we are not to settle for the affirmation or the empty dream of freedom, ... the historical ontology of ourselves must turn away from all projects that claim to be global or radical. In fact, we know from experience that the claim to escape from the system of contemporary reality so as to produce the overall programs of another society, ... another culture, another vision of the world, has led only to the return of the most dangerous traditions.

He specifies this as follows:

I prefer the very specific transformation that have proved to be possible in the last twenty years in a certain number of areas which concern our ways of being and thinking, relations to authority, relations between the sexes, the way in which we perceive insanity or illness; I prefer even these partial transformations, which have been made in the correlation of historical analysis and the practical attitude, to the programs for a new man that the worst political systems have repeated throughout the twentieth century.

He concludes:

I shall characterize the philosophical ethos appropriate to the critical ontology of ourselves as a historico-practical test of the limits we may go beyond, and thus as work carried out by ourselves upon ourselves as free beings (Foucault, 2003, p. 54).

Foucault was a radical protagonist of sub-culture, not of counter-culture.

The implications of this have been interpreted in profoundly different ways. While to James Bernauer and Michael Mahon

[h]is thought moved toward an ever-expanding embrace of otherness, the condition of any community of moral action,

testifying to

an impatience for … a freedom that does not surrender to the pursuit of some messianic future but is an engagement with the numberless potential transgressions of those forces that war against our self-creation. (Bernauer and Mahon, 1994, pp. 155f)

Tilman Reitz is more concerned with the neo-liberalist political implications of Foucault's ethics. Questioning Nancy Fraser's recent contention that Foucault's oeuvre belongs to the Fordist era and has thus become a matter for historians (see Fraser, 2003), Reitz argues that, on the contrary, Foucault is an eminently topical thinker, in that he has contributed to the expansion of a neo-liberal constellation from a leftist position. Foucault's opposition to the disciplinary powers of normalisation combine with his penchant for fragmentation to develop a brand of critique which, ultimately, exhausts itself in a mere affirmation of individual difference, diversity and particularistic identity, without due attention to hierarchical relations of power and domination. Although it could hardly be maintained that Foucault had intended to forge a coalition with the neo-liberal political milieu, especially his late writings would prove intellectually attractive in many quarters of academia where neo-liberal aspirations have come to the fore (see Reitz, 2003).[6]

Enjoying the symptom: masochism and the enacted utopia of the revolution

What emerges from our analysis of Žižek's approach to Foucault, is that the difference between an act proper (radical agency) and

[6] See also Cathren Müller's essay "Neoliberalismus als Selbstführung: Anmerkungen zu den 'Gouvernmentality Studies'", which demonstrates how governmentality studies, building on Foucault's work on technologies of the self, tend to "reduce social theory to a descriptive reproduction of neo-liberal ideologies", thus rendering invisible the elements of coercion and domination within neo-liberalist regimes. (Muller, 2003)

performative activity within a certain hegemonic structure, hinges on the way in which we position ourselves towards the excess produced by the discursive field. Radical agency is first of all conceived by Žižek in classic Hegelo-Marxist dialectical terms (also articulated by the Frankfurt School), as a way of

reading the troubling excess that occurs in the realization of some global [universal] project as the symptomal point at which the truth of the entire project emerges (Žižek, 2000, p. 347);

then, crucially, as a kind of endorsement (which the Frankfurt School did *not* subscribe) of this very "troubling excess", implying that the subject suspends its immersion in the socio-symbolic order (its alienation) by way of assuming the very abyssal negativity that structures such order. Thus the subject truly "identifies with the exception": the best way to undermine power, for Žižek, lies in overidentifying with the negativity (the structural exception/ excess) which (su)stains its space. What remains to be seen is what this act of endorsement actually (concretely) entails.

Žižek's argument on the fundamental difference between Foucault's and Lacan's notions of resistance/transgression to power might help us clarify the question. What qualifies a free act, according to Žižek, is an intervention whereby

I do not merely choose between two or more options WITHIN a pre-given set of coordinates, but I choose to change this set of coordinates itself (Žižek, 2001c, p. 121).

From this angle,

it is Lacan who allows us to conceptualise the distinction between imaginary resistance (false transgression that reasserts the symbolic status quo and even serves as a positive condition of its functioning) and actual symbolic rearticulation via the intervention of the Real of an *act*. [...] For Lacan, there is no ethical act proper without taking the risk of [...] a momentary "suspension of the big Other", of the socio-symbolic network that guarantees the subject's identity: an authentic act occurs only when the subject risks a gesture that is no longer "covered up" by the big Other (Žižek, 1993, pp. 262-64).

One of the most urgent questions that Žižek's radical formulation of the act poses is how to conceive of the relationship between the symbolic "big Other" (the discursive field) and the Real of the act, insofar as this relationship is mediated by the subject. This is evidently crucial for Lacan himself, who claims that the authentic act is a way to "treat the real by the symbolic" (Lacan, 1998, p. 15). As Žižek reminds us time and time again, Lacan's point is that the Symbolic alone guarantees our access to the Real (and, conversely, that only the Real allows us to truly resignify the Symbolic). The importance of the Symbolic-Real relationship implies that the act cannot be quickly dismissed as a violent, psychotic suspension of the subject's immersion in the socio-symbolic order, or else we miss the originality of Lacan's point and, consequently, of Žižek's argument. Rather, the intrinsically violent character of the act implies, strictly speaking, nothing but a repetition of what was always-already there, at the heart of the symbolic network. The act simply sanctions the existence of the foundational gap around which the whole socio-symbolic order is structured. This is also why the act is, in stark contrast to what today's multiculturalist ethical attitude suggests, the only way for the subject to truly "reach out for the other", in the precise sense of fully endorsing the radical otherness on which the functioning of the symbolic field hinges.

Perhaps the best way to approach the intricate theme of agency as developed along the lines of "subjectivity, violence and otherness", is by looking at one of the many examples on popular culture offered by Žižek's writing. In his recent *Revolution at the Gates*, he focuses on David Fincher's film *Fight Club* (1999) precisely to clarify the meaning of the act as the endorsement of the disavowed excess which sustains symbolisation. This example also allows us to focus on Žižek's main political concern, the critique of late capitalist ideology. The basic question posed by the film's hero (Norton) is extremely simple and yet absolutely pressing: how is the modern subject to break out of the futility of a life filled with failure and empty consumer culture (Žižek, 2002, p. 250)?

The suggested answer is equally simple, although apparently absurd: through self-beating. This strategy is epitomised in what is perhaps the most significant scene of the film, when the hero, whilst arguing with his boss over his salary, decides to enact his boss's repressed anger and suddenly starts beating himself up violently in his office. According to Žižek, this apparently masochistic act represents the only way "to suspend the fundamental abstraction and coldness of capitalist subjectivity", insofar as

we cannot go directly from capitalist to revolutionary subjectivity: the abstraction, the foreclosure of others, the blindness to the other's suffering and pain, has first to be broken in a gesture of taking the risk and reaching directly out to the suffering other – a gesture which, since it shatters the very kernel of our identity, cannot fail to appear extremely violent (Žižek, 2002, p. 252).

Radical agency is here linked to an apparently masochistic intervention "which is equivalent to adopting the position of the proletarian who has nothing to lose". In Žižek's Lacanian terms, the emergence of pure subjectivity coincides with an "experience of radical self-degradation" whereby I, the subject, am emptied

of all substantial content, of all symbolic support which could confer a modicum of dignity on me (Žižek, 2002, p. 252).

The reason why such a (humiliating and potentially perverse) position of self-degradation is to be assumed, Žižek argues, is that within a disciplinary relationship (between "master and servant"), self-beating is nothing but the staging of the other's secret fantasy; as such, this staging allows for the suspension of the disciplinary efficacy of the relationship by bringing to light the obscene supplement which secretly cements it. Žižek's central point is that the obscene supplement ultimately cements the position of the servant: what self-beating uncovers is "the servant's masochistic libidinal attachment to his master", so as the true goal of this beating is to beat out that in me which attaches me to the master (Žižek, 2002, p. 252).

Žižek's analysis highlights a fundamental political point: it is not enough to be aware of our state of subjection to change things, as that very subjection, insofar as it is part of a power mechanism, is inevitably "eroticised", sustained by the disavowed pleasure we find in being caught in it:

> When we are subjected to a power mechanism, this subjection is always and by definition sustained by some libidinal investment: the subjection itself generates a surplus-enjoyment of its own. This subjection is embodied in a network of "material" bodily practices, and for this reason we cannot get rid of our subjection through a merely intellectual reflection – our liberation has to be *staged* in some kind of bodily performance; furthermore, this performance *has* to be of an apparently "masochistic" nature, it *has* to stage the painful process of hitting back at oneself. (Žižek, 2002, p. 253)

Ultimately, for Žižek, the passage from "oppressed victim" to "active agent of the revolution" requires a move whereby the subject endorses that disavowed excess/symptom which "anchors" his identity in the socio-symbolic order *qua* power mechanism:

> *the only true awareness of our subjection is the awareness of the obscene excessive pleasure (surplus-enjoyment) we derive from it*; this is why the first gesture of liberation is not to get rid of this excessive pleasure, but actively to assume it. (Žižek, 2002, p. 254)

Žižek's reflections on masochism thematise one of his most recurrent theoretical argumentations: the question of the Lacanian superego as the bearer of a formidable command to enjoy. It is this understanding of superego pressure that brings him to state that

> psychoanalysis does not deal with the severe authoritarian father who forbids you to enjoy, but with the obscene father who enjoins you to enjoy, and thus renders you impotent or frigid much more effectively. (Žižek, 2000, p. 245)

Žižek often underlines the merciless character of the superegoic injunction to enjoy, as opposed to the external Law:

> Lacan's fundamental thesis is that superego in its most fundamental dimension is an injunction to enjoyment: the various forms of superego commands are nothing but variations on the same motif: "Enjoy!" Therein consists the opposition between Law and superego: Law is the agency of prohibition which regulates the distribution of enjoyment on the basis of a common, shared renunciation (the "symbolic castration"), whereas superego marks a point at which permitted enjoyment, freedom-to-enjoy, is reversed into obligation to enjoy – which, one must add, is the most effective way to block access to enjoyment. (Žižek, 1991, p. 237)

"Enjoy!" is therefore rightly regarded as one of the key terms in Žižek's dialectics. As such, it is the purely formal, unwritten, internalised, and thus all the more irresistible injunction to enjoy (i.e. to transgress) that secretly sustains the very space of the law.[7] More precisely, it coincides with the non-symbolizable, trans-historical excess which determines the condition of (im)possibility of a given hegemonic field.[8] Most of Žižek's writings are aimed at unmasking the nexus between superego transgressions and ideological formations, as a key to understanding regressive phenomena like nationalism and racism in our liberal democracies. Precisely because of superegoic pressure, there is no incompatibility between the post-modern, cynical and tolerant attitude of distance towards ideologies, of neutrality and non-identification, and the re-emergence of the nationalistic obsession with the ethnic Thing, or with New Right political populism. (see Žižek, 2001b, pp. 229-56; 1993, pp. 202-3; 1994, p. 57)

However, rather than just decry and/or attempt to repress the explosions of superego excess so as to revert to the precarious balance of the system from which they emerge, Žižek claims that

---

[7] Žižek (1994, p. 20) argues that "the superego is a Law in so far as it functions as an incomprehensible, nonsensical, traumatic injunction, incommensurable with the psychological wealth of the subject's affective attitudes".

[8] For the development of the notion of the "traumatic 'ahistorical' kernel" as the non-symbolizable excess which determines the difference between historicism and historicity, see Butler, Laclau and Žižek, 2000, pp. 111-12.

what is needed is the recognition of their symptomatic revolutionary potential. Drawing on the central theme of Walter Benjamin's *Thesis on the Philosophy of History*, he suggests that "symptomatic" events such as "the very rage of the anti-Semitic pogroms" down to today's "post-Communist outbursts of neo-Nazi violence" are to be regarded as

> a negative proof of the presence of these emancipatory chances. (Žižek, 2002, p. 256)

Ultimately, the strategy of endorsing superego excesses as a means to break out of the vicious circle of symbolic discursive practices, coincides with the politicisation of these excesses insofar as they are nothing but missed revolutionary opportunities.

Žižek, of course, knows very well that these acts of politicisation are risky, precisely because there is no guarantee that the superego obscenity which sustains power is actually turned into authentic revolutionary force. However, he holds on to his defence of redemptive violence in the form of the "enacted utopia" (Žižek, 2002, p. 261) of the revolutionary act:

> As Deleuze saw very clearly, we cannot provide in advance an unambiguous criterion which will allow us to distinguish "false" violent outburst from the "miracle" of the authentic revolutionary breakthrough. The ambiguity is irreducible here, since the "miracle" can occur only through the repetition of previous failures. And this is also why violence is a necessary ingredient of a revolutionary political act (Žižek, 2002, p. 259).

IV Therapy and politics: disturbing capital *qua* fundamental fantasy

Žižek's use of terms such as "violence" and "universality" alone is enough to explain the ambiguity of his position within today's left, best exemplified by the acrimonious confrontations with Judith Butler and Ernesto Laclau in *Contingency, Hegemony and Universality*. Particularly since the late 1990s, Žižek has progressively distanced himself from the official positions of contemporary leftist theory, both in their moderate and radical versions. On the one hand, he maintains that the moderates who endeavour to bring about a "capitalism with a human face" (from Third Way leftists to supporters of multiculturalism and identity politics) engage in an empty battle which only reinforces the global hold of capital; on the other hand, he claims that those radicals who bemoan the triumph of global capitalism as today's supreme evil are generally too inhibited to invest their thinking in a project which legitimises the excess of the revolutionary intervention ("the pious desire to deprive the revolution of this excess is simply the desire to have a revolution without revolution", Žižek, 2002, p. 261).

Within this framework, what remains absolutely unambiguous is that Žižek's theorisation of agency cannot be kept separated from his critique of late capitalism. In this sense, one can argue that his proposed solution is as extreme as the situation in which it intervenes. The originality of Žižek's anti-capitalism is rooted in his understanding of political struggle:

> politics is, in its very notion, the field of intractable antagonistic struggle.
> (Žižek, 2002, p. 268)

This means that a political intervention always and by definition "disturbs" the demarcation line between the field of legitimate agonistic confrontation (say, the parliamentary logic of party confrontation in today's liberal democracies) and what from that point of view is considered illegitimate (say, positions of the extreme Left and Right). Such a vision clearly dismisses the liberal notion of politics as a neutral, all-encompassing field; instead, it draws on the psychoanalytic insight that the emergence of (what we normally refer to as) "society" hinges on an act of fundamental exclusion.

Once the political domain is defined as antagonised by its inherent exclusionary logic, Žižek can focus on his leftist critique of today's constellation. The main argument revolves around a classic Marxian insight which, Žižek laments, is ignored by both contemporary political theorists of the left (Laclau, Badiou, Ranciére and Balibar, mainly),[9] and the proponents of today's Cultural Studies.[10] What Žižek strives to incorporate into an authentically progressive notion of "agency", is

> Marx's key insight into how the political struggle is a spectacle which, in order to be deciphered, has to be referred to the sphere of economics.

The problem, then, is that within the horizon of today's leftist engagement

> there is simply no room for the Marxian "critique of political economy": the structure of the universe of commodities and capital in Marx's *Capital* is not just that of a limited empirical space, but a kind of socio-transcendental a priori, the matrix which generates the totality of social and political relations (Žižek, 2002, p. 271).

From this angle, the act proper comes to coincide with an intervention on capital itself, the disavowed background without which our symbolic existence, today, would be impossible to conceive:

> the only way effectively to bring about a society in which risky long-term decisions would ensue from public debate involving all concerned is some kind of radical limitation of Capital's freedom, the subordination of the

---

[9] From a more general theoretical viewpoint, Žižek's reproach stems from what he regards as the secret Kantianism of these philosophers, i.e. their insistence on the notion of a regulative and unattainable Idea, the concept of empty universality which can never be filled by a particular content. What Žižek refuses, therefore, is "'the Kantian opposition between the constituted order of objective reality and the Idea of Freedom that can function only as a regulative point of reference, since it is never ontologically fully actualized. [...] the moment a political movement pretends fully to realize Justice, to translate it into an actual state of things, to pass from the spectral *démocratie à venir* to 'actual democracy', we are in totalitarian catastrophe – in Kantian terms, the Sublime changes into the Monstrous". The problem with this logic, which we may call of "self-inhibited agency", is that it "includes its own failure in advance" as it "sticks to its marginal character as the ultimate sign of its authenticity". In other words, it misunderstands the role and consistency of power: "it *needs* it as the big enemy ('Power') which must be there in order for us to engage in our marginal/subversive activity – the very idea of accomplishing a total subversion of this Order ('global revolution') is dismissed as proto-totalitarian." (Žižek, 2000, pp. 232-4)
[10] For Žižek's critique of Cultural Studies and their focus on struggles for recognition see, for example, the section "Theoretical state apparatuses." (Žižek, 2001b, pp. 225-29)

process of production to social control – the radical *repoliticization of the economy*. (Žižek, 2000, pp. 351-52)

From Žižek's perspective, Marxism and psychoanalysis combine to give shape to a rather rigorous definition of the political act:

> because *the depoliticized economy is the disavowed "fundamental fantasy" of postmodern politics* – a proper political *act* would necessarily entail the repoliticization of the economy: within a given situation, a gesture counts as an *act* only in so far as it disturbs ("traverses") its fundamental fantasy. (Žižek, 2000, p. 355)

In psychoanalytic terms, the traversing (disturbing) of the fundamental fantasy is nothing less than "the ultimate aim of psychoanalytic treatment" (Žižek, 2000, p. 266), as it amounts to bringing to light the primordial attachment upon which the consistency of the subject ultimately hinges. As illustrated in the section on masochism, this disavowed primordial attachment (excess) is

> none other than the primordial "masochist" scene in which the subject "makes/sees himself suffering", that is, assumes *la douleur d'exister*, and thus provides a minimum of support to his being. (Žižek, 2000, p. 265)

It is clear, therefore, that a Lacanian politicisation of the act,[11] implies the undoing of the ultimate passionate attachment at work in today's social constellation: capital itself. Žižek's point is that, in a way, politics should be submitted to therapy, in as much as today's power is sustained by the fantasmatic core of capital as the disavowed kernel which effectively runs our lives. By submitting capital to strict social control, the repoliticisation of the economy would necessarily entail a radical, painful (masochistic) act of dis-attachment from our own ultimate fantasy.

Žižek's call for the repoliticisation of the economy, however, does not amount to a psychoanalytic reading of the old Marxian

---

[11] "Lacan's wager is that even and also in politics, it *is* possible to accomplish a more radical gesture of 'traversing' the very fundamental fantasy – only such gestures which disturb this phantasmic core are authentic *acts*." (Žižek, 2000, p. 266)

adagio on the supremacy of the economy. In his recent *Revolution at the Gates*, he has refined his position by stating that the domains of politics (liberal democracy) and economy (late capitalism) are inextricably intertwined. Their inseparability ultimately means that there can be no endorsement of anti-capitalism (no struggle aimed at undermining the economic base) without a political intervention which problematises the very concept of liberal democracy, insofar as

> liberal democracy a priori [...] cannot survive without capitalist private property. (Žižek, 2002, p. 273)

In short, Žižek asserts that, today, parliamentary democracy constitutes nothing but the political form of late capitalism: attacking one (capitalism) without simultaneously intervening on the other (liberal democracy) is just a clever way to defy the very notion of agency.

V The unpredictability of the act and the Leninist freedom

What we encounter at the end of our critical enquiry is once again the very "bone in the throat" of Žižek's theory of agency, that notion of the act which makes his strategy so uncomfortable to many. Apropos of the empirical dimension of this notion, the first point to make concerns the relationship between the conscious symbolic activity of the subversive subject (say, the knowledge that the economy needs to be repoliticised) and the explosive, excessive, irreducible dimension attached to the act *qua* actual practical intervention. How are we to understand such relationship? Or, to put it in somewhat hystericised terms, what do we have to do when we know what we have to do? Significantly, Žižek keeps conscious activity separated from the act, insofar as the act "occurs *ex nihilo*, without any phantasmic support" (Žižek, 2000, p. 374), whereas activity is always secretly sustained by an underlying fantasy. Consequently, the act radically divides the subject, who is unable to

> assume it as "his own", posit himself as its author-agent – the authentic act that I accomplish is always by definition a foreign body, an intruder

which simultaneously attracts/fascinates and repels me, so that if and when I come too close to it, this leads to my *aphanisis*, self-erasure.

The paradox of the Žižekian act as the privileged form of agency becomes, at this stage, rather obvious: when we act, we are in fact acted, we enter a kind of "uncharted territory" where our gestures are performed blindly, as if we were guided by an invisible hand. The act, in other words, is not on the level of the subject, but of the object, insofar as the object in question is none other than the internalised excess, or surplus-enjoyment, which always-already parasitises any process of subjectivization:

> If there is a subject to the act, it is not the subject of subjectivization, of integrating the act into the universe of symbolic integration and recognition, [...] but, rather, an uncanny acephalous subject through which the act takes place as that which is "in him more than himself." (Žižek, 2000, pp. 374-75)

The second point to make, strictly related to the first, concerns the question of terror. In his (to many infamous) defence of "the Good Terror", Žižek reiterates that there is

> something inherently "terroristic" in every authentic act, in its gesture of thoroughly redefining the "rules of the game", inclusive of the very basic self-identity of its perpetrator.

Nevertheless, Žižek maintains a firm distance from terrorism. Despite acknowledging that the act is always "catastrophic (for the existing discursive universe)", he specifies that one should resist the temptation of willingly provoking a catastrophe (i.e. engage in terrorist activity), while at the same time resisting

> the opposite temptation of the different modalities of dissociating the act from its "catastrophic" consequences.

In short, he claims that despite the fact that

> the act always and by definition appears as a change "from Bad to Worse" (Žižek, 2000, p. 377),

we should not associate it to terrorism, for the latter is either a pseudo-radical activity sustained by a symbolic fiction or a "perverse" overidentification with the act, equivalent to

> a kind of hysterical acting-out bearing witness to their [the terrorists'] inability to disturb the very fundamentals of economic order (private property, etc). (Žižek, 2000, p. 270; see also p. 380)

To these mystifying forms of radical intervention, Žižek opposes "the Leninist act", which he locates in the space between the two Russian revolutions of 1917: the anti-tsarist revolt of February 1917, aimed at democratising society, and the second, decisive October revolution, which replaced liberal democracy with socialism. Lenin's great achievement was that of discerning the unique chance for a radicalisation of the revolutionary process:

> In February, Lenin immediately perceived the revolutionary chance, the result of unique contingent circumstances – if the moment was not seized, the chance for the revolution would be forfeited, perhaps for decades.

Despite widespread scepticism and open resistance within his own Bolshevik Party, Lenin was able to sustain "the abyss of the act" (Žižek, 2002, pp. 6-8), aware as he was that the revolution only legitimises itself by itself, irrespective of opportunistic calculations.[12]

The key issue is that, in his 1917 writings "between the two revolutions",

> what he [Lenin] insists on is that the exception (the extraordinary set of circumstances, like those in Russia in 1917) offers a way to undermine the norm itself. (Žižek, 2002, p. 10)

---

[12] As Žižek writes, Lenin knew that "those who wait for the objective conditions of the revolution to arrive will wait for ever. [...] Lenin's counterargument against the formal-democratic critics of the second step is that this 'pure democratic' option is itself utopian: in the concrete Russian circumstances, the bourgeois-democratic state has no chance of survival – the only 'realistic' way to protect the true gains of the February Revolution (freedom of organization and the press, etc.) is to move on to the Socialist revolution, otherwise the tsarist reactionaries will win." (Žižek, 2002, p. 9)

The force of Žižek's plea to "identify with the exception" of a given socio-symbolic order, i.e. to assume its excess, is thus perfectly embodied by Lenin's act, which combines the ability to read the "symptomatic" revolutionary potential of a certain historical situation, and the readiness to take the risk of a radical intervention without guarantees of a positive outcome. The violence implicit in radical agency is not that of a terrorist violation which simply breaks the legal norm, but, rather, that of an intervention which implicitly "redefines what *is* a legal norm":

> The act is therefore not "abyssal" in the sense of an irrational gesture that eludes all rational criteria; it can and should be judged by universal rational criteria, the point is only that it changes (re-creates) the very criteria by which it should be judged – there are no antecedent universal rational criteria that one "applies" when one accomplishes an act. (Žižek, 2001b, p. 170)

What is the significance of Lenin's act today? Or, more to the point, what does the invitation to "repeat Lenin" imply for our era of global capitalism? Žižek clearly warns us from a simple return to Lenin, to the "good old times of the revolution", since he knows full well that such a nostalgic ideological reappropriation would be utterly anachronistic and illusory. Nonetheless, he insists that today's state of affairs is, once again, exceptional, and as such it demands intervention. After the fall of the Berlin Wall and the end of Communism, and after the "ten-year honeymoon of triumphant capitalism" (Žižek, 2002, p. 296), what has emerged is the fundamental inability of the liberal-democratic state to tackle successfully crucial world issues such as the ecological and healthcare crises, the spreading of poverty, the role and power of multinational corporations, etc. According to Žižek, the only logical conclusion is that we urgently need a new form of politicization which will directly "socialize" these critical issues. Lenin, therefore,

> stands for the compelling freedom to suspend the stale existing (post) ideological co-ordinates, the debilitating *Denkverbot* (prohibition on thinking) in which we live – it simply means that we are allowed to think again. (Žižek, 2002, p. 11)

If the first seeds of this "thinking new forms of politicization" can already be discerned in the series of movements emerged since Seattle 1999, he claims that these social movements are symptoms of a profound malaise which needs to be given the form of a "universal political demand" (Žižek, 2002, p. 296), without which they remain caught

> in the vicious circle of "resistance", one of the big catchwords of "postmodern" politics [...] the last thing we want is the domestication of anti-globalization into just another "site of resistance" against capitalism.

Ultimately, the radicality of Žižek's theorisation of agency is encapsulated in his defence of the dimension of universality on behalf of the symptom, the excluded part:

> Today's dilemma is that there are two ways open for sociopolitical engagement: either play the game of the system, engage in the "long march through the institutions", or become active in new social movements, from feminism through ecology to antiracism. And, again, the limit of these movements is that they [...] lack the dimension of universality – that is to say, they do not relate to the social totality. (Žižek, 2002, p. 297)

VI Ways of Knowing: Some Conclusions

1. It goes without saying that the present article does scant justice to the complexity and ambivalence of Foucault's multifaceted work. Joan Copjec goes as far as to surmise the existence of a "Lacanian Foucault" who knows that

> there is indeed always something which in some way escapes the relations of power. (in Copjec, 1994, p. 2)[13]

However, she is right to emphasise that Foucault was, ultimately,[14]

---

[13] There are also various traces of this in Foucault's later work (e.g. Foucault, 1990, pp. 95 and 143). We shall explore this in more detail in the forthcoming book *Discourse and Beyond: Approaching Žižek through Foucault.*

turning away from the notion [...] of a surplus existence that cannot be caught up in the positivity of the social. (in Copjec, 1994, p. 4)

The point is that Foucault's thought has come to stand for a type of knowledge-making that construes any given system as a closed one, as a pneumatic world of power and counter-power, mutually anticipating, reinforcing and obliterating one another, a world as it is known from centuries of mechanist-determinist thinking from Newton to Luhmann. In such a world, there is

no rupture in the great chain of being through which freedom can enter (Deary, 2004, p. 25),

subjectivity is explained away, and paradigm changes must remain a miracle. It can neither be accounted for nor brought about since, as Foucault put it neatly in *The Order of Things*,

one does not know how an articulation so complex and so diverse in composition actually operates [...] I left the problem of cause to one side; I chose instead to confine myself to describing the transformations themselves. (Foucault, 1970, p. 8)

This captures in a nutshell what we might call the "will to contemplative self-effacement" which more often than not skews the insights Foucault has to offer.

2. Žižek's merciless drilling for a dialectical apprehension of the social, the subject and human agency results in the exposure of what he takes to be "the ultimate ideological operation" of deconstructionist criticism, namely,

the very elevation of something into impossibility as a means of postponing or avoiding encountering it. (in Daly, 2004, p. 70)

---

[14] As regards volume II and III of *The History of Sexuality*, which are often understood to have rectified the shortcomings of Foucault's genealogical work, see Žižek"s critique of the "phantasmic Beyond" (Žižek, 2000, pp. 251f). See also notes 2 and 4.

Rather than constructing social reality as "realtight", Žižek conceptualizes it as fissured and self-external, his wager being

> that reality itself is already based on some exclusion or inconsistency – reality is not-all. (in Daly, 2004, p. 102)

The Lacanian Subject he invokes is the name for this gap in the social (substance). A close relative of the Aristotelian soul, it is at once the driving force and limit of all forms of subjectivation, and thus correlative to the Real. It is therefore only consequent that, to Žižek, the proper space for theory

> consists of these very gaps and interstices opened up by the "pathological" displacements in the social edifice. (in Daly, 2004, p.53)

The true intellectual challenge and task on hand

> is not to recognize fiction behind reality – i.e. you experience something as reality and through the work of deconstructive criticism you unmask it as mere symbolic fiction – but to recognize the Real in what appears to be mere symbolic fiction. (in Daly, 2004, p. 102)

The Real, however, is not some kind of immutable Thing-in-itself "about which you can do nothing except symbolize it in different terms", Žižek never tires of reiterating; it is rather "freedom as a radical cut in the texture of reality", the point being

> that you *can* intervene in the Real. (in Daly, 2004, pp. 150, 166)

This brings us back to Foucault. Inside the deterministic system of the Foucauldian world, where the dialectical thought of an effect being "ontologically 'higher' than its cause" and thus escaping it (Žižek, 2000, pp. 256f.) is not entertained, human freedom appears as either mirage or miracle – it is "news from elsewhere" as Vincent Deary (2004) aptly put it. In contrast, the world that arises from Žižek's explorations allows for an Act to emerge through this "loophole in substance" (Deary, 2004) called subjectivity, which opens up the space for the symbolic reconstitution of social reality. The Act is *Real* insofar as it is not determined by the existing symbolic order and cannot rely on its normative support; it is *free*, for as a "mad" gesture it can only be made sense of retroactively; it is *ethical* inasmuch as "you assume that there is no big Other" (in Daly, 2004, p. 163), and *revolutionary* because it is the condition of possibility for any radical break with the generative matrix of global capitalism. The ethico-political Act, then, is the third manifestation (beside the Subject and the Real) of Žižek's key Hegelian motif of *absolute self-relating negativity*. As an emancipatory "answer of the Real" (Žižek, 2001a, p. 31), it is the keystone of Žižekian theory.

3. It is therefore surprising that, in his account of Alain Badiou, Peter Hallward comes to the conclusion that Žižek peddles "an effectively static or structural conception of the real" as opposed to Badiou's "essentially interventionist or activist approach" (Hallward, 2003, p. 150). What really bedevils Žižek's politics is rather the fact that the psychoanalytic Act is insufficient as a model for social transformation – if the latter is meant to be a *collective* emancipatory enterprise. His concept of the Act is indispensable, for it uncovers the crucial inconsistencies of poststructuralist resistance theories; if (mis)taken for a self-sufficient model of social transformation, however, it is wanting.[15] In fact, within the terms of Žižek's theory the question of how collective political practice could lead to a new type of society that, in Ian Parker's phrase, "realizes the full potential of open collective self-management" (Parker, 2004, p. 88) cannot even be framed. One of the reasons for this is his tendency to conceptualise social processes of identification/subjectivation as rearticulations of *primary* processes of identity formation. This results in an overly spontaneist conception of human agency and a reductive take on political practices, which prompted Judith Butler to pose questions regarding the price it might be worth paying for the ideals of a political project to be realized. Would Žižek's ideals justify

---

[15] For a perceptive analysis of this, see Parker (2004).

"any and all means of implementation?" (in Laclau, Butler and Žižek, 2000, p. 268).

"Deep down I am very conservative", he said once, "I just play at this subversive stuff" (in Boynton, 1998). Are we meant to take this seriously? He also endorsed Kurt Vonnegut's motto that

we are what we pretend to be, so we must be careful about what we pretend to be (Zizek, 2001a, p. x).

Žižek should know his favourite quotations.

Bibliography

Bernauer, J., Mahon, M., "The Ethics of Michel Foucault", in G. Gutting, ed., *The Cambridge Companion to Foucault*, Cambridge: Cambridge University Press, 1994, pp. 141-59

Boynton, R., "Enjoy your Žižek", *Linguafranca: The Review of Academic Life*, 7, 1998, http://www.linguafranca.com/9810/Žižek.html (accessed 8 February 2005)

Burchell, G. et al., eds., *The Foucault Effect: Studies in Governmentality.* Chicago: University of Chicago Press, 1991

Butler J., Laclau E., Žižek, S., *Contingency, Hegemony, Universality. Contemporary Dialogues on the Left*, London: Verso, 2000

Copjec, J., *Read My Desire. Lacan Against the Historicists.* Cambridge (MA): MIT Press, 1994

Daly, G., *Conversations with Žižek*, Oxford: Blackwell, 2004

Deary, V., "News from elsewhere", *Times Literary Supplement*, July 16, 2004, p. 25

Dreyfus, H., Rabinow, P., *Michel Foucault: Beyond Hermeneutics and Structuralism*, Chicago: University of Chicago Press, 1982

Foucault, M.:
- *The Order of Things* [1966], London et al.: Routledge, 1970
- *Power/Knowledge*, edited by C. Gordon, Brighton: Harvester, 1980
- "The Subject and Power", in Dreyfus, H. and Rabinow, P., 1982, pp. 208-26

Foucault, M.:
- *The History of Sexuality,* vol. 2, *The Use of Pleasure* [1984], New York: Pantheon, 1985
- *The History of Sexuality,* vol. 3, *The Care of the Self* [1984], New York: Pantheon, 1986
- "Technologies of the Self", in Martin, L. et al. (eds.), *Technologies of the Self: a Seminar with Michel Foucault,* Amherst, MA: University of Massachussetts Press, 1988
- *The History of Sexuality,* vol. 1: *An Introduction* [1976], London et al.: Penguin, 1990
- *Discipline and Punish* [1975], London: Penguin, 1991
- "What is Enlightenment?", in P. Rabinow and N. Rose, eds., *The Essential Foucault,* New York and London: The New Press, 2003, pp. 43-58
Fraser, N., "From Discipline to Flexibilization: Re-reading Foucault in the Shadow of Globalization", in *Constellations,* 10 (2), 2003
Hallward, P., *Badiou: A Subject To Truth.* Minnesota: University of Minnesota Press, 2003
Lacan, J.:
- *The Seminar. Book I. Freud's Paper on Technique, 1953-54,* New York: Norton; Cambridge: Cambridge University Press, 1988
- *The Seminar. Book XI. The Four Fundamental Concepts of Psychoanalysis,* New York, London: W. W. Norton, 1998
Lemke, T., *Eine Kritik der politischen Vernunft: Foucault's Analyse der modernen Gouvernemantalität,* Berlin and Hamburg: Argument, 1997
Müller, C., "Neoliberalismus als Selbstführung: Anmerkungen zu den Gouvernmentality Studies" in *Constellation,* 10 (2), 2003, pp. 98-106
Nixon, S., "Exhibiting Masculinity", in Hall, S., *Representation: Cultural Representations and Signifying Practices,* London et al.: Sage, 1997, pp. 291-336
Parker, I., *Slavoj Žižek: A Critical Introduction,* London and Sterling (VA): Pluto Press, 2004
Reitz, T., "Die Sorge um sich und niemand anderen: Foucault als Vordenker der Neoliberalen Vergesellschaftung", in *Das Argument,* 249 (vii), 2003, pp. 82-97.

Weedon, C., *Feminism, Theory and the Politics of Difference.* Oxford and Malden (MA): Blackwell, 1999

Žižek, S.:
- *For They Know Not what They Do*, London: Verso, 1991
- *The Sublime Object of Ideology*, London: Verso, 1992
- *Tarrying with the Negative*, Durham: Duke University Press, 1993
- *The Metastases Of Enjoyment: Six Essays on Woman and Causality*, London: Verso, 1994
- *The Ticklish Subject*, London: Verso, 2000
- *Enjoy Your Symptom*, London and New York: Routledge, 2001
- *Did Somebody Say Totalitarianism?*, London and New York: Verso, 2001
- *On Belief*, London: Routledge, 2001
- *Revolution at the Gates*, London and New York: Verso, 2002

Introduction to the Italian Edition of Glyn Daly, *Conversations with Žižek*[1]

Sergio Benvenuto

Keywords: Žižek's Hegelian Approach – Lacanian "Thing" – Ethics, Politics, Psychoanalysis – the Real – New Freudo-Marxism

Summary: *Žižek's great merit lies in his having recognized that Lacanian thought should be interpreted as a derivation of Hegelianism, which has dominated part of French philosophy since the 1930s. This introduction to Žižek's work allows the author to highlight the essential nodes of Lacanian thought, and in particular the notion of the Real. He discusses in particular the dual interpretation – Kantian and Hegelian – of the concept of the Real, and the ethical and political consequences which these two interpretations somehow imply.*

I "Sublime" pop

Paraphrasing Hegel's paraphrase of Martin Luther: *to recognize the rose of the sublime in the cross of everyday vulgarity*. S. Žižek, 2005, p. 67.

We want to introduce here an author who, despite his increasing popularity in Italy, remains less well-known here compared to other, especially English-speaking, countries. We are trying to overcome a general lag that characterizes Italy, a country where the trend of thought often (wrongly) used to classify Slavoj Žižek's work – "postmodernism", "post-structuralism", "French thought", etc. – does not enjoy the same success as it has in the Anglo-American world.

In fact, the very style of Žižek's writing, not to mention its content, seems specifically aimed at causing outrage in Italian academia. Case in point: the fact that he takes so damned seriously today's popular culture – Hollywood films, advertising, bestsellers,

---

[1] Žižek & Daly (2004).

fatuous fashions – in short, everything that intellectuals dismiss as Kitsch. One ought to examine the aesthetic references of twentieth-century philosophers, for whom citing Greek tragedies, the great Romantic poets, Shakespeare and Renaissance painting, the great Romantic poets, is considered *bon ton*. And while some went as far as quoting Proust, Rilke, Musil or Picasso (modernism having by then been established), rarely do they quote the film directors or musicians who form an important part of the lives of their sons and daughters. The cinema – which has produced great works in the twentieth century – is never cited by philosophers (apart from Deleuze, Nancy and a few others), as if it were some kind of idle hobby. In contrast, Žižek – who describes himself as a would-be *cinéaste* – continuously rattles off references to films, even those that can only be labeled as commercial or pop. In short, Žižek's style is *sublimis*, in the original sense of the term: it continually oscillates between the highest and lowest levels, reminding one a bit of Mahler's music. He nonchalantly moves from Schelling to Spielberg, from Wittgenstein's Vienna to Kinder chocolate eggs, from Hegelian dialectic to sexual references found in porn films. But this astonishing nonchalance in his choice of examples expresses a certain rhythm of thought that is peculiar to him, and which is one of the reasons his books have been so welcomed. I don't belong to any of the intellectual tribes with which Žižek so strongly associates himself – nineteenth-century German Idealism, Lacanian psychoanalysis, post-1989 neo-Marxism – and yet, I often enjoy reading him. Why? For *the music* of his thinking. Unlike other traditional philosophers, his writing evokes to us not Renaissance madrigals or Romantic symphonies, Brandenburg concertos or austere Webern's compositions, but rather, rock, funk and rap.

We have always been led to believe that what determines the success of a philosophical text is its content. But I wonder whether in the end it is instead the *music of ideas*. Some Romantic scholars who are so dear to Žižek did indeed seek to show that music is philosophical – but it is time to show in what way philosophy is, though not acoustical, musical. One may wonder whether what ultimately counts in philosophy is not the meaning of what one says, but *how* one says it, the argumentative strategy one uses (what Plato called *dialectic*). We continue to read Plato, Augustine, Descartes, Kant or Nietzsche, not because we are still Platonists, Cartesians, Kantian or Nietzschean, but because these masters' writings continue to seduce us. If we are today convinced that we see the limits to the conceptual content of their writings, what is it then that seduces us? I would claim that it is a rhythm or even a curvature of thought that is difficult for us to think about: a quality that does not fall into canonical distinctions (ethics, aesthetics, knowledge, know-how), a kind of lightness, or rather sensation given to us by real thinkers who dare to think of something heretofore unthought of, something new, that makes them so different from their followers, imitators and commentators, even from the best ones.

I don't believe that everyone who reads Žižek completely shares his way of thinking – one often gets irritated reading him. But one never gets bored. With Žižek, it's *worthwhile* disagreeing and arguing. In this introduction, I will not pass up the opportunity to question him. I wonder at times whether the highest praise one can offer a thinker is to say, "I don't much share your position, and yet *I'm interested* in arguing against it."

III The trees and the forest

Some find his continuous references to psychoanalysis, especially in its Lacanian form, as being rather inflexible. Although Žižek was a dissident in Slovenia, which at that time was still communist Yugoslavia, he remains – as he admits in these conversations – steeped in a Stalinist mentality. Isn't his need to *unequivocally take sides* part of the Stalinist legacy? Isn't his way of reading Freud and Lacan also Stalinist? And for that matter, wasn't the person who introduced him to Lacanian thought – namely, Jacques-Alain Miller – part of the Leninist-Maoist movement that pervaded the elite circle of philosophers at the Ecole Normale Supérieure in Paris in the 1960s? Clearly, for an anti-Leninist and anti-Stalinist, Žižek's positions at times have the distinctive aroma of Bolshevik Manichaeism. Anyway, even though I don't share this kind of politico-philosophical choice, I find Žižek's work regarding the politico-mental functioning of state socialism – which he experienced first hand – and its sudden disintegration to be among the most lively and lucid contributions in the literature on the Decline of Communism. Žižek is a "Stalinist", but a charming one.

Unlike many school-trained Lacanians, Žižek isn't boring. He always keeps in mind how Lacan's concepts – and those of psycho-analysis in general – were constructed: he doesn't simply dish out the warmed-up leftovers of a theory that's assumed to be true, but instead takes into account the costs of theory construction (and by costs I don't mean mental exertion, but the the scotoma, the blind spot that every theoretical construction – even the best – inevitably implies). What isolates so many Lacanians from the broader intellectual context is that, while they often have a Tarzan-like agility in jumping from one tree to another in the dense Freudian-Lacanian forest, they are unable to see the forest itself. But for someone outside, one has first to help him see the forest. As a philosopher, Žižek sees also the forest.

Žižek has understood a very essential aspect about Lacan: namely, that he made the only serious, sophisticated attempt at *rearticulating all of psychoanalytic theory in Hegelian terms*. More specifically, Lacan reread Freud through a filter taken from Alexandre Kojève in his famous seminars on Hegel,[2] a reading that drew heavily on the early Heidegger. Bataille, Lévi-Strauss, Merleau-Ponty, Klossowski, Breton, Aron, Koyré, Eric Weil, Corbin, Desanti, and more rarely Lévinas and Sartre – in fact, most of the personalities which later had a huge impact on French culture – all attended these seminars. And so it is that since the 1930s a certain unmistakable style (which its opponents label as dandistic) prevails in the French (and not just French philosophical) way of writing. So, all of French culture, from the 1930's to the present, was shaped by Hegel and Kojève – it is all *Hegejevian*, so to speak. All

---

[2] In the 1930's, Kojève held a seminar on *The Phenomenology of Spirit* that marked a fundamental turn for all of French culture, an event from which it has not yet recovered (Kojève 1969).

of Lacan's thought up to the 1960's develops a number topics and notions that were already present in Kojève's seminars, such as the desire for recognition, the desire of the Other, the dialectic of the subject and its constitutive alienation, and so forth. In short, in order to thoroughly understand Lacan, one needs to have first understood Hegel and Heidegger, and to understand them as Kojève did. If one doesn't know them or understand them, then Lacan's assertions and graphs will remain catechisms for disciples to recite. Lacanian theory is a Hegelian and phenomenological psychoanalysis: this is both its strength and, in my opinion, its shortcoming.

The shrewd reader will ask, "How can one construct today a philosophical discourse upon a discipline that is now in crisis, as is psychoanalysis? Isn't Žižek's exuberance a kind of Indian Summer of the Freudian theory?" Žižek's confinement to the fringes here in Italy, for example, is probably the result of the increasing mistrust of psychoanalysis among many Italian intellectuals. Žižek's story is an eloquent symptom of the change in the status of psychoanalysis over the last twenty-five to thirty years (a change that has been more marked in the US than in Europe). Psychoanalysis has, for the most part, been abandoned by psychiatrists and more generally by the "sciences" (biology, neurosciences and cognitive science now dominate psychiatry); psychoanalysis has lost a large part of its academic-scientific respectability. Despite this, it has not disappeared. It has instead become a theory of reference in humanities departments, including those new fashionable disciplines such as the history of art and film, comparative literature, cultural studies, gender studies, queer studies, communications, etc. The university students and professors, as well as the so-called public intellectuals, who lead this kind of *koiné* forward, are often fans of Žižek. Psychoanalysis is less and less something belonging to psychiatrists and psycho-therapists, and more and more something belonging to feminists, literary critics, "continental" philosophers, historians of film and lifestyles, Geertzian anthropologists, to name a few.

There is an accompanying further change in the ethico-existential function of analytic treatment. One goes to the psychiatrist or cognitive psychotherapist in order to be quickly cured of unbearable symptoms, and one undertakes a lengthy analysis as part of a journey of *metanoia* – as St. Paul called it – that is, spiritual conversion or reconversion of one's own being in the world. Although journalists often write that the psychoanalytic cure has by now been replaced by psychotropic drugs, this isn't the case: very often those in analysis also take such medication, so that psychopharmacology and psychoanalysis mutually, though secretly, support one another. Psychoanalysis in the West is tending to transform itself from specialized therapy, as it once was, into a tool, rhythm and support of a lifestyle and of a way of being-in-the-world.

The Specter of Hegel

In this context, how is one to understand Žižek's Hegelian revival? In fact, Hegelianism has enjoyed a new vitality in recent decades in fields far outside of philosophy. I am not referring here only to the acclaimed Return to Hegel among American neo-pragmatists such as Richard Rorty, who underlined the Hegelian matrix of American pragmatist thought, from Royce to Dewey. The most widely cited epistemologist and historian of science today, T.S. Kuhn, presented a Hegelianized theory of the progress of science that has left a lasting impression on our times.[3] I. Lakatos' reconstruction of the development of mathematics and scientific knowledge is explicitly Hegelian, as is the anti-epistemological anarchism of P. Feyerabend. And it is not difficult to make out the extension of Hegel's shadow behind the very interesting developments in the sciences of evolution and biology (Gould, Eldredge, Oyama, and especially Lewontin). More than Marx, it is Hegel who seems to be the specter that wanders about the West.[4] Lacan's work can thus be inscribed within a broader movement of *Hegelian Challenge*. And those who disdainfully reject Lacan because they find him abstruse, obscure,

---

[3] Kuhn and Lacan had a same teacher: the philosopher and historian of science Alexandre Koyré. The links between Kuhn and Lacan remain completely unexplored. About Koyré's influence see in particular Kuhn (1977).
[4] Following Derrida's *Specters of Marx* (Derrida 1994), very few still doubt the fact that Marx lives, albeit from a spectral life.

mystical – in short, a charlatan[5] – are in fact turned off, even if they don't know it, by the Hegelian, or rather, *Hegejevian*, style of his way of thinking.

Lacan re-transcribed psychoanalysis from the point of view of transcendental philosophy, that is, along the line that goes from Kant to Hegel, Nietzsche, Husserl and Heidegger. This transcription inevitably placed Lacanian thought in conflict with a large part of the psychoanalytic establishment, which is currently dominated by an Anglo-American orientation, one that is traditionally a more empiricist-positivist way of thinking – Locke-Hume-Bentham-Mill line all the way up to the recent philosophy of mind.

Lacanians will say that the core of Lacan's theory is that "the unconscious is structured like a language": an exquisitely Hegelian sounding apothegm. What Lacan says is, if psychoanalysis essentially works by way of speech (all psychotherapy is, by definition, *logotherapy*), and if this linguistic process is able to have notable effects on the life of the analyzand,[6] why should one then think that language is only a tool for working on the unconscious? Isn't the unconscious instead made of the same substance as the tool we use upon it, that is, language?

A similar argument was put forward by Bishop Berkeley,[7] who hated materialism: why should one think that perceptions are a way of entering into contact with reality (the material world), as opposed to thinking that what we call reality is, in the end, nothing other than our perceptions themselves? But Hegel's speculative idealism went further: our approach to perceptual reality is always by way of concepts – we can talk about this table only because we have developed the concept 'table'. Thus, concludes Hegel, we

---

[5] The accusation of charlatanism against Lacan is by now a commonplace in certain cultural circles, the best known one being made by Noam Chomsky (1989, pp. 31-40).

[6] Lacanians use the term *analisant* [the analyzing one] in place of the more traditional *patient* in order to distinguish analysis from any kind of medical act, and in order to highlight the active role of the analyst's client.

[7] Lacan has recognized the influence of Berkeley on his own thinking: Lacan (1975, ch. II, p. 93).

philosophers can settle for the concept 'table' and needn't consider the contingent, concrete table. Lacan carried out a similar operation in the area of psychoanalysis: since the analyst works by way of language, he concludes that the unconscious is essentially language. The unconscious is *ça parle*, which is a way of saying *ça pense* – in short, the unconscious is thought. It is not something one thinks about, it is what thinks. It is Objective Thought, *Objektive Geist*, in the Hegelian sense (a thought with no specific subject, or as W.R. Bion would say, "thought without a thinker").

Idealism, from Hegel to Lacan, is irrefutable: clearly, anything we can say regarding even the most contingent, singular or, to us at least, extraneous reality, will always be said by way of concepts, and hence by way of language. Even if we claim that language is not important, that we are still animals, etc., we can only say this linguistically. It is on this basis that the subject of language came to dominate Western thought in the latter half of the twentieth century – what came to be called the *linguistic turn*. In fact, language has a less "spiritualist" connotation compared to the Hegelian *Geist* (Spirit). This logocentrism of the second half of the twentieth century reveals a fundamental *decision*: that of excluding contingent things from theoretical considerations. The contingent – "the bone", as Žižek calls it ("the spirit is a bone") – doesn't matter.

The philosopher Krug, who was a contemporary of Hegel, challenged Hegel to deduce from the logical movement of the Absolute the pen with which he was writing in that precise moment. Hegel answered that his speculative philosophy made room for the notion of "absolute chance", and already included contingency in the notion of essence. "Contingency, not the contingent, is necessary. For this reason a given contingent is not the object of much interest,"[8] and hence, not even Krug's pen is of much interest. This indifference towards the contingent, which in turn is swallowed up in the concept that determines its possibility, is repeated by Hegel.[9] We will see

---

[8] D. Henrich, p. 168. See Žižek, 1988, 2.2 & 2.3.

[9] "Not in the infinite drive to dissolve the contingent in the concept, but precisely in abandoning such an endeavor does one find the right attitude of the subject towards

below how this idealist indifference towards the contingent poses critical problems when Žižek conceptualizes the notion of the Real. Those who are not Hegelian think that it is ultimately the contingent – precisely because it has been "left free from the idea" – *that makes a difference*, that is, that makes History.

IV A Romantic denunciation

In any event, this psychoanalytic neo-idealism becomes somewhat twisted and contorted at a certain point. If, on the one hand, the unconscious according to Lacan is structured like a language – that is, human reality is structured *a priori*, even before stupid and contingent human beings flesh it out–on the other hand, what counts for Lacan is the *loss* that the irruption and primacy of language produce. Human beings are alienated creatures precisely because they are creatures of language. Our mother (the Other) teaches us to speak; that is, when we as babies desperately cry out, our mother tells us, for example, "You want the pacifier!" She gives a signifier – the pacifier – to the desire that makes us cry out. From that moment on, we know that what we desired was that signifier, a kind of knowledge that comes from the Other. But what did we really desire *before* we were *told* what we desired? What dark, primordial object caused us to be so agitated? We will never know. Language humanizes us, but at the price of a basic distortion that polarizes our existence: the actual thing we sought will always be over and beyond the language that humanizes us. As we will see, this Hegelian psychoanalysis rests on a kind of *Romantic* denunciation.

Many adherents to this type of psychoanalysis will certainly look down at the "Romantic" qualification given to it. When I refer to a number of important currents in Western thought as being Romantic, it is not to belittle them. I myself am (to some extent) incorrigibly Romantic – otherwise, why would I read Žižek? For that matter, we

---

chance. The latter, as naturalness left free from the idea, is already overcome and seen as indifferent" (Henrich, op. cit. p. 169).

are all Romantics to some extent,[10] perhaps not in philosophy, but in our aesthetic tastes, in our sentimental lives, with our children, in politics, etc. One doesn't live by bread and Reason alone. And isn't Freud's basic message also quite Romantic, "*le cul a ses raisons que la Raison ne connaît pas*"? Aren't the libido's reasons Romantic? Romanticism today is the view that human beings essentially lack something that can never be had, that they live their own humanity as an exhilarating, incurable sickness.

Lacanian Romanticism differs from the hermeneutic approach precisely because it thematizes a real, extra-subjective lack as the origin and fulcrum of subjectivity. Hermeneutics, in contrast, adopted Nietzsche's (ironic) motto, "There are no facts, only interpretations," in order to proclaim the (in my view, maniac) triumph of subjectivity: the Real and Being are dissolved in the historical – and human, all too human – dynamic of interpretations. Hermeneutics thus turns into an endorsement given to each and every *current* ideology and belief, the only condition being that it have *kairos*, that it is timely and historically successful. This view triumphs today in a wide range of fields in contemporary psychoanalysis – a view that is referred to as "narratological", "relational", or "hermeneutic", in accordance with Shafer, Spence, Stolorow, Renik, *et al.* In short, the unconscious is reduced to an inter-subjective relation, or rather, to a relation between discourses: the analyst does nothing more than help the subject find for himself a better narrative, to interpret himself according to a new and happier story. As can be seen, the dimension of the Real in this case is permanently removed: analysis is simply a discourse that deviates, modifies, and develops other discourses. Analysis is nothing more than a *transformation*; that is, it gives new forms to our own interpretative lives.

---

[10] But the Romanticism that contrasts itself with, or ignores, science is completely foreign to me. This Romanticism slips into the usual obscurantism of chic superstition. I am surprised by how many psychoanalysts today, coming from any number of schools, are so inclined, as individuals, towards such naive, cheap beliefs, by how many embrace various forms of questionable alternative medicines. The first generation of psychoanalysts wanted to be at the avant-garde of the scientific spirit; after just one hundred year, analysts have tended to become gullible and irrational, adapting to mainstream pop and New Age culture.

I have always considered Lacan's Hegelianism as being much more insightful compared to the hermeneutic molasses. Paraphrasing the basic hermeneutic motto, Lacan would instead say, "There are no facts, only interpretations of the Thing." The Real is not removed; to the contrary it becomes the very fulcrum of subjectivity. Whence the importance Lacanians place on trauma: they bet on the fact that every subjectivity is constructed and formed around a trauma, around something that breaks our subjectivity, that disrupts it and forces it to reconstitute itself and find a new balance (and by 'trauma' is understood above all the experience of excessive, devastating pleasure). Thus the narratological soap opera – in which treatment consists in substituting a happy myth that the subject will recount to himself for an unhappy one (neurotic or otherwise) – sidesteps the fulcrum of the Real with which every subjectivity must sooner or later come to terms. The theory according to which "the unconscious is structured like a language" paradoxically turns into a kind of, trans-psychological, transcendentalist view, and as a result every subjectivity revolves around a Real that can never be symbolized nor rendered in discourse. It is what Lacan called his "mysticism".

V Talking about things that are better left unsaid

Western culture over the past two hundred years seems to be roughly divided between two trends. One is generally called *positivist* (or "scientistic", according to its opponents), and includes methodological rationalism (e.g., Popper). It is positivist since it doesn't accept that the negative operates in the world – and negativity is brought into the world by the (thinking, desiring, speaking, suffering) subject. Positivism certainly grants that everything that we may think or know is linked to an *I* that remains transcendental: all knowledge is knowing-for-someone. But the point is that, for positivism, this transcendental *I*, which is presup-posed, can never be posed by any meaningful discourse. This commitment was expressed apodictically by Wittgenstein in the last sentence of his *Tractatus*: "Whereof one cannot speak, thereof one must be silent."[11] What one cannot speak about, above all, is the subject for which the world appears and who thinks of it as a world – *one must remain silent about this*. Lacan says that this view implies a *Verwerfung, forclusion*, a foreclosure of the subject: consequently, the subject cannot be, as such, the object of *meaningful* knowledge or discourse.

Positivism's self-foreclosure from the possibility of thematizing subjectivity has become even more evident in recent decades as positivism now dares, with the help of neuroscience and cognitive psychology, to ascend to the Heavens: to develop a *science of the mind*. Cognitive science is the attempt to make thought the object of scientific thought.[12] But terminological preferences are never irrelevant: cognitive scientists always speak of the *mind*, upon which a verifiable or falsifiable theory can be constructed – but they never speak of a *subject*. Speaking of it remains foreclosed. The mind is, in short, subjectivity in so far as it becomes the object of science. But clearly, if the scientist wants to remain positive – that is, be one who has a good head on his shoulders – he can never thematize himself as a subject who studies, and makes conjectures about, the mind.[13]

The other current – which includes Lacanian psychoanalysis – can in fact be defined as Romantic and transcendental, despite a certain flag-waving materialism on its part. This current poses what must be presupposed in every act of thought and knowledge, i.e., the subject–upon which it has no intention whatsoever of

---

[11] Wittgenstein, 1921, p. 7.

[12] I leave aside here what Žižek calls the "third culture" along the lines of John Brockman, that is, a philosophical popularization of the "hard" sciences that offers non-reductionist interpretations of them (a nebula that ranger from Hawking to Capra, from Dawkins to Varela, from Gould to Mandelbrot and Minsky, etc.) This "third culture" clearly expresses an increasing need to step out of the constrictive dichotomy that characterized twentieth century culture. See Žižek, 2005b, pp. 87-117.

[13] The cognitive sciences tend to be self-referential – to the extent that have to do with minds studying minds – and from Russell we know how every self-referential discourse continually risks getting caught in antinomies. But the disquieting paradoxes of self-reference are avoided insofar as the cognitive sciences always separate the subject as (the unspeakable) premise, from the mind taken as object – they distinguish *types* of mind, to use Russell's terms.

remaining silent. But not in order to present it as a mind or brain, that is, not as its own object of knowledge. From Kant up to Lacan, one counted on the fact that one could rigorously thematize transcendental subjectivity (the *absolute, self-referring negativity* of the idealists) without reducing it to an object of knowledge. But this belief leads to an image – or rather, eulogy – of subjectivity as the eternal, drifting mine in the order of being (in the ontic order). It is precisely because the Romantic refuses to consider the subject as a presence among presences, a thing among things – even as a thing of a special substance, *cogitans* and not *extensa* – that the subject is exalted as that which seamlessly introduces the lack, negativity, the void, the unpredictable, the abyss, the night, the ineffable (the divine? is subjectivity divinity for us moderns?) into the positive dimension of things. We have here a number of keywords of Lacanian theory.

In fact, when Žižek and others[14] note that Lacan's theory is a Hegelian reformulation of Freud, one shouldn't take this Hegelianism in a literal, pedantic sense: it is not an application of the triadic thesis-antithesis-synthesis form. The Hegelian *Aufhebung* – as overcoming, cancellation, conservation of what is cancelled – is resized. The Lacanian dialectic is a dialectic of the lack and its representation – but it is always a dialectic. In this psychoanalytic neo-Hegelianism the original lack is never overcome-cancelled-retained in some higher synthesis: it produces the subjective story as an attempt, an epic, to overcome it. Lacan is certainly much more Romantic (more modern) than Hegel: the subject as event introduces the lack into the dense, voidless world of things – and for this reason the subject will always be defined as a split one. The subjectivity that positivism fails to thematize is instead described by modern Romanticism as something that will always lack something, especially itself as a "thing" to grasp and possess.

This Hegejevian Romanticism which has seduced non-positivist intellectuals from both sides of the Atlantic was expressed quite

---

[14] Myself included (Benvenuto 1995).

well by the journalist Massimo Nava (2005) in an obituary for Paul Ricoeur. For Ricoeur, he writes,

> man is distinguished from animals by his own cruelty; he nurses sad passions like envy and hatred. And man is the only living being that has freed itself from the instinct for survival.

Such a statement, with its journalist's cheek, describes the basic thought underlying contemporary Romanticism: *that the human being is not just a natural being.*[15] And man is not just such a being precisely because of his "sad passions". The aim is not to return to an outdated spiritualism, but to lay out a project that is at once ethical, aesthetical and political, namely: that human beings are dysfunctional, they are not darwinianly fit – they are a Romantic animal species. There follows from this an entire view of animal nature as a kind of Lost Innocence: of the animal as an imaginary harmony, as a being that lacks nothing, that always fits with its environment and so forth.[16] Having been chased away from its terrestrial paradise of animal nature, human subjectivity – in Lacan as in this form of contemporary thought – always appears not only as a lack of this animal harmony, but also as *manque à être*, as lack of being.

But this was the fundamental point of Kojève's seminars. And the Hegejevian Sartre had already written in *Being and Nothingness* that the "for-itself" (the subject) "is what it is not, and is not what it is":[17] a quite Hegelian statement. We can say that Lacan always sought to describe the subject in so far as it "is what it is not, and is

---

[15] Žižek repeats similar things in these conversations: "Something goes terribly wrong in nature: nature produces an unnatural monstrosity and I claim that it is in order to cope with, to domesticate, this monstrosity that we symbolize" (Žižek & Daly 2004, p. 65).

[16] This idyllic view of the animal – like the Eden lost by human subjectivity – seems completely mythological to those who know animals well. Derrida had criticized this view in recent years – and made Lacan the target of this criticism as well. See Derrida (2002a; 2002b, pp. 50-3). For a critique of the Heideggerian view of animal nature (that essentially inspires the Lacanian criterion of humanity) see Agamben (2004).

[17] On the similarities between Sartre and Lacan, because of their common Hegelianism, see Van Haute (1989): M. Borch-Jacobsen (1991, in part. pp. XIII-XVI, p. 228-9).

not what it is," that is, through a dialectic between being and representation, between recognition and alienation.

In the case of Žižek, this human specificity is linked not only to language, but also to the Freudian death drive (the journalist's "sad passions"):

> Death drive is not something that is in our genes; there is no gene for death drive. If anything, death drive is a genetic malfunction.[18]

The death drive, *Todestrieb*, is the presence of the unnatural in nature.[19]

VI From the Symbolic to the Real

Those who are not up to date see Lacan almost exclusively in a Hegelian light due to the primacy he affords the signifier and language. But things changed following his death, and Žižek is an eloquent example of this: a less logocentric form of Lacanian theory took shape, in which what counts is the Real and that which summons it (the small *a* object, the Thing, enjoyment...). The more updated Lacanians now read the master in a more *real*-ist register. This is due in part to a more general climactic change in Western thought in recent years: the decline of the *linguistic turn*. As noted earlier, Western thought from the 1950's to the 1980's was focused on language – and Lacan ably expressed this focus. In line with the latter Wittgenstein and Austin, Anglo-American analytic philosophy had for decades identified philosophy with linguistic therapy: the philosopher deals with neither the world nor with the

---

[18] Žižek & Daly (2004, p. 94).
[19] One could object to this Žižekian identification of the death drive with that which denies natural determinism – the opposite instead seems to me to be true. For Freud, *Todestrieb* was in fact a repetition compulsion, the inertia of pleasure that leads us to Nirvana or death. Today we would say that it is the entropic tendency inherent to every natural, closed system. I would rather expect to see in Eros, in the life drive, that which denies and contrasts the inertia of natural life: it is what escapes the *Lustprinzip* (the principle of desire-pleasure) and inexplicably leads us toward the other.

subject, but only with language games. Likewise, phenomenology seemed to have turned into hermeneutics, so that the philosopher does nothing more than interpret texts. In short, the heirs to the positivists and phenomenologists followed a parallel convergence, to use an oxymoron, towards language. This logocentric spell has by now been broken. Analytic philosophy is practically coming to a close as it merges with the new philosophy of mind, which instead takes up the grand metaphysical questions of the seventeenth and eighteenth centuries: the mystery of consciousness, the relation between the mind and the world, between thought and body, etc. But continental philosophy is also ridding itself of hermeneutics and – as in the most recent work of Derrida or Agamben[20] – is re-examining the question of animal nature, for example, denouncing the sacrificial abandonment of the biological, corporal dimension of humanity. Today, for the more open-minded Lacanians, the Real predominates.

But for Lacan, what is the Real? Many do not understand what he means since they think of the Real in terms of external things, of the table in front of me or the pen with which Krug writes, but clearly, this is not what is at issue. The table, the pen, everything that makes up the domestic world we live in – exhaustively domesticated by science and technology, which have transformed nearly everything into tools for us – is the *Umwelt*, our environment, or rather, the *Heim*, the home in which we live, of which we are a part because it is also a part of us. It is the reality of recognizable and predictable things which end up being in our image and likeness. The Real that Lacan discusses is instead all that is outside our subjectivity: it is unthinkable, unknowable, something that radically threatens our subjectivity even while it attracts it. It is that which is experienced in the so-called *de-realization syndrome*: we no longer feel a part of the familiar reality, and we finally perceive the real as…Real.

In *The Ethics of Psychoanalysis*,[21] one of Lacan's most fascinating seminars, he discusses *das Ding*, the Thing: each of us is attracted by something obscure, unique and unnamable, which guides our

---

[20] See footnote 17.
[21] Lacan (1986).

life and calls for a kind of unconditional loyalty on our part. Although Lacan gives several names to this real thing around which we revolve – later he uses the Platonic term *agalma*,[22] or the small *a* object – he is always discussing the same thing: a thing-lack that is beyond any linguistic representation. But doesn't this hypostasis of an extra-subjective Thing – even if it constitutes the eye of the hurricane of subjectivity – conflict with the underlying Hegelian optimism that inspires the Lacanian theoretic endeavor?

If the Real is in fact what subjectivity excludes, is the Real then that which *any specific* subjectivity excludes from itself, or is it that which is excluded by all subjectivities? In the first case, we remain within a Hegelian logic: the Real is always Real-for-a-subject. The Real would be a necessary, yet always specific, aspect that every subject implies and creates. My Real needn't be your Real.

It is not by chance that Lacan attributes to the Real the modality of the *impossible*.[23] We typically think of the Real in the same way as we think of the contingent, like this table I'm writing on which is blue and made of wood – *Die Welt ist alles, was der Fall ist*, "The world is all that falls."[24] The real world is contingent, it falls from the sky. Then, why is the Real, according to Lacan, impossible? Is it impossible in the same way that a square circle is impossible, or that two plus two is equal to three? It is impossible because Lacan thinks of the Real in a Hegelian way, that is, always from on the basis of subjectivity: the Real is what is impossible *for* a subject... and yet it happens, it falls on top of him! We can say at any rate that the contingent (not contingency!) is impossible for an Hegelian, that which is impossible for him to integrate into his system.

"The Real is impossible in the sense that we cannot symbolize it or accept it," says Žižek. Just as when someone dear to us dies, and our first, incredulous response is to exclaim, "It's not possible!" – but it is real for this very reason. Some time for mourning is needed

---

[22] *Agalma* is something dazzling inside Socrates that attracts and seduces young people (*Symposium*). See Lacan, 1991b.
[23] Lacan uses the distinct modes of classical logic: the contingent; the necessary and the impossible (but he excludes the possible).
[24] Wittgenstein, 1921, p. 1.

in order *to realize* that such a loss has occurred, that is, in order to inscribe this lack within ourselves, and hence to take it out of the Real. What is an ordinary contingency from an objective point of view – the fact that someone dies – turns out to be impossible for a subject. As Žižek points out in these conversations,

> For Lacan, the Real is not impossible in the sense that it can never happen – a traumatic kernel which forever eludes our grasp. No, the problem with the Real is that it happens and *that's* the trauma. *The point is not that the Real is impossible but rather that the impossible is Real.*[25]

VIII The ethical real

But the crucial point is this: if the Real is always the Real-for-a-subject, if the Thing is not the Kantian thing-in-itself, but *my Thing* that attracts me and not someone else, don't we fall back into an objectivist psychology? That is, since my Real is not that of another, I can consider the Real of another in an objective manner, from the outside, as something I can study as a moment of the other's subjectivity. Doesn't subjectivizing the Real (extricating it from any Kantian dimension of the Thing's unattainability) result in a "psychological" objectivization? When Žižek says, for example, that for the Nazi the Jew was the abject Real to be evacuated, isn't he just doing social psychology, with which any researcher on the "mass psychology of fascism" could agree?

When one says that the Real is that which is excluded by the subject, one is in fact using a subtly ambiguous term, since *exclusion* has both an *active* sense (eliminating something that was once included) and a *passive* sense (leaving something outside of a positive act of selection). It seems quite insignificant, yet this distinction forms the basis of the reading that the radical left, on the one hand, and free market conservatism, on the other hand, give to third-world poverty. For the former, the poor are excluded in the active sense, they are the products of capitalism; for the

---

[25] Žižek & Daly, 2004, pp. 69-70.

latter, the poor are excluded in the passive sense in that they remain outside of capitalism – they were unable to become part of the game. Contrasting solutions follow: if exclusion is active, then capitalism is the sickness to be cured; if exclusion is passive, then capitalism is the remedy. Žižek seems to give an active sense to exclusion: the Real is that which was excluded by a subject, to the extent that it is always relative to a subject. The Real is a product of subjectivity, even if this latter is in some ways the product of the Real. A paradoxical consequence of this dialectical subjectivization of the Real is the belief, expressed by some Lacanians, according to which only psychotics are able to come into actual contact with the Real with "a bare mind", insofar as that which they foreclose from the Symbolic returns to them from the Real.

But let's consider the (very objective) work of astronomers. We can certainly say that in studying the stars they are attracted by a Real that is shared only by those who have that same passion. So, when they speculate on black holes, for example, are they thus representing the Thing that attracts them? And yet astronomers make up a community that shares rules and professional ethics. And is it not the case that they form an ethical community precisely because the thing they seek is not the Thing of this or that astronomer, but a thing-in-itself that draws them and compels them? Of course, black holes are themselves a representation that has been constructed through the history and game of astronomy, something that the community of astronomers as much invented as discovered; thus, a naively objectivist reading of the objects of astronomy is not sufficient. This example of the famous black holes was not chosen by chance: they are so fascinating because they seem to be a prototypical phenomenalization of the thing-in-itself – they indicate the entry into a universe that by definition is unknowable (*it is impossible* for someone to return to our universe and tells what is inside a black hole). I wonder whether the Thing is simply that from which a subject is excluded and around which it constitutes itself, or whether, more radically, it is not something from which *every* subject, without exclusion, is excluded insofar as it is a subject. We can think of the Thing as something that can never be objectified for anyone else: it is that exclusion which universally unifies us and makes it possible to construct community and solidarity among ourselves. Any other approach is idealist: it amounts to saying, "Black holes are only a construction of astronomical subjectivity." They are certainly a construction, but they are not *only* that. The hypothesis of black holes says in fact that there exists – to use the scientists' terminology – a *singularity* in the universe that is radically excluded from our known universe, and this is precisely the Real, singularity itself. We can therefore say that the Real is always in some way a black hole. It is not so much something that disrupts a determinate order of reality, a specific *domus* or domestication of the world, but rather, it is that which is beyond anyone's reach, which in turn is the very aspect that draws and attracts us.

An even richer example is death itself. As Heidegger showed, given that my death can only be *mine*, it is my most authentic, most proper possibility. But in saying that true death is only mine, i.e., is always subjective, we universalize its place: each of us deals with one's own death as subjective. What is more real than death? And isn't it a thing-in-itself since it unravels from a Hegelian dialectic that poses the ever Real as a product of the subjective story?

Now, only this de-subjectivized externality of the Thing – that is, its Kantian dimension – can explain why, for Lacan, this loyalty to our desire, our remaining subject to the Thing, has to do with what we commonly call ethics. Historically, the ethical paradigms have been quite diverse, but in general what we refer to as ethical are those actions in which the other counts. And what is the other subject if not, quite simply, the fact that... it excludes me as a subject? Isn't the subjectivity of the other something that radically excludes mine? Isn't every subject for the other something that is absolutely real insofar as I can never be the other subject, and hence can never live its death? What is ethical is my looking after the other as a subject in itself and for itself – it is precisely in excluding that, *as a subject*, s/he is *my* object.

Žižek reminds us (as do various religions) that ethics always implies transcendentality. But Žižek does not say that this also implies a universal exclusion, in the sense that we are ethically bound to that from which we will always be excluded.

From a Kantian approach, the Real is the impossible for everyone – and it is this universality that makes it an ethical stake. By *everyone* I don't mean the unanimous "everyone" in the sense of the statistical unanimity of human beings: I mean the others to the extent that each one will be excluded by every other subject. For us, aren't others the Real *par excellence*?

An hypothesis of universality (like brotherhood among all human beings) is based, not on a least common denominator between all human beings, but on what each subject is *devoted to*, namely, to a care for the Real. For monotheistic religions, universal sisterhood or brotherhood is based on a devotion to God – but the Real cannot be enthroned in the Supreme Being.[26]

The Lacanian dialectic thus finds itself before a critical junction: if the Real is always complementary to a subject, to each subject, it cannot be what brings us together universally since everyone would be excluded. Thus, the Real is reduced to a halo that accompanies subjectivity, a kind of blind spot in subjective life. In contrast, if the Real falls from the sky, so to speak, then it is not subjective and hence marks something completely external to the subjective order which is the domain of psychoanalysis. One needs to return to Kant: the Real is the thing-in-itself that we must always presuppose (without ever being able to pose it as an object) and that anchors us ethically. Even if Žižek clearly opts for the "subjectivist" solution, he does not preclude the reference to Kant.

On the other hand, Lacan himself seems to give us another view of the Real, according to which the Real cannot be reduced to a correlate of a subject. It is no coincidence that in the seminar on ethics Lacan takes on the Kantian *thing*. At a certain point he refers to the debate between Goethe and Hegel over Sophocles'

---

[26] If we identify the Real with God (as religions do) one always ends up contrasting *my God* with that of the others, and universalism ends up in cultural clashes. God is always the God of Abraham and Isaac; the Real, instead, belongs to no one, it is never "mine" or "yours".

Antigone, concerning Antigone's embarrassing declaration that she buried her brother Polyneices' body just because he was her brother! Antigone curiously states that a brother is unique: "I can never have another one." Lacan shows that it is not just a silly remark, as Goethe thought: for Antigone, the brother is her *thing* precisely because he has this unique character.[27] Now, every uniqueness is inexpressible. Language and knowledge can never express the uniqueness, the pure event: the *unicum* is unthinkable for a speaking subject who inevitably categorizes.[28] But is Antigone's Thing, the uniqueness to which she is devoted, is it a Thing only for Antigone? After all, what do we care about Polyneices? It's Antigone's business. But if this were the case, the tragedy wouldn't move us, and instead it does.

But in the end ethics has precisely to do with this: what counts is not a generic other, a member of my same species *homo sapiens*, but the other who is *him* or *her*. Ethics socializes us on the basis of the asocial, absolute and unthinkable singularity.

VIII "Unutilitarian" ethics

It would be a mistake to think that the questions raised by Žižek concern only Lacanians. Even those who don't take part in this philosophical-psychoanalytic slang encounter similar problems, although expressed in different terms.

The appeal to the Real has ethical and political implications that are just as important. For example, it lies behind the rejection – on Žižek's part – of the doctrine that has largely inspired the legal, political and ethical organization of modern societies: namely, utilitarianism. This is the theory according to which the essence of human beings resides in their seeking to maximize their own

---

[27] J. Lacan (1986, ch. XIX, pp. 296-8).

[28] In fact, proper names that indicate single individuals are only *indexes*, like a finger pointing towards that specific thing; they are not real concepts.

pleasure and/or happiness.[29] We can say that modern utilitarianism marks the triumph of Greek sophistry in our culture. The sophist proposed useful, successful tools for convincing one's fellow citizens: "Given that every human being seeks pleasure, offer them pleasing prospects!" Utilitarianism thus offers a kind of technology of seduction; at one time it was the eristic of sophists, now it is advertising, the mass media industry, technologies of consensus, ads... Utilitarianism is in the end the theory of flattery: "If you flatter others, and offer them the image of what they want to be, they're yours!"

There is little to say: a large part of our communal life is utilitarian. Utilitarianism has been perspicuous from time immemorial. The central point for Žižek, however, is that human beings *are something more*: the essentially utilitarian interpretation that a great number of Anglo-American analysts have given to Freud's theory is an unjust appropriation.

In the same way that ancient philosophers countered the sophists, Žižek relies on the fact that human beings are not simply machines for maximizing pleasure and/or happiness. Human beings – of which philosophers would be the most sensitive and high-strung examples – are also bound by a need for truth. But I would ask at this point, what is truth if not the fact that other real subjects – and not just my own pleasure to be maximized – count?

Human beings are not completely objectifiable since, despite all the technologies for flattering and exploiting them (that is, for making them happy), there is a part of them that looks after the Real. In short, it is not enough for them to be happy. Indeed, Žižek states,

---

[29] As part of utilitarianism I also include so-called contractualism, which is today quite fashionable thanks to J. Rawls and his theory of justice. Contractualism is a kind of marginalist utilitarianism (similar to the so-called marginalist economics): we call a society *just* when those who are worst off can say, "In an unjust society I would be even worse off."

What is missing is precisely a theory of – as Kant already put it in his *Critique of Pure Reason* – why human beings are destined to ask themselves questions which they cannot answer.[30]

Why is it that, like hysterics, they seek a satisfaction they can never have? Human beings have this anti-utilitarian vice of asking useless questions. And this is because they don't want to be just "happy fools": happy, yes; but fools, no. This willingness on the part of human beings not to be simply happy, is pompously, and Kantianly, called freedom. Žižek restores the concepts of *freedom* and *autonomy*. Curiously, he has a Hegelian conception of the Real, and a Kantian conception of ethics.

We say that the ethical act is Real, Real is not this kind of thing-in-itself that we cannot approach; Real is, rather, freedom as a radical cut in the texture of reality.[31]

But isn't this the heart of Kantian ethics, i.e. "noumenic freedom"? Human beings aren't just machines that follow the law of maximum pleasure (or least pain), but are able to impose the law by themselves. Subjective transcendence transcends utilitarianism. "You were not born to live like brutes, but to follow paths of… the Real."[32] Žižek reminds us that "life is not simply life." In short, life is acceptable if one has a Cause. This seems to me to be the basic concern of the Žižekian take on Freud and Lacan.

Now, this Žižekian emphasis on autonomy and freedom seems to overturn an important aspect of the Lacanian "campaign", and in particular, his attack on the various conceptions of the *autonomous Ego*, of the liberal ideology of the free and entrepreneurial Ego. Clearly, the Lacanian ironies regarding freedom marked his distance with respect to the existentialist themes that were pervasive in Paris

[30] Žižek & Daly, 2004, p. 58.
[31] Ibid, p. 166.
[32] Paraphrase from Ulysses' words in Dante's *Divine Comedy*: "Considerate la vostra semenza:/ fatti non foste a viver come bruti/ ma per seguir virtute e conoscenza" [Consider what you came from:/You were not born to live like brutes/ but to follow paths of excellence and knowledge] (*Inferno*, XXVI, 118-120).

during the 1940's and 1950's – one need only think of the Sartrian exaltation of "unbounded freedom". Lacan apparently wanted to oppose the Freudian disenchantment to an essentially catholic, consciousness-oriented view derived from the Cartesian axiom regarding the free will of a thinking being. But over time, the savvier Lacanians realized that, in the end, their doctrine was based on a fundamental assumption: that it is possible to speak of the subject – not minds – only if there is ethical freedom in the background.

In fact, ethics – whether in Descartes or Kant – is inseparable from freedom: a subject is ethical only if it is in some way *autonomous*, that is, if it gives itself *nomos*, the law, without being naturally subject to it: autonomous, at least in certain crucial aspects of life, from the *dictat* of the pleasure principle. ("An ethical act," says Žižek somewhat romantically, "[…] signals a rupture, a break in the causal network or structure of the universe. Freedom is this break – something which begins out of itself."[33]). It is not because some human beings are able to make duty prevail over pleasure; rather, it is because our pleasure in the end is not our only duty. And it is in this ethical autonomy that we finally find, beyond the cozy cocoon of reality, contact with the Real.

For Žižek, the ethical dimension – without which there is no subjectivity – makes the Real sensible. This will certainly surprise those who think that ethics is a question of norms, prescriptions, commandments, rules, etc., and analysts themselves usually think of ethics as something normative, super-egoic.[34] Lacan's novelty, which is taken up by Žižek, consists instead in having spoken of ethics as a relation to an original *thing*, to which we can remain more or less faithful, to an irreducible Real that attracts us and pulls us in. Lacanian thought grafts uncannily a Kantian ethics onto a Hegelian dialectic of the subjectivity and the Real.

---

[33] Žižek & Daly, 2004, p. 124.

[34] The (dialectic?) paradox of ethics is that, if it's identified with norms and laws, it runs into its own stalemate. Maybe someone who is good follows a norm, but unconsciously. If the law says, "Do not kill!" it means that the subjects strongly desire to kill. The commandments are like the ditch that was once the riverbed, when the river ran dry.

IX Marxism of beautiful souls

A final note needs to be added regarding Žižek's commitment as a political writer. While Žižek is innovative in his analysis of culture and in philosophy, he is politically rather conservative: he follows the Freudian-Marxist tradition. As is well known, Freudian-Marxism or Marxist-Freudianism began early in the 20th and cut across the entire century with its phosphorescent lights: from W. Reich and S. Bernfeld, to E. Fromm, H. Marcuse, L. Althusser, E. Fachinelli, J.F. Lyotard, E. Laclau, A. Badiou and others. Žižek thus continues the glorious tradition that tried to combine Marx and Freud – and Nietzsche, and sometimes also Heidegger and Derrida. The Marx-Nietzsche-Freud trinity was the paradigm of Modernity itself for a large part of the last century (the three "masters of suspicion", as Ricœur labeled them). The Marxist analysis of the fetishism of commodities seemed to many generations as the socio-economic *pendant* not only of the Freudian hypothesis of fetishistic perversion, but of the psychoanalytic theory of alienation *tout court*. It is precisely because combining Marx and Freud is so tempting, easy, and inevitable, that I personally have always deeply distrusted Freudian-Marxism. I have always distrusted alliances that present themselves with the inviting smile of the obvious.

I have the impression that, for the generation that both Žižek and myself who writes belong to, the ideal of socialism or communism was in the end a mask for the more basic ideal of the Revolution. That is, our desire to shake up the society in which we live was much stronger than the desire for a new society, that was being vaguely sketched out. Our real enjoyment was deconstructive; the outcome that the change was supposed to bring about was only a pretext (proof of this lies in the fact that all the forms of socialism that were *real*-ized were simply horrific for us). Today, believing in the Revolution is like believing in God or in the soul's immortality: it is not something one can argue for or against. One either has faith or one doesn't. It thus makes no sense here to raise objections to Žižek's faith. And yet, some remarks must be made.

It doesn't seem to me at all irrelevant that Freud was not seduced, not even for an instant, by Bolshevism,[35] which he considered a secularized application of religious utopia, a promise of a paradise on earth as an ersatz of heaven. Freud instead thought that human beings would never succeed in freeing themselves from their own unconscious, from that which grants dissatisfaction and suffering regardless of a society's setting. I always read the *Future of an Illusion* (Freud 1932) as a critique not only of religion, but also of a socialist millennialism. And one cannot simply get around it by saying that Freud was naïve about politics and hardly Freudian: on the contrary, I see his distrust of the Dram of a Wonderful Future, of political Messianism, as a corollary to his theoretic position. At least in this regard, I am more an orthodox Freudian than Žižek.

Lacan's own "environmental" sympathies for the Left are well known, but he *never* formulated any kind of Freudian-Marxism, Leftist doctrines remained outside of his teachings. Rather, he never attempted, for example, a dialogue with Althusserian Marxism. He often said "The social is always a scourge". This could be a blindness on the part of the Master, but I share the arguments he used to respond to those young opponents he encountered in Vincennes' University and Louvain: he exposed the illusion of the Revolution as a solution to the human *manque à être*. To the *gauchistes* students of Vincennes, he quite rightly said, "The regime shows you and tells you, 'Look at how they enjoy themselves!'"[36] Žižek certainly does not contest Lacan at all, but couldn't one give the same reply to his Freudian-Marxism?

Of Žižek's leftism I would say the same thing that he himself says quite rightly in this book regarding the hard-line Left, especially its Trotskyist variant:

---

[35] "And although practical Marxism inexorably cleared away all idealistic systems and all illusions, it has in turn created illusions that are no less questionable and free from the former. It hopes to change, in the course of a few generations, human nature. [...] But such a transformation of human nature is unlikely" (S. Freud, 1937; *SE*, 22, p. 179; *GW*, 15, p. 194).

[36] Lacan, 1991a, p. 240.

When I speak with some of my orthodox Marxist friends of all the recent disturbing events [...] they are always telling the same story [...]. So the story goes that there was always a chance of an authentic workers' revolution, but [...] I think that the standard idea that in all these cases we had a missed opportunity for socialist revolution is a deep delusion. It doesn't function in this way.[37]

I would extend that judgment of illusion from paleo-Marxism even to neo-: the world doesn't function in a Marxist way.

But in excluding the power of the contingent, doesn't Hegelianism lead sooner or later to dogma? And in order to get out of the dogma, the medicine, for centuries, has always been the same: the Kantian beyond-the-horizon of the Thing. In identifying the real and the rational, doesn't every Hegelianism inevitably lead to a *loss of reality*?

In short, the reasons I reject Marxism-Leninism are the same for which Žižek rightly rejects ideologies: they seek to *give meaning* to suffering and to history. In fact, we find here the two sides of exclusion, the active (Hegelian) and passive (Kantian). It seems to me that when one dies of hunger or AIDS in Africa, and says, "I am a victim of Western capitalism!", that is when he or she opts for the active sense of exclusion, his or her belief gives meaning to their pain: they feel like a victim to be avenged, since the "deep" responsibility for their misery can be precisely identified and named. In other words, blaming the West for one's own poverty gives meaning to one's own misery (isn't anger the triumph of meaning?), but Žižek himself tells us that giving meaning to suffering is the greatest illusion. Aren't countries like China or India now emerging from misery (of course, with enormous inequalities and abuses to be overcome) and threatening the West's supremacy precisely because they have finally stopped giving meaning to their misery? Just because they stopped complaining about the West's exploitation?

What is much more Real-istic, much more intolerable, is the passive interpretation of exclusion: people are often poor because...

---

[37] Žižek & Daly, 2004, pp. 145-146.

they are superfluous. If today hundreds of millions of people in the poorest countries in the world simply disappeared, our wealthy societies would hardly notice. One part of humanity is excluded in the sense that it is not needed by capitalism or anyone else. Isn't this senseless, unbearable contingency of human beings – if they didn't exist, everything would go on as before – perhaps the most intolerable thing, from which Freudo-Marxism has often tried to distract us? And yet, doesn't Freud's Oedipus say something that is quite un-Marxist? It is not that a parent tried to sexually abuse a child, but simply that the child is excluded from the sexual life of his parents. The thing that is difficult to tolerate is the non-guilt of the parents. Today, a number of "revisionist" psychoanalysts and psychotherapists tend to place all the guilt on the parents, overturning Freud's approach: If I have problems, it's the fault of my abusive, incestuous father, of my mother who wasn't good enough, of my lecherous uncle, etc.

A flood of novels and films unceasingly tell us that Oedipus is innocent while Laios and Iocasta are guilty. But Oedipus' Complex is terrible since every subject in the end – whether in analysis or in life – must recognize, at Colonus, that that good-for-nothing parent was not the final cause of his malaise.

And this, applied to social and political life, opens up for us a simple and tremendous evidence: that every human being is fortuitous, that he or she had no right to be born; and if we find a meaningful place in the world, this means that we have created it.

Bibliography

Agamben, G., *The Open. Man and Animal*, transl. Kevin Attel, Palo Alto, CA: Stanford University Press, 2004

Benvenuto, S., "Lacan's Dream", *Journal of European Psychoanalysis*, n.2, Fall 1995-Winter 1996, pp. 107-131

M. Borch-Jacobsen, M., *Lacan, The Absolute Master*, Palo Alto, CA: Stanford University Press, 1991

Chomsky, N., "Noam Chomsky: An Interview", *Radical Philosophy* 53, 1989

Derrida, J.:
- *Specters of Marx*, New York: Routledge, 1994
- "E se l'animale rispondesse (Finte e tracce)", *aut aut*, 310-311, 2002a, pp. 4-26
- *Fichus*, Paris: Editions Galilée, 2002b

Freud, S.:
- *Future of an Illusion* [1927], *GW*, 14, pp. 325-380; *SE*, 21, pp. 5-56
- *Introduction to Psychoanalysis (New Series)* [1932], *GW*, 15; *SE*, 22, pp. 5-177

Henrich, D., *Hegel im Kontext*, Frankfurt/M.: Suhrkamp, 1981

Kojève, A., *Introduction to the Reading of Hegel*, New York: Basic Books, 1969

Kuhn, T. S., "Concepts of Cause in the Development of Physics", in *The Essential Tension*, Chicago-London: The University of Chicago Press, 1977, pp. 21-30

Lacan, J.:
- Le *Séminaire, livre XX. Encore*, Paris: Seuil, 1975
- Le *Séminaire, livre VII. L'éthique de la psychanalyse*, Paris: Seuil, 1986; trans. D. Porter, *The Ethics of Psychoanalysis 1959-1960*, New York: W.W. Norton, 1997
- Le *Séminaire, livre XVII. L'envers de la psychanalyse*, Paris: Seuil, 1991a
- Le *Séminaire, livre VIII, Le transfert*, Paris: Seuil, 1991b

Nava, M., "Il filosofo della metafora", *Corriere della Sera*, 23rd May 2005

Van Haute, P., *Psychoanalyse en filosofie*, Peeters: Louvain, 1989

Wittgenstein, L., *Tractatus logico-philosophicus* [1921], London: Routledge and Kegan Paul, 1961

Žižek, S.:
- *Le plus sublime des hystériques. Hegel passe*, Paris: Point Hors Ligne, 1988
- *Distanza di sicurezza*, Rome: Manifestolibri, 2005a

- "Lacan between Cultural Studies and Cognitivism", in *Interrogating the Real*, London-New York: Continuum, 2005b

Žižek, S. & Daly, G., *Conversations with Žižek*, Cambridge: Polity, 2004 (Ital. Ed.: *Psicoanalisi e mondo contemporaneo*, Bari: Dedalo, 2006)

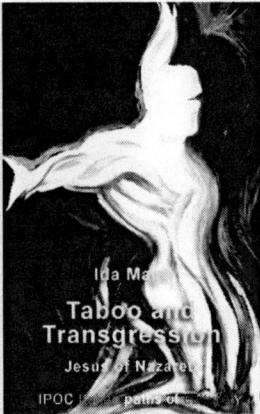

TRANSFERENCE
&
COUNTER-TRANSFERENCE I

René Major,
Love of Transference and Passion for the Signifier

Fabiano Bassi,
Evolution in the Clinical Use of Counter-transference

Cristiana Cimino,
Transference and Bare Life. Defencelessness

Giampaolo Lai, Pierrette Lavanchy,
Disidentity Shock in Transference and Counter-transference

Antonio Maiolino,
Transfert: A No Man's Land

Italian paths of culture

*An outstanding work, but however written with
an aphoristic light touch.* **Massimo Cacciari**
*It deals with topics that stand deep in the heart of the world we are
living in, and with our chances of freedom.* **Claudio Magris**

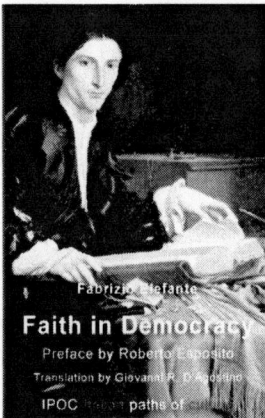

Fabrizio Elefante
Faith in Democracy
Preface by Roberto Esposito

Book: ISBN 9788895145402 – pp. 220
e-Book: ISBN 9788895145846 – pp. 104
Custom-made Book: chapter(s) – Keywords
and/or Loci Sections

Italian Edition:
Fabrizio Elefante
La fiducia nella democrazia

Book: ISBN 9788895145068 – pp. 212
e-Book: ISBN 9788895145501 – pp. 100
Custom-made Book: chapter(s) – Keywords and/or Loci Sections

IPOC Italian paths of culture
159, V.le Martesana – I - 20090 Vimodrone MI Italy
Ph. +39-0236569954 – Fax. +39-0236569954
e-mail: ipoc@ipocpress.com
www.ipocpress.com

Love of Transference and Passion for the Signifier

René Major

Keywords: Tranference love – Erotic transference – Love of transference – Jung – Spielrein – Freud

Summary: *The author examines the circoumstances that led Freud to write about Transference love (*die Ubertragungsliebe*): Sabina Spielrein's analysis with Jung in which the erotic transference (*die Liebesübertragung*) is induced by the analyst. In this case the Interchange of signifiers emerges as a reality of thought transference on a scene of fiction. while the analytic situation, as a scene of fiction, allows some effects in reality by the significant articulation of the veracity of the subject's relation to the truth. A comparison is made between the analytic and the literary scenes.*

The ethics of psychoanalysis can best be measured on the cutting edge of its relation to truth.[1]

It is around this central theme that Freud builds his entire discussion on what he considers the major stumbling block of analysis, in its historic development as well as in the course of each treatment: namely, the case in which a woman shows unmistakable signs or declares straight away that she has fallen in love with the doctor who is her analyst.

I am deliberately retaining Freud's terms of transference-love (*die Übertragungsliebe*) and erotic transference (*Liebesübertragung*),[2] in the context of this specific case – and *this* case only – that is, that of a woman in love with a male analyst who is also a doctor. The context, of course, must be taken into account. Freud's remarks on transference-

---

[1] This paper has first appeared in *Etudes freudiennes*, 19-20, Paris, Evel, 1982.
[2] The English translator makes the following distinction: *Übertragungsliebe*, transference-love; *Liebesübertragung*, erotic transference. In French, the translation of these two terms is closer to 'transference-love' and 'transference of love' ('*amour de transfert*' and '*transfert d'amour*').

love were written in 1915, and the concept of *Laienanalyse* (lay analysis is practised by non-doctors, i.e. it is a discipline unrelated to medicine) would only emerge eleven years later. But above all, it appears at once that this is the only type of situation that arose clearly enough, or of which Freud had become aware up to that point:

> It has come to my knowledge that some doctors who practise analysis frequently (*haüfig*)[3] prepare their patients for the emergence of erotic transference[4]

or even incite it, he adds, in order for the treatment to advance.

> I can hardly imagine a more senseless proceeding [...] There is no doubt that the outbreak of a passionate demand for love is largely the work of resistance.[5]

A change of scene takes place: *Wie wenn ein Spiel durch eine plötzlich hereinbrechende Wirklichkeit abgelöst würde.*[6] Reality suddenly erupts onto the scene of fiction. And resistance plays the role of *agent provocateur*[7] in the context of analytic work.

What relation could there be between this induction of the 'real' and the analytic context operating as a fiction capable of producing this induction (this is Freud's major argument) regardless of the 'reality' of the analyst? And since erotic transference is no less authentic than any other love, what is this fiction which, in analysis, elevates the truth to the level of the real, or this reality which raises to the level of fiction? What exactly would it be an analysis carried out in the truest tone, nearest to its truth?

Ultimately, more than the relation between the ethics of psychoanalysis and the truth, it would be a question of the veracity of this relation to the truth. Here, the truth becomes something of a different nature from historic or subjective truth. Its nature can no

---

[3] The first edition uses the word *frühzeitig*: 'early on' or 'prematurely'?
[4] 1914/1915, p. 161.
[5] Ibid, pp. 161-162.
[6] Ibid., *GW*, p. 310; *SE*, p. 162.
[7] In French in the original.

longer be determined by choosing between two alternatives: stay true to your desire or consume your *Dasein*.

The Freudian text maintains a close relation of veracity between its subject, held to be scientific, and the style which shapes this subject; between the narration of a story, always other when scripted, and the analytic scene, locus and lack-of-locus where this story arrives at the truth; between the language thoughts (*die Sprachgedanken*) of the dreamer and the transferential inscription of the reader. The style becomes the mark *(stilus)* of the object. So much so that a talented writer would be able to convey all of its truth-fiction[8] from the unique perspective of the writer.

The *agent provocateur* that love insistently places, through its repetitive character, in the service of resistance to this *veracity*, is also seen by Freud as the signal of a tendency towards what he has already named counter-transference (*Gegenübertragung*) that can be present in the analyst's mind. He does not, however, conclude that there can be counter-transference love. Freud in no way conceives that the analyst could be in love with his patient. He merely elaborates all the hypotheses concerning the responses or non-responses that can be given to the demand for love of a woman in analysis. His reflections, reviewed and reconsidered, follow upon what he had called in *Studies in Hysteria,* the false relation and the *mésalliance*,[9] reflections inspired by Breuer's misadventure with Anna O., at the beginnings of psychoanalysis.

Freud had spoken of counter-transference five years earlier at the Nuremberg conference, but had already used the term before this conference in a letter to Jung, in reference to the Sabina Spielrien 'affair'. These experiences, he said, have the character of a *blessing in disguise*,[10] an unexpected blessing.

---

[8] D.M. Thomas, *The White Hotel*, 1981.
[9] In French in the original.
[10] In English in the original.

It is true that this has never happened to me, but I have come very close to it several times and I have had a *"narrow escap"*[11] [...] The fact is that I was ten years older than yourself when I came to psychoanalysis.[12]

Jung later wrote:

I deplore the sins I have committed, because I am largely to blame for the high-flying hopes of my former patient [...] I imputed wishes and hopes entirely to her without seeing the same thing in myself [...] Caught in the delusion that I was the victim of the sexual wiles of my patient, I wrote to her mother.[13]

We are now familiar with this letter to the mother and, to a certain extent, with what followed.[14] Given that Jung's letter is akin to a confession to the father, as he himself puts it – a confession enacted by Sabina Spielrein – and implying a plea – addressed and sealed – that Freud maintain his love for him,[15] can we say that this letter gives a glimpse of the cutting edge of the relation to truth, of which Freud was to speak, in retrospect, in 1915?[16]

The love of transference, admitted or denied to varying degrees, sustains the analyst both in his role as interpreter and in the place from which he interprets, the two often becoming indistinguishable. We have only to see how analytic filiations are legitimated by this love to the point of obscuring its indissociable opposite. For the love of transference is always love of *Liebesubertragung (transference-love)* and rarely, to my knowledge, love of *transference-hate*, which undeniably also exists. "Judith loved Holopherne and had to kill him." It is Sabina Spielrein herself – whose name in German is

---

[11] Also in English.

[12] *The Freud / Jung Letters,* The Hogarth Press, London, 1974, p.230.

[13] Ibid, p. 236.

[14] J. Nobécourt et M. Guibal, *Sabina Spielrein, entre Freud et Jung*, Aubier, Paris, 1981.

[15] "That my patient and you (Freud) understand *my perfect honesty*". Much can be said about the use of a foreign language here.

[16] "[...] *dass die psychoanalytische Behandlung auf Wahrhaftigkeit aufgehaut ist*" (G.W. X, p.312), "that psychoanalytic treatment is based on veracity" (SE, 12, p. 164).

heard as the injunction to "play in the true tone"[17] – who reminds Freud of this, in reference to Jung.

Called upon to make a judgement, in the sense of a "slicing in two (*trancher*, in French)",[18] the father – in Jung's words – is careful not to pay a personal price in this affair. Without attempting to better understand the role of the stranger, of the Jewess, between the Christian and himself, Freud suggests Sabina to give up, to accept her losses, and to adopt the "endopsychic" solution: gather into her own psyche the feelings that survived, keep for herself this treasure of signifiers. This, until "the project of fighting the tyrant through a psychoanalysis with Freud" would take another form, namely that of marriage.

> Now I would like to contribute a word to your decision [...]. An analysis immediately after marriage would severely limit the rights of the man of whom you have said so much good. He must first try to find out to what extent he can cause you to be attached to him and make you forget old ideals. Only that which will elude him belongs to the domain of analysis.[19]

Either wise advice or judicious avoidance.

It might as well be said that on this occasion Freud thinks that transference-love consists of the love that eludes love. It would be an endless endeavour to untangle the Freudian paradoxes woven around this question that remains omphalic for psychoanalysis, since it clearly poses again the question of origins, indeed of the non-originary nature of the origins, and supposes nothing less than this: that the analytic relation is rooted in such an asocial, a-transferential, auto-analytic radicality that it can both untie all pre-existing bonds and untie itself.

Dreaded and desired, transference-love and transference-hate can only be tempered by a passion for the signifier. But this passion alone cannot guarantee the ethics of speech because, although it claims

---

[17] As Michel Guibal points out in "Les fils de la dissimulation", in *Sabina Spielrein, entre Freud et Jung*, op. cit.

[18] Or a '*tranche-fert*' as Derrida says, in "Du tout", *Cahiers Confrontation*, v.1, Paris, Aubier, 1979.

[19] Letter dated August 30, 1912, in *The Freud / Jung Letters*, op. cit., p.264.

to be totally true to the virtual expression in words of the enigmas of sexuality, the coming to light of the latter supposes a borderline locus of enactment: the place where the sexual reality of the unconscious is enacted in speech. It is at this limit that the determination of the subject, having crossed the interwoven desires of the analysand and the analyst, is deported out-of-place: into interpretation, where it is less a question of seeing oneself than, in fact, of *making* oneself heard, unerringly.

We must admit hypothetically that if Freud's remarks on transference-love only concern one specific situation, it might be because all the other can be brought down to this. Considering mainly the sphere of narcissism that shelters this love which eludes all love, transference-love concerns essentially the desire to be loved. And wanting to be loved – no doubt beyond love – is to want one's desire to be recognized at last. I am also speaking of the analyst whose desire resides just as naturally in the network of double affinities woven by the sexual and the signifier. Thus, the limit is located at the crossroads of transference-love and the love of transference, precisely where the subject of the unconscious opens and closes to the effect of the interplay (*interprêt*) of signifiers.

If, in the analytic space, it happens that the 'wanting to be loved by the one who wants to be loved' creates a mirror situation – double transference effect or effect of transference of the double – this situation is predicated, at the very least, upon the placing in reserve, if not the placing under guard (guardianship) of a signifier.

The Spielrein affair – as it is portrayed in the correspondence between Jung and Freud – is very instructive. As they are busy telling each other stories about the politics of the psychoanalytic movement and its fictional plot, Freud and Jung overlook their passion for signifiers. This is what allows the commentators of the French edition of the Spielrein file to present it as a "Freudian fiction" rather than an analytic story.

What does Sabina Spielrein have left to help her find the privileged signifier of what can sustain her desire? To take up this passion that transference has left pending, to perceive herself as being heard by the Other, and to inscribe these signifiers in the fiction that the story relates. Although fragmentary, the file found in the cellar of the Geneva Institute of Psychology shows that she pursued this task with some talent; fate intervened and erased the trace of it, along with her name in the history of psychoanalysis, her disappearance in Odessa during the Stalinist Purges, as well as the trace of her role in Jung's life and work.

> For over three months, I analysed everything: I retired to the countryside to try to preserve myself and my ideal; in the end, I spoke of it to one of my colleagues and showed him each one of his letters. As a result, I felt even more alone than before, because my lover could not be exonerated […]. This is why I resorted to the only life-raft left to me: to speak to the man who loves him deeply and who respects him […] Freud loves him! May he understand me!

As for Jung, two women played an essential role in his life: of course his mother, who was always considered a clairvoyant, a figure of the night who would disappear several months at a time for a stay in the hospital, when he was only three years old; and a black-haired servant girl who took care of him and belonged to him in some mysterious way. Jung had loved a young girl, a hysteric, dark-skinned, named S.W., who had herself called "the Jewess".

> Dr Jung and I were perfectly able to read each-other's thoughts. One day, in a state of great excitement, he gave me his diary and asked me to open it at random. When I opened it, I fell on the exact passage where he recounts how one night S.W. appeared before him dressed in white. This young girl was deeply entrenched in him, and she served as my prototype.

When Jung admits to her that he is experiencing a transfer of feelings to Freud's daughter, Sabina, Jewish like the latter, foresees that she and Freud would soon suffer the same fate in Jung's feelings.

> I tend to think that he has lured himself, she would write to Freud, and that he was seeking your protection and wanted your love. […] Now I would like my lover to have the courage to admit that, although he was attracted to Miss Freud, the roots of his love for me are to be found elsewhere. […] Who knows how can he explain that his libido was transferred from Miss

Freud to me? [...] No doubt, he and I are, like it or not, married to Professor Freud!

As far as the Spielreins are concerned, Sabina's mother feared falling in love with a Christian or being loved by one, since her father, because of his own father, had to give up his plan to marry the daughter of a Christian doctor. Inevitably, a Christian, a highly respected Saint Petersbourg doctor, fell in love with her. Since she could not marry him, he killed himself. Sabina's father was imposed by the grandparents because of his piety and his belief in predestination. Let us review the sequence from the beginning: Sabina's great-grandfather opposes his son's marriage to the daughter of a Christian doctor, and chooses a Jewish wife for him. The grandfather, in turn, forbids his daughter (Sabina's mother) to marry a Christian doctor, and designates a heretic to become her husband: figures that Sabina embodied in Jung and Freud.[20] It is in the context of this family story with multiple unfulfilled loves that Sabina conceives her erotic transference to Jung, the son of a priest, who confesses his attraction to Jewish women, particularly black-haired ones.

> He had two daughters and, inside him, the outline of a little boy, which my unconscious recognized in its *premonitory dreams*.

This imaginary child would become a solid certainty. He would be called Siegfried. His name had always been Siegfried. Since the father or the grandfather had so often repeated in dreams: "A great destiny awaits you, my child", the name of the Wagnerian hero was associated with the idea of passion and anarchy. But the signifiers of the name Siegfried are also tied to Jung's and Freud's privileged representations. So much so that the analytic relation between Jung and Sabina Spielrein is built on real connections by thought transference.

---

[20] See *Sur ce nom-là*, by Jacques Nobécourt, in *Sabina Spielrein, entre Freud et Jung*, op. cit.

Our souls were very close for a long time; for instance, we never discussed Wagner, and then one day I came to him and started to describe what differentiates Wagner from the composers before him, explaining that his music is profoundly psychological: the same sentimental tonality is accompanied at once by the same melody; and just like an emotional tone connected with the same memory is at first uncertain in the depths where it lies buried, in Wagner's music the melody is at first barely distinguishable from other tonalities, only to emerge later in all its clarity, before being transformed finally and blending in again with all the others. [...] Dr. Jung had tears in his eyes: "I will show you, he said, that I was just writing the same thing".

For what concerns Freud's Siegfried – indissociable from the Sieg/mund too amply commented upon to need further discussion here, its early evocation in *The Interpretation of Dreams* indicates the weak point – the umbilical point – around which a whole language structure is woven.

For Sabina, this "Siegfried" was becoming a *problem* – the very heart of the problem – to which solutions could be found at different levels. But these solutions were not all independent from transference modalities. First, the solution took the form of a veritable child made believable by Jung's response to Sabina's transference. Disregarding this possibility would have been a resistance to what was producing, between them, reciprocal signifiers to be interpreted. However, this does not mean that the effects of interpretation had, for the subject, such a value of truth that they deformed reality. What emerged in this situation was the non-relation to the truth, or the analyst's hate of transference.

This is no doubt what Freud, who had never been analysed himself, had difficulty recognizing: that the analyst could inflict such a narcissistic wound. This is what Sabina keeps testifying, while trying to preserve Jung as an object of love. Freud can only reply: "I imagine that you still love Dr Jung so deeply because you have not brought to light the hate you bear him". As far as the *real Siegfried* is concerned:

Of course, I wish that you could discard like useless clutter the infantile ideal of the Teutonic hero and knight, which disguises all your opposition to your milieu and your origins; and I hope that you do not expect this misleading image to provide you with the child that originally you no doubt wanted your father to give you.

In fact, it was a matter of submission, of subjection to an unrealized desire that nevertheless transmitted through generations as the signifier of an ideal child. Freud takes a stand, as always, on the side of the word of the father.

Thus, Sabina had to deplete the "Siegfried" complex of its energy, as she herself says, in order to put this energy to another use and create a sublimated version of "Siegfried".

Echoing with profound irony the solutions suggested, Sabina replies that her problem could have found a solution in a "symbolic Aryan-Semitic child, the fruit, for instance, of the union of Jung's doctrine with that of Freud".

Writing to Jung, Sabina says:

This is how, as you were saying, you killed the *real Siegfried* (proof that you also had a 'real' one). [...] I, on the contrary, killed in my dreams the man who should have been his father, to replace him later, in reality, with another one.

For Jung, "Siegfried" had become the symbol of a heroic disposition. For Freud, the "Siegfried" fantasy represented merely the accomplishment of an infantile desire. For Sabina, "Siegfried" was in turn: a book project, a series of dreams, and a piece of music. And later, it was also an insistent question: how to discern, in analysis, an indication as to whether Siegfried should be an ideal or a real child?

During her pregnancy, she had almost lost her daughter after having a violent dream on Siegfried. There is only one way to discard a psychic content, she would say, and that is to destroy it. She named her daughter Renata.

We know nothing about Renata Scheftel who lived, and perhaps still lives, on the Black Sea coast, in Odessa: neither if "she came into her own" as Freud wished for her, nor if she made her own the legend of the blond Siegfried.

Sabina's story seems so strange that it is easy to believe that what is considered reality could be pure fiction, in the context of the scene where the real of the unconscious comes into play.

The story of Frau Anna G. is completely different. This twenty nine year old woman consulted a Viennese analyst in the fall of 1919, because for the preceding four years she had experienced severe pain in her left breast and in the pelvic area. These symptoms were associated with a chronic respiratory ailment.

Second child and only daughter of a father who came from a Jewish family in Russia, and of a mother who came from a Polish Catholic family established in Ukraine, Anna had a happy childhood in the pleasant port of Odessa. Her father had a luxurious yacht and every summer, along with the prospect of excursions at sea, Anna enjoyed the visit of her uncle and aunt. The latter, her mother's twin, had married a languages professor in Vienna. She herself was a very talented pianist and, doubtless because she had no children of her own, showered great affection upon her niece. Later, when Anna separated from her husband, she went in Vienna to live with her aunt.

Anna's happy childhood years came to an end when she was five. A terrible accident put an end to the idyllic family life she had known. Her mother, who used to break the monotony of winter by making brief trips to Moscow, always returning with armfuls of gifts, did not return that year, or ever again. It was shortly before Christmas. A telegram arrived to announce that she had died in a fire at the hotel where she was staying.

Overwhelmed by pain, her father buried himself in his work. Anna was left to the care of her nanny and her governess. The uncle and aunt no longer visited them. By a tragic twist of faith, Anna's uncle died shortly afterwards from a heart attack. Neither her father nor her aunt ever remarried and, a part from a scant exchange of letters, they practically lost touch.

Motherless, abandoned by her uncle and aunt (as it must have seemed to her), abandoned by her father who showed only indifference (except toward his son), thanks to the affection of her governess Anna was nevertheless able to learn several languages and to develop her musical talents.

At the age of fifteen, an unpleasant incident deeply affected her. She had ventured onto the port with two friends to watch a political demonstration that turned violent. Because of the elegant clothes they wore, the three girls were insulted and threatened by a group of demonstrators. The girls were frightened, but suffered no actual harm. What affected Anna the most was her father's attitude when she returned home. Instead of comforting her, he coldly blamed her for having exposed herself to danger. After this event, she treated her father with coldness and reserve. Shortly afterwards, she left Odessa for Saint Petersburg. There, she took dance classes and quickly gained the affection of one of her teachers, a young widow who invited Anna to live with her. Mrs. R. became her mentor as well as her friend.

The ease and comfort of this situation came to an end when Mrs. R. suddenly decided to remarry. The man in question became a good friend of them both, and Anna did not suspect that a special bond could threaten the serenity of their shared existence. Of course, she could only be glad that Mrs. R. encountered happiness. Although Mrs. R. and her new husband insisted that she continued to live with them, Anna did not want to interfere in the life of the couple in any way. It was then that she received a letter from her aunt announcing the death of Anna's grandfather, who had been living with Anna's aunt for several years. She was alone again, and was inviting her niece to live with her.

When she saw her aunt again, Anna felt a strange mixture of happiness and sadness.

Her first impression was that she was being greeted by her mother who, had she lived, would have been the same age and would have indubitably looked the same. The two women were, in fact, identical twins. At the same time, the aunt was struck to see in Anna the acute sensibility and sharp intelligence her sister had in her twenties.

Encouraged by a friend of her aunt, the young woman quickly became a master cellist, member of a professional Viennese orchestra, and she became engaged with a young lawyer she had met at the Conservatory.

The only cloud on the horizon, for the young couple, was the rumour that war was imminent. When the hostilities began, the husband was luckily assigned to a combat unit stationed near the city, so that he knew he could make regular visits home.

The day before her husband's first leave, Anna was sized again with shortness of breath and pain in her breast and abdomen. She lost her appetite and had to stop playing music. She informed her husband that she had fallen ill and that she knew she could never make him happy. Therefore, she returned to her aunt's. Despite her husband's pleas, she remained steadfast in her decision, pleading her husband to forgive her.

This was the patient's history when she went to seek psycho-analysis. While Sabina's love story is predicated on the persistence of a kind of foreign body in her head, that she struggles to extract with all her might, the story of the unfortunate Frau Anna hides under its transparency the secret of an enigma to be deciphered.

For several weeks, Anna's analysis seemed to be at a standstill. Although she was not a prude, the young woman was very reluctant to discuss her past or present sexual feelings. She often denied them categorically or remained silent. Experience has shown that the patient's silence usually indicates thoughts concerning the analyst. For example, when Anna recounted her meeting with a Saint Petersburg student, she spoke in the most neutral terms except for her insistence that it had been a "white" (platonic) relationship. This adjective attracted the analyst's attention. When he asked Anna what associations came to her mind, she spoke of the white sails of a yacht: which could be related to childhood memories of time spent with her father. She said she was thinking of a week-end at sea with this student and other friends. She had been very much in love with him, but their relation had not gone beyond mutual affection; their souls had remained as white as the sails in Odessa or the nights in Saint Petersburg.

What might have appeared as a lack of honesty, and could have irritated the analyst, testified instead to a transference-love that had to remain pure: the situation could facilitate the search for a signifying thread in her discourse and her history, without an explosion of feelings that risked distracting attention, but with the advantage of granting the analyst the latitude for any interpretation he might be tempted to inscribe on the white page. Once this situation rose, the question remained as to whom, in this configuration, had to be cleansed of all suspicion.

The analyst suggested that in Saint Petersburg she must have had an affair. She admitted this, saying that she eventually "gave" in to the student's repeated insistence. The use of this verb suggested, in turn, that she had even become pregnant and lost the child. She specified that this happened as a result of a bad fall at the dance studio, and wondered how the analyst could have guessed this secret. Afterwards, she seemed relieved to have shed an unreal perfection. Not without humour, she said that she felt like if she had been in a free fall.[21] A few days later, she recounted the following dream:

> I was travelling by train and found myself seated across from a man who was reading. He started a conversation and I felt his tone was becoming too familiar. The train stopped in a station in the middle of the countryside and I decided to get off, to get rid of him. I was surprised to see many other people getting off the train as well, in this deserted place. But the panels on the platform said Budapest. I threaded my way stealthily through the crowd to avoid the ticket inspector, since I didn't want him to see that I was supposed to continue on farther. I crossed a bridge and found myself in front of a house bearing the number 29. I tried to open the door with my key but, to my surprise, the door did not open. I continued on to number 34. Although my key did not turn in the lock, the door opened. It was a small hotel. There was a silver-handled umbrella drying in the hall, and I thought: "my mother is staying here". I went into a white room. A rather aged gentleman appeared and told me: "the house is empty". I took a telegram out of my coat pocket and gave it to him. I felt sorry for him because I knew what was in the telegram. His voice filled with pain, and he said: "My daughter is dead". He was so distressed that I had the impression that I no longer existed for him.

---

[21] She used the verb "*niederkommen*", suggesting either "falling" or "giving birth". But about her deep secret she remained totally "unforthcoming".

The first number in the patient's dream corresponded to her age, and the second to the age of her brother, who was five years older. The desire to have been the boy in the family was quite clear, but it also implied the desire to have stayed near her father, as her brother had done. The latter had visited her recently in Vienna, with his wife and two children. The situation in Russia had made them decide to immigrate to the United States. Naturally, Anna was thinking about her father, who was now alone in his old age. In the dream, he was, at last, distressed by the news of his daughter's death, while in fact he expressed only the most conventional regret when she left home.

Several elements of the dream remained unexplained, including those at the beginning of the dream. Anna did remember a train trip during which a young man showed vivid interest in her, but this memory did not really contribute anything significant. The analyst asked himself if she found his remarks about her affair in Saint Petersburg too familiar, and was secretly planning to stop the analysis in order not to go any further. This would leave the door open to another interpretation of the dream's ending. Perhaps she perceived that her analyst might have been suffering for personal reasons, and that she no longer existed for him.

Lost in these considerations, he was surprised to hear that his patient had suddenly recalled a forgotten fragment of the dream:

> I was telling the man on the train that I was going to Moscow to visit the T. family; he replied that they would have no room for me and that I would have to sleep in the summer house. It would be very hot, he added, and I would have to undress.

The T.s were distant relatives on her mother's side, who had kept affectionate ties with her aunt and her mother, but whom she did not know personally. The analyst interpreted this additional part of the dream as a nostalgic desire to return to the lost paradise of her childhood. She agreed with this, and they remained at a considerable distance from what was devouring her.

The analyst had just suffered the tragic loss of one of his daughters, who was only twenty-six and mother of two young children. But during the previous hour he had been able to do what was needed to insure that *la séance continue*.[22] The patient had decided to make a trip to Bad Gastein[23] with her aunt, and wrote him from there:

> I was troubled and distressed by the element of prediction contained in my dream. I would not mention it if I was not sure that you were aware of it yourself. I was already half convinced that the man who receives the telegram in my dream is you (at least in part), but I was afraid of tormenting you unnecessarily. [...] I have always thought that, in addition to my other infirmities, I am afflicted with what is called double vision.[24]

Anna returned from Gastein in a veritable state of exaltation. With joviality and exuberance, she held a dream monologue as if she was in a hypnotic trance. She brought her Gastein diary, which testified to feverish literary activity and unrestrained imagination. This was in sharp contrast with her guarded manner of speaking during the sessions. A poem called "Don Juan" began with these lines:

> I dreamed of a love affair
> With his son, in a train, somewhere
> In the darkness of a gloomy tunnel,
> His hand had slipped under my dress, between my tights,
> I was breathless. He took me to a white hotel on the edge of a lake. [...]

It would be indecent to reproduce the rest. Her fantasy involved the son of the analyst – whom she had never met, needless to say – with whom she indulged in every possible erotic dalliance. This clearly expressed her desire to take the place of the deceased sister (which one?). Certainly, the white hotel represented her mother's body. She insisted:

> The white hotel is the place where we were. Crowds of people were staying in this hotel, horrible, selfish people who would willingly have

[22] In French in the manuscript.

[23] Resort in the Austrian Alps, frequented also by her analyst.

[24] It would be useful at some point to examine this question of the dream and telepathy [note in the margin of the original manuscript].

continued to write their postcards even if the hotel was on fire, provided the fire did not affect them […]

The contents of the patient's diary were striking in that they provided a wealth of details concerning her sexual fantasies. Considering that her sex life was comprised of a brief affair at the age of eighteen, and of a few months of married life, it is easy to understand that her ardour could only find expression in imaginings or in her symptoms.

Since her return from Gastein, Anna was free of her physical suffering, at least to some extent, and it was possible to take advantage of this reprieve to explore more fully the truth about her intimate life that, as it turned out, had been a real nightmare from the start of her marriage. The disasters described in her diary returned in the form of hallucinations each time she had sexual relations: the house caught fire, she was pushed from a cliff into the void, or else there was an earthquake. She now dreaded even caresses, which she used to like, because they foreshadowed these hallucinations. Moreover, she interpreted these terrifying visions as the unquestionable sign that she should not have children. All this could explain the fact that her relationships with men had always been short-lived, and that she only had stable relations with women.

However, was this enough to deduce that this was her way of perpetuating her relation to her mother, and that it was only from her – or from Mrs. R. – that she could have accepted a child? Anna persistently denied this interpretation. Of course, she had (no doubt unjustly) accused the Saint Petersburg student of being in love with another girl whose presence she could have hallucinated when they were in bed together. She blamed this jealousy – or interest? – on a memory in which, at the age of four, she might have seen – but she was not sure – her uncle and her mother exchange a passionate kiss, alone in the garden. In retrospect, she felt that the gifts her mother brought back from Moscow were proof of her guilt. In fact, she did not believe that her mother went to Moscow. Her uncle probably arranged to meet her somewhere between Vienna and Odessa, no doubt in Budapest, where he was a professor of languages. Anna even reinterpreted the mockery of the sailors, when she was fifteen, as saying that everyone knew her mother had died in the arms of her lover in Budapest. This left her free to imagine that perhaps her uncle had not died a few months after her mother, but that this story was invented by her father and her aunt to prevent gossip. Naturally, she had never questioned her aunt about this, not wanting to awaken her sorrow.

Frau Anna certainly sensed that her analyst doubted that these suppositions could have any foundation, and that he felt they were more closely tied to fantasy than to reality. This did not exclude, in the mind of the analyst, the possibility that unconscious guilt tied to her mother's death, aside from explaining her father's coldness, might have been keeping alive an infantile desire that the person who gave birth to her should give her a child, placing her in a position identical to that of her mother, and making her the sister of her own daughter.

On her last session, Anna brought two photographs that she showed somewhat triumphantly to her analyst: one, in tones of sepia, showed her mother's tomb; the other, more recent, showed that of her uncle. After a long search, Anna had found the cemetery where he was buried. There is always an element of surprise in this type of situation, where what was strange for the patient becomes familiar to her, and what was familiar to the analyst becomes strange to him. The same date was inscribed on both tombs.[25]

The reader might have guessed by now that Anna's analyst was none other than Freud himself. The 1931 manuscript bears a footnote specifying that the author had dedicated the account of this case to his own mother, who died on September 12th, 1930. This text – condensed here to its essential content – was to be published by the organisers of the Goethe Award, following a homage to Freud for his literary talent, at least according to the person who provided us with the unabridged text. These circumstances explain the paragraph attached to the text:

---

[25] This being so, Anna inevitably asked herself if her father's coldness, after her mother's death, was caused by the legitimate doubt he might have had as to his daughter's paternity. Anna's interest in foreign languages could possibly find its source here.

On this occasion, I thought it appropriate to contribute the account of a case where reason and imagination become partners in the search for the truth, as they were in the mind and heart of the genius we are honouring. In fact, I believe that Goethe would not have been surprised to learn that in the domain of the libido, what is most high and what is most low are intimately linked and, in a certain way, depend on each other: "From Heaven, through the world, right down to Hell."

Of course, it is obvious that the entire account is literary fiction.[26] In this I include the diary, correspondence, and other documents – of which I used only a portion, modified as is befitting, by the interjection and projections of my own interpretations in the text. The author attempts, with a mastery inadequately brought to light here, to reproduce the style of narration of Freudian cases, and the force of conviction inherent to this style. He sees these as having to be counted among the most important phenomena of 20th century consciousness. At the same time, he displays extensive knowledge of Freud's work and of various known letter exchanges. And he even shows knowledge of unknown exchanges, unless he is dabbling in divination. For instance, in the letters exchanged between Frau Anna and Freud after the analysis (regarding the publication of her case), D.M. Thomas attributes it to Freud to have lent Anna telepathic knowledge of a tragic event that took place in Budapest in 1919, an event known only to Freud and one or two of his closest colleagues: the day when Ferenczi finally married the woman he courted for eight years, and who did not want to divorce her husband before her daughters were married, was the very day when the husband died. I was able to confirm this by examining the *unpublished* correspondence between Freud and Ferenczi.[27] Naturally, by corroborating these facts,

---

[26] Thomas, 1981, p.104. I am grateful to Octave Mannoni for bringing the book to my attention as soon as it was published.

[27] This correspondence was still unpublished when the present text was written in 1982; it has been published afterwards (Paris, 1992-2000). It must be added that Ferenczi loved not only Gizella Palos, but also one of her daughters, Elma, who was in analysis alternately with him and with Freud. In other spheres of activity, such a situation might have a merely anecdotal value. But in psychoanalysis, given the transference-generated filiations of the analysts, this truth-fiction relation in the story has incalculable consequences sometimes translating into *telepathy* over several generations.

I find myself in the same position vis-à-vis the incredulous reader as Anna (which one?) vis-à-vis Freud.

My interest in this fiction[28] is sparked by Thomas's implicit theoretical position. His position concerning transference is founded on two principles: that the interchange of signifiers is constitutive of transference, and that transference is linked to thought transference.

The first principle governs the veracity of the relation to truth. The revelation of the analysand's unconscious knowledge is subjected to a process involving the unconscious discourse of the analyst in its sexual reality. This supposes an intermediary space where the collusion between the knowledge of the one and the discourse of the other are dis-placed in relation to the Discourse of Truth: a discourse drawing on an infinite reserve of signifiers, compared to which any other discourse is always lacking. The misadventures of transference-love as they relate to the love of transference represent moments of immobilisation of a process made of continuous projections and introjections. These moments, which show how the object comes to be constituted, also show how the signifier can stick to the skin, adhere to the voice or to the gaze. Sabina Spielrein's diary and letters before her marriage testify to this. The same adhesion does not take place in Frau Anna's correspondence. Its absence elevates Thomas's fiction to the level of "analytic truth". In this process, the identification of the signifiers in the enigmas of sexuality justifiably intersect with fantasies of desire belonging to two unconscious discourses. This highlights the relation of the subjects to the truth at stake (hence to subterfuge), which the analytic function guarantees, being itself the scene where this truth is put on trial. The interchange (*inter-prêt*) of signifiers is constitutive of transference inasmuch as it maintains the subject in a relation of non-relation to these signifiers. It is the subject who transposes himself into the other, to hear from this other place what he is not saying; in other words, to hear himself there.

---

[28] Here, the fiction is given an extra turn by changing the position of the narrator. Thomas has Freud tell the story in the first person, and I retell the same story in the third person while interpreting it.

The relation of transference to thought transference, on the other hand, concerns the subject's relation to knowledge. While the *word play* (*double hearing*) is the necessary condition for the knowledge of the unconscious, the language of transference, like a noise in communication, disrupts this knowledge and, at the same time, brings an element of order to it. This language presumes that the communication of unconscious knowledge can be established through *double vision*; which would lead us to think that in addition to the unconscious logic that advances from experiences to axioms, in the psychoanalytic field there exists a modality of knowing thanks to which a psychic action in one individual can induce the same psychic action in another. This would then suppose that between these two actions a physical process is created, in which each of the two psychic actions is in turn transformed.[29] In such a case, we would be dealing with knowledge of thoughts or events through the intermediary of something resembling a foreign object in the head, which occupies the psychic space.

It must be apparent to the reader that the element of telepathic knowledge in Frau Anna's dream *overshadows* transference-love by introducing thought transferences imbued with *a passion for the signifier*, while *the analyst's* love of erotic transference temporarily suspends Sabina's search for essential signifiers whose working through alone makes love limitless.

Is it not profoundly strange to have to conclude that love shared in the analytic situation can only be an *agent provocateur* that disturbs the veracity of the subject's relation to truth?

Translated from the French by Agnès Jacob

---

[29] This is what Freud calls the telepathic process (see "Dreams and the Occult", 1933). Patrick Miller and myself developed the concept of foreign object in the head (referring both to transference and the telepathic nucleus of the dream, and to telepathy in psychoanalysis), in "Empathy, Antipathy and Telepathy in the Analytic Process", in *Psychoanalytic Inquiry*, Int. Univ. Press, 1982, vol. I, 3.

Bibliography

Derrida, J., "Du tout", *Cahiers Confrontation*, v.1, Paris : Aubier, 1979

Freud, S.:
- *Observations On Transference-Love* [1914/1915], *GW*, 10; *SE*, 12, pp. 159-169
- *The Question of Lay Analysis* [1926], *GW*, 14; *SE*, 20, pp. 209-292
- *Dreams and the Occult*, *GW*, 15; *SE*, 22, pp. 31-53; oe 1933

The Freud / Jung Letters, London: Hogarth Press, 1974

Sigmund Freud, Sándor Ferenczi Correspondance, Paris: Calmann-Lévy, 1992-2000;

The correspondence of Sigmund Freud and Sándor Ferenczi, Cambridge: Harvard University Press, 1994-2000

Major, R., Miller, P., "Empathy, Antipathy and Telepathy in the Analytic Process", *Psychoanalytic Inquiry*, New York: International University Press, 1982, vol. I, 3.

Nobécourt, J., Guibal, M., *Sabina Spielrein, entre Freud et Jung*, Paris: Aubier, 1981

Thomas, D. M., *The White Hotel*, London: Victor Gollancz Ltd., 1981

Evolution in the Clinical Use of Counter-Transference

Fabiano Bassi

Keywords: Counter-transference – Intersubjectivism – Theory Technique

Summary: *The author traces the development of the concept of counter-transference in psychotherapeutic theory technique and attempts to highlight the theoretical motivations, beginning from Freud and continuing with the schools of thought that came after him, underlying the modifications and extensions suggested to "correct" the very nature of the conceptualization of counter-transference. The second part of the article reviews the points of view of two contemporary authors, Jacobs and Renik, who in their own distinctive ways and with different stresses, have actively put forward innovative points of view for the understanding of this concept. An assessment on Renik's positions brings the author to his own considerations on the intersubjective point of view, which has strongly asserted itself in recent years.*

In the ever-changing theoretical landscape of clinical psychotherapy counter-transference is probably the one concept that has undergone the most changes. Initially considered the main obstacle to conducting a correct psychotherapy, counter-transference, even if through a series of rather controversial phases, has more and more taken on the aspects of a tool crucial to understanding the patient. The history of the evolution of its use is also a summary of the history and evolution of the theory and technique of clinical psycho-therapy: reconstructing it is an opportunity to review many of the most important turning points that have occurred in the conceptualizations that have been emerging in our discipline over the last century or so and to see particularly clearly how the vision of psychotherapy as a unipersonal experience has been gradually replaced by a bipersonal model.

   This article intends first of all to describe concisely the development of countertransference in psychotherapeutic theory and technique, attempting to bring to the foreground the theoretical motivations behind the various re-propositions as expressed by the several authors of the different schools;[1] secondly I shall introduce recent contributions by two north American authors who, in their own distinct ways and with differing degrees of radicalness, have recently tried to develop a further evolution of countertransference.

   I also bring to the reader's attention that, following Friedman (1988), I shall always refer to "psychotherapy" to mean both "psychoanalytically oriented psychotherapies" and "psychoanalysis": I shall not go into the details of this choice, which derives from my feeling that any attempt to draw a clear boundary between psycho-analytically oriented therapies and psychoanalysis is impossible (and artificial), in these pages for obvious problems of space. Another author whose thinking perfectly sums up my own position is Wallerstein (1989), to whom I refer the reader who wants a fully exhaustive examination of this point.

From Freud to the '70s

Freud came upon the phenomenon of countertransference in the early 1910s, at a time when the propulsive force of his progresses in defining the technical aspects of his psychotherapy were proceeding with the fullest intensity. In the same years Freud started to become aware of the huge potentials of the creature he had just conceived and his main concern became to arrange as rigidly as possible the technical dictates at the basis of his therapy. Both in his personal practice and, even more amazingly, in that of his top followers, Freud had seen the high risk of the insurgence in the doctor patient relation of phenomena that could escape the therapist's control: his experience with Dora's case (1905) had introduced him dramatically to the transference phenomenon, which

---

[1]An excellent text for a very exhaustive assessment of the concept of countertransference is the not so recent volume edited by Albarella and Donadio (1986), which collects a series of classical crucial contributions on this aspect of technique theory.

he had initially considered a lethal factor for the economy of treatment (and the cause of young Dora's abrupt and unidirectional abandonment of therapy), but then quickly reintroduced to the set of potentially useful medical tools and thus, in a few words, raised to the status of key element for the progress of any therapy.

With regard to countertransference Freud moves in the same way: in describing it for the first time (in his contribution to the Second Congress of Psychoanalysis, held in Nuremberg in 1910), he talks about it as a new obstacle to the healthy conduct of treatment. Being a reaction of the therapist's to something that has been evoked within him by the transference emanating from the patient (thus the choice of the term *Gegenübertragung*, with the preposition *gegen*, "against", to identify the clear cut counterposition between transference and this new concept), countertransference stirs inside the doctor a storm of unconscious feelings that risk clouding his vision, making it impossible for him to read the motions occurring in the patient. Countertransference, moreover, may be responsible for those "blind spots" in the therapist, i.e. those areas where an unsolved conflict in the therapist colludes with a similar difficulty in the patient, preventing both from registering what happens behind that area of functioning.

The only way to ward off the terrible effects of counter-transference is self-analysis. But at the Nuremberg Congress, Freud, in the wake of the danger found in the failures countertransference may have on the inexperienced therapist, following the advice of Jung (the real rising star of the 1910 Congress), came up with the idea of introducing a training analysis as a requirement for anyone wishing to become a professional psychotherapist. This training analysis was to be managed by the newly set-up International Psychoanalytical Association.

However, in a paper written not much later, Freud (1912) makes a small opening in favor of countertransference: while insisting on the founded danger that it may be responsible for those black spots in the practician, Freud also stresses that counter-transference may be used as a useful tool allowing the therapist to tune his unconscious to that of the patient (here Freud uses the famous metaphor of the therapist's unconscious as a telephone receiver of the patient's unconscious), thus improving his knowledge of the patient's inner world. It seems to me that it is important to remember that this paper, "Advice to the practician in psychoanalytic treatment", is one of the Freudian texts that is more markedly characterized by an "indoctrinating" intent, having, amongst its more explicit aims (and this is a feature of all of Freud's technical works), that of functioning as a sort of list of "don'ts" in analytic treatment rather than as an actual technical text book.[2] But despite this important concession, Freud was never to further develop the potentials of countertransference, which was never to enjoy, in Freud's writings, the same triumphant destiny as the evolution of transference, elected with honors by Freud to the status of highly valuable technical tool for optimal treatment. In Freud's works, therefore, countertransference holds an ambiguous position, seen at once as a lethal danger to be wary of, *but also* as a potential tool. As we know, after drawing up several papers on technique between 1912 and 1915 (which he meant as chapters to an actual volume on technique, which never saw the light), Freud practically never dealt with technical theory again in the nearly twenty-five years he was to live. Thus, at the time of his death, countertransference was left in this ambiguous position.

Followers of Anna Freud and of Melanie Klein were to fight over Freud's heritage with riotous disputes. The former, prevailing in North America, were to form the school known as Ego Psychology, which had (and in part still has) its strongholds in the Psychoanalytic Institutes of New York and Boston and in Hartmann and Rapaport at first, and in Brenner and Arlow later, the most diehard *defensores fidei* of the purity of Freudian thinking. The almost paralyzing strictness of Ego Psychology in its entirely political attempt to defend the power of the Freudian tradition was, as from the '40s, to drive the authors of this school (and the teachers of the Institutes that drew their inspiration from it) to propagate a theory of psycho-therapeutic technique completely stuck on the primacy of the triad based on the anonymity of the therapist, neutrality and abstinence.

[2] Friedman, 1994.

The uncritical adherence to this absolute *Trimurti* has produced results that would be grotesque, if only they weren't so tragic: therapists who refused to shake hands at the beginning or end of a session so as not to communicate anything of themselves through their grip, therapists who practiced in totally bare rooms to avoid transmitting their personality with their choice of furnishings, therapists who would not say a single word to their patients session after session and would indicate the end of the session by standing up, but still without uttering a single word (Jacobs, personal communication), therapists who would let their own houses be burgled, even though they heard noises coming from the nearby rooms, to avoid interfering with their patients' free associations (Lai, personal communication). In the precepts of Ego Psychology technique and theory, the emergence of counter-transference is *always* the symptom of something wrong with the therapists, who are then called on to work on these interferences self-analytically and, when they are not able to solve them, are asked to undergo a fresh period of personal analysis. The same goes if therapists find themselves constantly thinking about their patients outside sessions or dreaming about them: indeed, in cases like this the "counter-transference disease" is considered particularly serious.

Somehow surprisingly, it seems that the followers of Melanie Klein were the first to be responsible for the healthy rehabilitation of the concept of countertransference, largely on the wave of their interest in phenomena related to introjection, projection and projective identification, for the understanding of which countertransference seems potentially to be the most efficient tool the therapist has. The article destined to make history as the manifesto for the recovery of the importance of countertransference was written by Paula Heimann (one of Klein's pupils and patients) in 1950. In this contribution Heimann emphasizes the role of therapists' feelings in understanding their patients: she thought that too often therapists allow their tendency towards "reason" to prevail as far as the materials provided by their patients are concerned, instead of leaving their emotional perceptions to act freely, and when this happens their understanding of patients will prove heavily penalized.

From this point of view countertransference then rises to a fundamental role as a both a diagnostic and therapeutic tool and is at last put back in a prominent and central position. In a way, however, with her intuition Heimann echoes Freud's invitation to the therapists never to give up an attitude of "freely fluctuating attention", which he found to be the optimal state of mind to allow the doctor to capture the widest possible range of contents offered by patients: indeed, the way Heimann would have liked to see countertransference being used echoes the attitude of freely fluctuating attention already precisely indicated by Freud.

Another author, who operated a few years later and who has given an essential contribution to the progress of the concept and use of countertransference in clinical psychotherapy, comes from the ranks of the Kleinian analysts: Heinrich Racker, a therapist operating in Argentina, trained with the Kleinian school, but who ended up developing positions not entirely standardized to this school's beliefs. In his classic contribution, Racker[3] distinguished himself as the first author to connect back the fundamental conspiracy of silence reserved by psychoanalytical literature to the issue of countertransference to a precise, so to speak, political intention. That is to say, the intention to leave the "myth of the impersonal analyst" intact, the myth, in other words, of the therapist's neutrality. Racker felt ready to hypothesize that the therapeutic relation should no longer have been understood as an intrinsically unbalanced relationship between a healthy person (the therapist) and a sick one (the patient), but preferred to interpret it as a common effort in which both participate with their personal contribution. With this premise it was a short step to introducing a broader conceptualization of the phenomenon: countertransference, therefore, was no longer considered something brought about by the patient's transference, something that in a normal situation the therapist ought not to have, not to experience, but became the therapist's normal transference towards the patient, within a perfectly specular situation to the one that inevitably leads the patient to have a normal transference with the therapist.

[3] Racker, 1957.

Dealt with within these terms, countertransference turns more and more into a tool of unequalled importance to achieve progress and success in the therapeutic enterprise: far from considering any of the therapist's possible countertransferential "deviations" an obstacle or an element of confusion, or in any case an impediment to therapeutic progress, Racker sees in the so-called "countertransference neurosis" a compelling useful phenomenon to help therapists find their way among the twists and turns of the internal world patients present to them, laying the foundations for the definition of the phenomenon that Jacobs would later systemize, giving shape to the concept of "countertransferential enactment". In his description of how the contribution of countertransference can lead to success in the therapeutic process, Racker is so precise that he even defines two modes of countertransferential response, which when spotted can help therapists clarify their vision of the current state of their relationship with a patient. Indeed, there are two types of counter-transference: "concordant countertransference" (a situation where, in their countertransference, therapists move in unison with the movement described by the patient, thus maximizing their understanding of and sharing in the patient's internal world) and "complementary countertransference" (where therapists find them-selves resounding with the position of the object the patient is describing instead of with the position of the patient, in a situation where therapists receive a clear and explicit signal of temporary disgregation of their tuning into the patient and of their unlawful distancing from it).[4]

We're now in the height of the sixties and, as can be seen from my story so far, the contribution of Northern American psychotherapy to

---

[4] I shall put forward a very simple clinical example to further clarify these concepts. The patient comes into the consulting room and starts inundating the therapist with stories of how aggressive and unfair his boss is with him, never forgiving the slightest mistake and always trying to undermine him at every opportunity. When concordant countertransference prevails, the therapist will immediately share in the patient's sense of frustration and injustice and put it immediately into perspective. When complementary countertransference prevails, on the other hand, the therapist will find him/herself thinking that the boss must have his good reasons for treating such a heavy and boring person, as the patient can often come across as, in this way, and so on. The importance of the therapist's ability to recognize these two forms of countertransference as far as diagnosis is concerned, is clear, as well as its connection with the progress of the therapy.

the progress of the use of countertransference is still practically non-existent, despite the fact that the supremacy of classical psychoanalysis had already been put into question, for example by Gill's suggestion to find and place side to side to psychoanalysis an expressive psycho-therapy considering three modes of treatment, both to be considered as placed on a *continuum* and differentiated only by their gradient of "analytical purity" (basically, use of transference and interpretation of resistance). The first fundamental North American contribution to broadening the concept of counter-transference, even if so guiltily belated, can, I think, be found in the work of Kohut and Ego psychology, which, though it doesn't deal with counter-transference directly, assigns to it (or rather, reassigns) a central role in the theory of empathy technique. I stress "reassigns" because, in fact, the idea that among the therapeutic factors of psychotherapy, together with the intellectual component represented by interpretation, one should include, in a role of equal importance, the component of attachment to the therapist, i.e. the relation component, was already present in Freud (see, for example, 1913). Therefore, with his centralization of empathy (and what derives from it in terms of countertransference) as a principal therapeutic factor, Kohut merely reemphasizes an element the preeminence of which, already unequivocally defined by Freud, had been roughly cancelled, specially by Ego psychology.

As we know, Kohut has never put his thinking down on paper in a systematic way. What writings we do have are in fact collections of scattered contributions put together merely for publishing interests and are mainly theoretical in content. It would be in vain to try and find in any of his works direct considerations on theory of technique, with the partial exception of his famous text on the analysis of Mr. Z., where Kohut (1979), taking advantage of the rhetorical instrument of the tale told to another, tells us the story of his personal analysis and his subsequent self-analysis, carried out following the dictates of the developing Self-Psychology. It is, however, quite possible to deduce from his works the technical considerations that derive from his thinking, a task which various authors (e.g. Ornstein, 1979) have taken upon themselves. How does theory of technique then change in the light of contributions coming from Self Psychology? It changes because of how it promotes empathy[5] to the position of core technical element of any psychotherapy. Empathy alone, Self Psychology upholds, can help the therapist catch that part of patients' mental content, that is to say their feelings and needs, which remain largely unconscious: by employing the method of empathic understanding therapists use themselves as a responsive instrument capable of reflecting patients' emotions and needs. The empathic approach to the patient (which we could translate as counter-transferential attitude asked of the therapist) consists in a prolonged empathic immersion in the relation and is certainly not resolved in the mechanical automatic presentation to the patient of ready-made sentences aimed at supplying the patient with a superficial and fundamentally fake interest ('I know how you feel;' 'that must have been really depressing for you;' 'I really understand how much that must have hurt,' and so on): any attempt at a deep understanding on behalf of the therapist must of necessity be preceded by such a prolonged empathic immersion, which is the *conditio sine qua non* of any subsequent explicatory hypothesis. As Kohut clearly stated, psychotherapy is a science that explains what was initially understood empathically. Even though empathy is certainly not the equivalent of counter-transference, I think I have made it clear enough why I think I can consider the centralization of Self Psychology as a crucial passage in the process of enriching the clinical use of countertransference, the various phases of which I am here trying to retrace.

The last author I want us to remember in this historical outlook is a representative of the British school of object relations, or better still, of that component of object relations originating from the *middle group* of which Balint and Winnicott were the first representatives. Joseph Sandler is an author of immense clinical sensibility, as well as being an extremely important rearranger of a good part of psychotherapeutic theory and theory of technique.

---

[5] I am well aware of the controversies the concept of empathy can stir up: this is of course not the place to try and disentangle them. One particular author, among many, who deals with this operation with extreme detail is Paul Ornstein (1979, 2003), to whom I refer the reader.

In a 1976 essay, Sandler drew new attention on a particular aspect of countertransference which is brilliant in its simplicity. First of all Sandler immediately shows his willingness to consider counter-transference something that coincides with the therapist's attitude, therefore not specifically deriving from the patient's transference: in his way of seeing things, countertransference is made up of a mix of the therapist's personal characteristics and the patient's requests. The patient, fully entering these dynamics, gets used to modulating requests taking these personal characteristics of the therapist's into account.[6] The therapist's destiny, therefore, is to respond to the patient in a far more complex way than that of mere freely fluctuating attention: the therapist's answers will derive chiefly from the way she/he tunes into the system of requests and needs put forward by the patient, a tuning in which tends under many aspects to remain unconscious. To refer to this tuning in Sandler chose the term "role-responsiveness".

A choice of more recent contributions

At this point I would like to focus on the contributions by two North-American authors, Jacobs and Renik, whose activities began in the eighties and nineties respectively. Writings on counter-transference by North-Americans have only recently undergone a consistent quantitative development, largely for the reasons I previously mentioned, concerning mainly an utter banishment of the wider vision of therapy propagated by Ego Psychology, especially in its most conservative strongholds, the New York Psychoanalytic Institute and the Boston Psychoanalytic Institute, responsible until recently for training a large number of therapists.[7] Though this

---

[6] This data can be easily confirmed with work on any patient who has undergone more than one personal therapy: it becomes immediately apparent that all personal therapies differ, for the simple reason that the therapist is different, and thus the system of contents and perspectives the patient brings are also different (as well as the answers the therapist is capable of giving). This happens precisely because of factors connected with the role-responsiveness.

[7] In actual fact the number of candidates in the New York Psychoanalytic Institute for 2002 was 0 (zero) and this data sums up as explicitly as could have been possible the crisis

opening occurs with a certain delay compared to progresses already introduced decades ago by authors from other geographical areas, I still believe it should be welcome, if only because it implies a tacit recognition of a finally corrected blind-spot.

Theodore Jacobs trained with the New York institute, and his positions are therefore an attempt, within this severe bulwark of the most classic form of Ego psychology, to promote a progress of this school's positions towards theory of technique. Jacobs is the author of the introduction to the concept of "countertransferential enactment". In actual fact, the way Jacobs came up with this term is a classic case of serendipity: in his attempt to describe what can happen to the therapist at work the author wanted a different term from "acting out", which he considered to be too linked to an acceptation of a pathological nature, immediately bringing to mind by association the phenomenon that leads certain patients (especially those in the severest diagnostic categories) to act out their symptoms or emotions, turning them into impulsive, uncontrolled and often very serious actions. Wanting to clearly distinguish the concept he was developing from this strictly psychopathological acceptation, Jacobs checked the dictionary to find a different term for a similar phenomenon: the phenomenon is that by which the therapist at work finds her/himself "putting into action" a particular behavior (in the form of actions, verbalizations, silences, expressive modalities, etc.) in an impulsive way and as a consequence of a temporary loss of control due to pressure from something the patient is pushing her/him towards and/or something emanating from her/his own unconscious. The term "countertransferential enactment" seemed very useful to describe a universally recognized phenomenon which still lacked a systematic delineation, and was therefore adopted by the literature to eventually become a key word which featured in many an article dealing with theory of technique.

In the essay where he introduces the concept of counter-transferential enactment, Jacobs (1986) reviews the not too vast

"classical psychoanalysis" is undergoing in North America, while it pays today for its mistakes, connected to its uncritical resistance to the discipline's evolution.

literature on the subject to prove that even if the concept had already been signaled out and described by a small number of authors, their attention was, however, focused mainly on the more macroscopic aspects of the enacted behaviors the therapist can express within therapeutic technique, those enactments that usually cause a dramatic loss of balance in the treatment and which usually end up breaking it. Such occurrences are fortunately rare: much more common are the losses of balance and of the therapeutic alliance produced in treatment by a far more subtle counter-transferential enactment, even perhaps by an enactment the influence of which the therapist only realizes a long time after its actual occurrence, and usually because the patient has somehow stressed it. Jacobs is an extremely sensitive author and in his writing he always supplies very illustrative clinical presentations, useful for fully appreciating his position. In the essay we are discussing, therefore, he leads the reader to taking note of the way in which the therapist's most diverse and slightest shades of acting (or non-acting) can become points where countertransferential enactment can express itself. So, for example, the *attention* the therapist gives to the story told by the patient can become an opportunity for enactment to take place, whether the therapist is finding it difficult to concentrate on the story, or whether she/he is applying to it an exaggerated stenographer-like attention. The same applies to the technical instrument of *silence*, which can be an important resource during work but that can quickly turn into a means of punishing the patient or of containing the unrecognized aggressiveness of the therapist towards the patient. It follows from this that an other component of the therapist's tool box, i.e. the use of *neutrality*, can hide a countertransferential enactment somewhere; acting as a means of escape the therapist can use to hold back aggressiveness, or, on the contrary, the fear of being too unbalanced in favor of the patient. Furthermore, the modes determining the negotiation of *treatment completion* offer ideal potential docking grounds for counter-transferential enactment, with completion being either accelerated to get rid of a boring, annoying or in any way disturbing patient or deferred *sine die* for some sadist purpose of the therapist's, or because of an unrecognized falling in love with the patient. Finally, not even the *careful monitoring of transference*, which is apparently a fine guarantee against the risk of counter-transferential enactment, is exempt form becoming in turn an opportunity for enactment to take place: this is just what happens in therapies where a continuous drawing on transference interpretations prevents the therapist from reading anything else within the contents the patient produces and in any case ends up mummifying the therapy with an equidistance which is of no use when it comes to understanding the patient. In another interesting contribution, Jacobs (1991) has also shown how another common phenomenon capable of inducing counter-transferential enactment is represented by "analytic secrets", i.e. by those situations whereby therapist and patient unconsciously collude to keep the secret on a passage or event in the patient's life the emergence and analysis of which would be something too emotionally unbearable for both: the way the therapist, sometimes for years on end, continues to let her/himself be "deceived" by the patient, thus avoiding to help the latter disclose the secret at issue, is in every way a case of counter-transferential enactment. In this essay too, the range of clinical illustrations Jacobs provides for his intuition is absolutely exhaustive to the understanding of his argument.

According to Jacobs, however, countertransferential enactments, though they represent a risk any therapist can stumble upon at any time, can be avoided, or fundamentally contained, thanks to the auto-introspective work therapists must constantly carry out on themselves. We might say that this is the most substantial toll the author pays to the positions of ego psychology, which were the daily bread of his personal training. But Jacobs gets away from ego psychology's more extreme considerations, for example when he denies that the therapist's tendency to think of a certain patient with particular intensity, or to have dreams about her/him, is always and necessarily a sign of countertransferential neurosis on which the therapist must immediately work, even resorting to a *surplus* of personal analysis, if necessary. With these positions Jacobs differentiates himself markedly from the next author whose thinking I shall now sum up.

Owen Renik works at the San Francisco Psychoanalytic Institute, in a city and an area, California, which has traditionally favored the more progressive and least conservative positions compared to the main trends of the rest of North America, in the field of our discipline too. Furthermore, with an operation that caused loud protests in North American psychotherapy, Renik held from 1992 to 2001 the position of editorial director of the historic *Psychoanalytic Quarterly*, as well as being elected in charge of the scientific and research activities of the American Psychoanalytic Association: these two prestigious platforms have thus given extreme prominence to his very eclectic, and in certain aspects absolutely iconoclastic positions, making him a favorite target of all the vestal virgins of the sacred fire of psychoanalytic purity. I shall sum up Renik's thought with reference to four of his articles (Renik, 1993, 1995, 1996, 1999) which I consider to be the most representative of this authors positions on countertransference and its employment in psychotherapeutic technique.

In the first relevant passage in of his revision, Renik (1993) condemns the ideal of the analyst's subjectivity: starting from the consideration that therapists can only capture their own counter-transferential enactments after these have led to a particular action or behavior, Renik states that the therapist's point of view must be considered inevitably subjective and adds that therapists have to accept the fact that they must give up on the possibility of knowing their patients' thoughts and only "make do with" knowing their own thoughts about their patients' thoughts. The author doesn't shun the fact that the acceptance of this point must be difficult for supporters of the classical positions, as agreeing with this perspective implies scaling down the role of interpretation in psychotherapy, a role which has historically always been considered crucial in the economy of the therapeutic enterprise.[8] Renik, however, does not

---

[8] In actual fact, those who are more aware of the evolution of psychotherapeutic technique had already pointed out the occurrence of this phenomenon in our discipline (see Galli and Rigon – 1988 – and their considerations on the shift in psychotherapy from the centrality of interpretation to the centrality of setting, a shift that Renik's thought extends to the field of psychotherapeutic technique).

consider this shift in favor of the inevitable subjectivity of therapists neither dangerous nor inauspicious, so long as therapists are prepared to give up their ideal role of haruspices of a whole range of objective truths and learn to deal with their irreversible subjectivity: in this way it then becomes possible, for example, to give up on the impossible enterprise of filtering all countertransferential enactments and the task of therapists will be rather that of registering these enactments as they take place and to include them within their relationships with patients, discovering, with the latter operation, a valid instrument to develop their knowledge of patients' dynamics. On the contrary, in their possible choice of protecting their supposed objectivity at all costs, therapists run the risk of surreptitiously encouraging the patient to endorsing an unnecessary idealization of the therapists themselves to the detriment of patients' and therapists' freedom with respect to the operation making up the aim of therapy itself, i.e. the enrichment of the patient's self-knowledge.[9]

The next passage of this progression leads Renik (1995) to attack the technical defense of the therapist's anonymity in support of the introduction in therapeutic technique of the therapist's self-disclosure. He immediately makes it clear that his is not an invitation to adopt a self-revealing naturalness (in other words, the analyst talking freely about his private matters), but a technical position he sees as necessary and urgent because of several considerations:

a) the absolute impossibility for the therapist to maintain even the slightest degree of *true* anonymity;

b) the very widespread and ingrained tendency of therapists working with children, adolescents and with seriously ill patients to use the self-disclosure tool to variable degrees;

c) the data, strongly emerging from the literature, showing the strong propulsion given to treatments when therapists happen to reveal to their patients something about themselves (just think of those cases in the literature on the therapist's illness or pregnancy).

---

[9] In this passage Renik recognizes his debt to Hoffman (e.g., 1983).

Thus the therapist's problem is no longer deciding what to hide, but rather beginning to understand the best way to manage what we reveal about ourselves to the patient: it is a question of learning to manage, to the best effect, an inevitable and ever-present element in any treatment.[10] A zealous defense of the therapist's anonymity has the only apparent aim of producing a collusion in the wake of which therapist and patient disown the former's subjectivity and fuel the delusion of the therapist's omnipotence and the perpetuation of this idealization on the patient's behalf. As a consequence the main aim the therapist believed to be achieving by relying on anonymity is completely distorted: far from leaving the stage, the therapist gets stuck in the middle of it like a marble statue surrounded by a halo of mystery and relentlessly pushes the patient to thinking about the therapist and not about himself. The destiny of therapists who go out of their way never to disclose themselves is that of becoming not anonymous, but ambiguous. A sincere self-disclosure on the therapist's behalf is a much faster and cleaner tool to lead the patient to working more coherently and effectively on the transference relationship, which is constantly fuelled by the therapist's frank, and obviously respectful, self-disclosures. Furthermore, in this way it is also possible to finally do away with the other ancient ideal of the therapist's infallibility (so similar to that of the Pope's) which created the technical measure of advising therapists never to admit their own mistakes before their patients, limiting themselves, possibly, to bring them to a later phase of self-analysis or a new *tranche* of personal analysis. This, needless to say, is not an *a priori* denial of the potential therapeutic value of patients' idealization of their therapists: the main difference is that this development becomes just one of many possible developments, one the therapist must be aware of in case it becomes useful to make the therapy progress. Clearly Renik duly defines in some way the field of self-disclosure and stresses the fact that the therapist's should constantly assess which self-disclosures may be useful to a more thorough knowledge

---

[10] One cannot help thinking back to the classic case of Greenson (1967) and his patient who had discovered the therapist's political sympathies on the basis of how the latter interpreted the material when politics was discussed.

of the patient and which not, and should therefore be avoided: among the very first self-disclosure to avoid we obviously find those which are made for the sole purpose of giving the therapist narcissistic satisfaction, using the patient as a complaisant audience. According to Renik, a sincere recourse to self-disclosure gives the therapist the opportunity to found a relationship with the patient based on respect and the taking on of particular responsibilities on behalf of the therapist, two values which it is of the utmost importance to transmit to the patient.

After attacking and demolishing the ideal of the therapist's anonymity in this way, Renik (1996) deals with the subject of analytic neutrality. The concept of neutrality the author is against should be intended in the broadest sense: neutrality both in the sense of therapists not interfering with their own points of view on the patient's situation and in the sense of an obligation not to take sides with respect to patients' conflicts, keeping an equidistance between Id, Ego and Super-ego. As we can now expect, after revealing the impossibility for the therapist to affirm an objective point of view on the patient and the vainness of the attempt to preserving anonymity, Renik is ready to unmask the idea that the therapist may *really* keep an attitude of neutrality towards patients and their lives and conflicts: on the contrary, even where this becomes possible, the author believes that such a technical tool would in any case be counterproductive. Indeed, Renik cannot imagine effective treatment in the absence of a form of participation by the therapist that also includes an open willingness to exchange views with the patient on her/his situation: being the therapeutic relationship a condition finalized to the improvement of the patient's self-knowledge, our author refuses to see such a process taking place in the absence of a confrontational, inevitably subjective, attitude on behalf of the therapist as realistic. Patient and therapist must necessarily compare points of views on what the patient is describing and together they must negotiate a new point of view capable of making the patient progress in his path of self-inquiry. Countertransferential enactments (clearly inevitable) must also give their contribution to this shared investigational process. Renik, therefore, fails to see the use of a precept such as neutrality, the chief aim of which ought to be that of filtrating the affections the therapists invests on the patients and on the treatment. In his opinion, the therapists interventions are always and only personal judgments formed in a situation of emotional involvement: taking this into account helps the therapist know where both he/she and the patient are standing and to discourage the unnecessary overrating of the figure of the therapist and her/his taking on an illicit authority.

The last contribution I wish to discuss, Renik (1999), is in fact a summary of his positions where he introduces the idea of "playing one's cards face up" with the patient. He also tries to give a more systematic definition of when and how the therapist can proceed with self-disclosure. and what with. The basic idea is the one already expressed: the need to make the therapist's points of view on the clinical events and on her/his participation as open as possible to the patient and a ready willingness on behalf of the therapist towards a non-filtered self-disclosure. In this Renik sets himself apart from what Jacobs suggests, i.e. a "selective self-disclosure", limiting the use of self-disclosure only to those situations where it is the only way, according to the therapist, to solve a contingent passage in her/his work with the patient. Renik, on the other hand, supports establishing in therapy an atmosphere where patients can always feel free to request additional explanations if they deem it necessary, or even less intervention if they feel the therapist's presence to be too strong: thus it becomes necessary to authorize the patient to become an assistant of the therapist's. For this idea Renik obviously feels he is in debt with Sullivan, whose thought we know to have been surgically annihilated from the history of psychotherapeutic theory and technique, but which has made a vigorous comeback in the positions of authors such as Renik, who are often referred to as "interpersonalists". Renik takes care to explain to patients, from the very first sessions, that he expects them to actively take part in monitoring the evolution of the therapeutic relationship, hinting that the most important issue one may cover during therapy is the therapy itself. Vice versa, those who do not apply the self-disclosure technique, who do not play their cards face up with their patients, tend to communicate more or less directly to the patient that the therapist is not available (even if verbally he/she states the contrary) for a true interpersonal exchange: usually the patient adapts, and the therapy becomes a dull broth with unbalanced flavors and the only game the therapist is prepared to play with the patient is a tiresome, sterile and a little sadistic pastime that Renik calls: "Guess what I'm thinking."

Renik's thoughts and positions are regularly attacked from various fronts and his papers never fail to cause, quite literally, an outcry among therapists of the most diverse traditions, finally united in defense of the sacred rigor of classical technique. At this point I would like to point out some of these criticisms and the defenses one can put up against them. The first of these criticisms obviously comes form the defenders of the supremacy of classical technique (or of "Technique" tout-court and with a capital "T"), concentrated in North America, especially in the Institutes of New York and Boston (Brenner and Rangell are among the most famous of these veterans): according to them everything that moves away from classical technique is worse than classical technique and risks producing potential degenerations in treatment. These authors do not only attack Renik's positions, but oppose the whole long evolutional path I have attempted to summarize in these pages. They personally remind me of those Japanese soldiers who, stranded in some atoll in the Pacific, were rescued several decades after the end of WWII , which they believed was still being fought. More specific and refined are those objections pointing out the risk that the technique put forward by the supporters of intersubjectivity risks rationalizing a personal style and gratifying a therapeutic form of behavior which they consider even deontologically reprehensible: ideally these criticisms come alongside the positions of those who consider self-disclosure too invasive and intrusive and destined to interfere heavily with a correct transference/countertransference interaction. It seems to me that both these lines of criticism can be effectively rejected by the care taken by Renik, particularly in his most recent contributions, over better systematizing self-disclosure technique, stressing the need for the therapist to scrupulously monitor every single occasion when self-disclosure is employed, so as to be as sure as possible that one is avoiding the employment of such a tool based only on narcissistic gratification or unlawful intrusion dynamics, something which is far from the only goal that every form of self-disclosure intervention must seek: improving the patient's self-awareness. Concerning the fuelling of work on transference, it seems undeniable to me that the use of self-disclosure represents an accelerator and multiplier of work on the transferential relationship, with its ability of directly stimulating the patient to compare her/his own positions with those of the therapist: the patient, furthermore, is always free to warn the therapist of any unease he/she may be feeling due to the self-disclosure, which thus appears as a tool which is intrinsically retroactive and which can be improved and refined with time. As for the risk of a deontologically reprehensible degeneration, this seems to me more of a risk in those endless silent therapies carried out by the defenders of neutrality and anonymity (as so often patients who come to us for a second therapy tell us), with those pauses which seem to exist only to make the therapeutic technique eternal, to the advantage exclusively of the therapist's bank account.

Another pertinent criticism comes from Eagle (2000), who dedicated a good deal of his ponderous essay to attacking Renik. Thinking back to certain clinical passages that Renik uses in support of his claims, Eagle believes he can most certainly affirm that the same result could have been reached without self-disclosure but by abiding to analytic neutrality. Without even going to the heart of the sensation expressed by Eagle (to reason over what has actually gone on in a clinical passage is an operation so open to subjective judgment that it more resembles the appreciation of a film or book as good or bad), the following point does seem important to me: if you do decide to play cards face up with a patient one is always free to think that, in particular passages of therapy, the best way to improve a patient's self-awareness may be that of letting her/him proceed alone, without too much help or of frustrating the need to feel that the therapist is close, thus favoring an attitude very similar to what neutrality prescribes; vice versa, therapists who embrace the centrality of anonymity and neutrality armor themselves with the assumption of a rigid monolithic attitude, which deprives them of the possibility of drawing on other modes that could contingently reveal themselves to be more effective for favoring the end of a deadlock in a patient's condition. Thus, self-disclosing therapists are always free to choose, when they consider it necessary, to draw temporarily on a more neutral attitude, while neutral therapists totally deprive themselves of this opportunity. If, on the other hand, a therapist who embraces anonymity and neutrality feels even a tiny bit free to adopt a more elastic attitude occasionally, then she/he is also using self-disclosure (perhaps without admitting it to her/himself or to others) and may as well be prepared to include self-disclosure in her/his technique. To disclose oneself (i.e. to abandon neutrality) is like being pregnant: you can't do it only partially. On the other hand, being neutral is like being a virgin: you can only be a virgin as long as you stay so. In the same essay Eagle goes on to accuse Renik's positions of being a product of the ever-present spread of post-modern thinking, which concentrates entirely on overcoming authoritarianism and on promulgating democracy, sanctioned by the universal attention to "political correctness". To this Renik simply replies, with his apparent naivety, but one steeped in common sense, that his own way of working seems to him to work more effectively than the system promoted by classical technique and that's why he employs it. This reply is undoubtedly aligned with the philosophical positions of "weak thought".

Finally, we have to account for the criticisms moved against the modern intersubjectivists by the progressive wing of the psychotherapeutic field: indeed, according to some representatives of the latter there is nothing new in Renik's positions, nothing that wasn't already being carried out decades ago, first and foremost, for example, by Sullivan. Now, on the one hand I cannot remember the name of a single author who has expressed, as clearly and simply as Renik, the idea that it is possible, necessary even, to draw systematically on self-disclosure: perhaps some of these critics have already been discussing something similar in their coteries, daring not to make their positions known to the vast public. Sullivan's works have certainly been available for a long time, but, as chance would have it, have been banned by the control system of institutionalized psychoanalysis, like those of so many other authors who fought for the beginning of a more modern conceptual system to interpret therapeutic technique:[11] the works of those who, like Renik, set about posing such questions once more to the psychoanalytic institution seem to me to deserve support. My experience as educator of young psychotherapists, however limited, leads me to confirm, among other things and contrary to those who believe Renik's technical suggestions to be equivalent to the discovery of hot water, that the young who begin approaching our profession, even when they are not trained by one of the more conservative institutions, are imbued with the belief that a therapeutic treatment should be conducted respecting anonymity and neutrality, but feel relieved when I suggest to them to use their affective system as a tool to employ and share with the patient during any type of therapy.

Conclusive Considerations

Freud treated his earliest patients one hundred and ten years ago. About twenty years later (i.e. ninety years ago) he composed his few detailed writings on psychotherapeutic technique. It is difficult to imagine a scientific discipline whose rules can hope to remain valid for such a long time: this is more a characteristic of theological construction. Psychotherapeutic theory and technique have changed and are still changing and the conceptualization and modes of employment of countertransference seem to me to represent the two aspects that are changing more quickly. Moreover, such a modification had become even more necessary, because the classical technique drafted by Freud was only a list of "what not to do", which he was encouraged to make after becoming aware of the endless flux of situations whereby some pupils of his anxiously resorted to his master's wisdom as a remedy for more or less serious messes caused

---

[11] It doesn't seem to me appropriate here to delve into the fortunately well-known discussion of the various vile, and often criminal, acts that have been perpetrated in the years by so-called official psychoanalysis: for less expert readers I can suggest Roazen (1975, 2002) and Cremerius (1987, 1989).

by a management of transference/countertransference they had completely lost control over.[12] This list of prohibitions and warnings was then adopted by Freud's heirs as the Freudian Gospel on technical questions for political reasons. It then became inevitable in time for certain authors to come up with the idea of also defining the "things to do", or the "things that may be done" as part of a treatment. From Paula Heimann onwards, therefore, we have come across a range of authors who have committed themselves to such an operation, and Renik can be considered the latest, and most audacious, follower of this tradition.

It therefore seems that finally, for psychotherapy too, it is becoming possible to go beyond the crushing phenomenon of the non-obsolescence of the various theoretical stratifications, brilliantly identified and described by Galli (e.g., 1996), a phenomenon that made psychotherapeutic theory and technique embarrassingly unique among all adjacent disciplines: we may finally declare the obsolete nature of many of the theoretical and technical ideas of the pioneers, without necessarily transferring them to the trashcan of history, but rather to the museum of the origins of science, where they will rest gloriously next to the astrolabe, the spy glass and Foucault's pendulum, possibly ready to be studied by historians. The ideal of the therapist's subjectivity, alongside anonymity and analytic neutrality, seem to me the first concepts to deserve this peaceful retirement. With this movement psychotherapy finally accepts the opening to a more relativistic conception of its dimension, an opening that even a much harder science than ours, such as physics, already developed long ago when it accepted the introduction of Heisenberg's indetermination principle and the advent of quantum mechanics which followed (see Hawking, 1988, pp.73-74).

I am absolutely in tune to Wallerstein (2002) in my belief that the abdication of classical psychoanalysis has been accelerated, in these last decades, by the progressive worsening of the psychopathology of patients who turn to psychotherapists (patients with borderline

---

[12] Ferenczi and Ernest Jones (but classically Jung too) were two of the most "diligent" setting violators in relation to a bad management, above all of erotic transference.

or narcissistic personality disorders, with serious depressive or post-traumatic stress disorders), i.e. of those patients who are absolutely incapable of bearing the depriving atmosphere imposed to the relation by those therapists who still insist on using anonymity and neutrality. The only "patients" who still accept the harshness of the classical analytic setting seem to be young doctors and psychologists training in our field, but they too will learn, the hard way, the advantages of creating an elastic, empathic, shared and communicational relational atmosphere, within which a careful and well geared use of self-disclosure represents one of the most important therapeutic factors.

Bibliography

Albarella, C., Donadio, M., *Il Controtransfert*, Naples: Liguori, 1986
Cremerius, J.:
- "Alla ricerca di tracce perdute. Il 'movimento psicoanalitico' e la miseria dell'istituzione psicoanalitica", *Psicoter. Sc. Um.*, XXI, 1987, 3:3-34
- "Analisi didattica e potere. La trasformazione di un metodo di insegnamento-apprendimento in strumento di potere della psicoanalisi istituzionalizzata", *Psicoter. Sc. Um.*, XXIII, 1989, 3:3-28
Eagle, M. N., "Una valutazione clinica delle attuali concettualizzazioni su transfert e countertransference", *Psicoter. Sc. Um.*, XXXIV, 2000, 4:5-44
Freud, S.:
- "Fragment of an analysis of a case of hysteria" [1905], *SE*, 7:7-123, London: Hogarth Press, 1953
- "The future prospects of psychoanalysis" [1910], *SE*, 11:139-151, London: Hogarth Press, 1957
- "Recommandations to physicians practicing psycho-analysis" [1912], *SE*, 12:111-120, London: Hogarth Press, 1958
- "On beginning the treatment" [1913], *SE*, 12: 121-144, London: Hogarth Press, 1958

Friedman, L.:
- *The Anatomy of Psychotherapy*, Hillsdale: The Analytic Press, 1988
- "Fascinazione e richieste in psicoanalisi: l'aspetto delle richieste", *Psicoter. Sc. Um.*, XXVIII, 1994, 3:5-40

Galli, P. F., *La persona e la tecnica*, Milan: Il Ruolo Terapeutico, 1996

Galli, P. F., Rigon, G., "Dall'interpretazione al setting: i fattori terapeutici in psicoanalisi", Relazione presentata alla IX giornata scientifica della fondazione "Centro Praxis", Santa Maria a Vico (Ce), 1988

Greenson, R. R., *The Technique and Practice of Psychoanalysis*, Madison: International Universities, 1967

Hawking, S., *A Brief History of Time*, New York: Bantam Books, 1988

Heimann, P., "On counter-transference", *Int. J. Psycho-Anal.*, 31, 1950

Hoffman, I. Z., "The patient as interpreter of the analyst's experience", *Cont. Psychoanal.*, 1983, 19, pp. 389-422

Jacobs, T.J.:
- "On countertransference enactments". *J. Amer. Psychoanal. Assn.*, 1986, 34:2
- "Notes on the unknowable: analytic secrets and the transference neurosis", in T. J. Jacobs, *The Use of the Self*, Madison: International Universities Press, 1991

Kohut, H., "The Two Analyses of Mr Z", *Int. J. Psycho-Anal.*, vol. 60:3, 1979

Ornstein, P. H., "Notes on the central position of empathy in psychoanalysis", *Bull. Assn. Psychoanal. Med.*, 4:95-108, 1979

Ornstein, P. H., Ornstein, A., "The function of theory in psychoanalysis: a Self-psychological perspective", *Psychoanal. Q.* LXXII: 2, pp. 157-183, 2003

Racker, H., "The meanings and uses of countertransference". *Psychoanal. Q.*, 26, 1957

Renik, O.:
- "Analytic interaction: conceptualizing technique in the light of the analyst's irreducible subjectivity", *Psychoanal. Q.*, 4, pp. 553-571, 1993
- "The ideal of the anonymous analyst and the problem of self-disclosure", *Psychoanal. Q.*, 3, pp. 466-495, 1995
- "The perils of neutrality", *Psychoanal. Q.*, 3, pp. 495-517, 1996
- "Playing one's cards face up in analysis: an approach to the problem of self-disclosure", *Psychoanal. Q.*, 4, pp. 521-540, 1999

Roazen, P. :
- *Freud and His Followers*, © Paul Roazen, 1975
- "L'esclusione di Erich Fromm dall'Ipa", *Psicoter. Sc. Um.*, XXXVI, 3, pp. 23-64, 2002

Sandler, J., "Countertransference and role-responsiveness", *Int. Rev. Psycho-Anal.*, 3, 1975

Wallerstein, R.S.:
- "Psychoanalysis and psychotherapy: an historical perspective", *Int. J. Psycho-Anal.*, 4, pp. 563-591, 1989
- "La traiettoria della psicoanalisi: un pronostico", *Psicoter. Sc. Um.*, XXXVI, 4, pp. 5-32, 2002

Transference and "Bare Life". Defencelessness

Cristiana Cimino

Keywords: Bare life – Real – Claustrophilic area – Uncanny – Trauma.

Summary: *The hypothesis of this work is that the psychic life is marked from the beginning by the exposure to a Real that is by definition extraneous, uncanny, undomesticated and not subjective. In some circumstances the quota of Real exceeds that which is sustainable for the subject, in such a way that contact with this Real assumes traumatic connotations. This gives rise to a primary experience of "defencelessness", "Bare Life" according to some of today's philosophy. From this basic experience, that can be assimilated only in part to the Freudian Hilflosigkeit, the drive to merge with the other originates in the attempt to recuperate the state of indifferent well-being/bliss, similar to that described by Winnicott, brutally interrupted by trauma. The attempt to "make whole" with the other assumes various forms, from that described and called by the Italian psychoanalyst Elvio Fachinelli as "co-identity", to one that tends toward an actual fall from boundaries, inducing confusion of identities between patient and analyst. In the present work, these psychic movements are traced in the dynamic of transference and counter-transference and are illustrated with the evidence of a clinical case.*

I Introduction

In the essay "Terminable and interminable analysis", Freud (1937) warns us about an indefinite prolongation of the analysis. On this track, Elvio Fachinelli[1] (1983, 2001) theorized that the analytic

---

[1] Of Elvio Fachinelli (1928-1989) have been translated the following articles on *Journal of European Psychoanalysis*: "On the beach", 2, 1995; "Lacan and the Thing", 3, 4, 1996-1997; "The psychoanalyst's money", 18, 2002. "The impossible training of Psychoanalyst.

treatment, by its very nature, tends to direct us toward what he described as "claustrophilic area", or "area perinatale" (the psychic area of time before, during and just after birth), characterized by a relationship of dual unity between the patient and the analyst that reverts to the mother-baby relation at birth, if not *previous* to birth. In these terms the therapeutic relationship can, effectively, reveal itself to be particularly difficult to resolve, risking an indefinite prolongation. Nevertheless, this particular dimension gives rise to extremely interesting phenomena, from both clinical and theoretical psychoanalytic perspectives. The area that Fachinelli called "claustrophilic" is manifested in dreams, at times even away from the analytic setting, in states of altered consciousness of various nature*s,* and in the patient as well as in the therapist. In the analysis of some patients, this tendency seems to be particularly potent. Fachinelli describes phenomena of "absorption of the other", of "co-identity" and of "sisterhood" (because in these phenomena it is always the maternal-feminine side in play) relived in the dynamic of transference and counter-transference, in the field in which the paradoxical situation is created of being two persons, the same and separate, at the same time. In such conditions, the sensation of temporal suspension can be strong and *a* "coincidence" or telepathic phenomena between patient and analyst can occur. But, above all, the tendency to co-identity, that is, the search on the part of the patient for "affinity, familiarity, communality" (pp. 156-157) with the therapist, is strong. The patient's "search for precise co-relationship, for identity at the limit" (p. 157) in which co-identity is verified, would have as its aim the identity of the mother, which is what the patient is trying to reach. All these phenomena belong to the "as if" category and therefore concern the symbolic sphere.

My impression is that in certain patients – not necessarily in psychotic ones, but on the contrary, often in those who present ample functioning zones of the neurotic type – this continuous, infinite dimension, takes on different characteristics and modes of

A conversation with Sergio Benvenuto", in Sergio Benvenuto and Anthony Molino, *In Freud's track's*, New York: Jason Aronson, 2008.

expression. Indeed, what takes place is a temporary and more or less important fall of the boundaries and, in fact, an actual confusion of identities between patient and therapist. In the therapist, this generates phenomena of altered consciousness of varying degrees, which also have a communicational valance and originate from the patient's impulse to merge into the other, in an attempt to rebuild an ultimate unity in transference. I have collected these phenomena in a category I have called "continuous" (Cimino 2002), using again, with a broader meaning and an attempt of systematization, a term already used by Fachinelli (1983). All these phenomena, those described by Fachinelli and also those that lead to an actual confusion of identity in the dynamic of transference and counter transference, can, in different ways, be precious indicators, if gathered by the therapist, of the undifferentiated or particularly "fluid" zones of the patient's identity.

The urge to merge with the other is common to a varying degree in all human beings and has its origin in their initial condition of impotence-defencelessness. As Freud taught us, at the beginning of our lives there is a physiological supremacy of the other, who is the actual omnipotent one who underlies actual limits and is the dispenser of life or death. Defencelessness can be brought back to a condition of brutal exposure to the Real, that is by definition foreign, alien, un-domesticated and unable to be domesticated, eluding signification, as Jacques Lacan would say "not registered in the symbolic". The Real is not the domestic, known environment, not what accompanies our daily life and gives form to it, but its exact opposite. It is not *the Heim* (the house), but its very contrary, the *Unheimliche*, that which perturbs, radically escaping our grasp and every instance of subjectivation (Lacan 1966; Benvenuto, 2008). The encounter with this Real, which all of us experiment with from time to time, fortunately in a fleeting manner, constitutes instead, for some subjects, a central experience and assumes traumatic connotations. Trauma, then, is the contact with an excessive quota of the Real in an encounter with the other, who is experienced from the beginning as too Real. There exists an inevitable, traumatic quota tied to the primary object, in its reality (but we can say with reality in general), which makes it in part inaccessible, not able to be subjective, and which keeps us at its mercy. In some conditions this physiological dimension assumes traumatic characteristics, tied to an excess of Real, which makes the other irreparably foreign, unable to be decoded, but above all painfully "present". This presence interferes with the state of unconscious well-being-bliss necessary to make structural the living "benign omnipotence", similar to what is described by Winnicott (1971, 1984). The break into the state of well-being lets the "uncanny" (*Unheimliche*) emerge, that is, bare life in defencelessness that gives space for the symptoms.

The symptom in its widest sense is the agency aiming to dissolve the boundaries between self and non-self. It is an attempt to enter (or return?) to a condition of non differentiation, to a sphere in which every tension and every painful knowledge of one's own existence ceases: this is the "continuous". One must repair the tear, reestablish the indifferent well-being, utilizing the concrete presence of the other by trying to become "one" with him.

III The encounter with Lorenza

Lorenza is an intelligent and gracious young woman, student in an artistic faculty. She is twenty-six years old. She came for consultation because of a general impasse in her life. Only two exams and her thesis remain for her to graduate, but she is no longer able to follow her studies. Things are not any better in her private life, since, in spite of some attempts, she appears to be unable to establish any emotional ties with a man nor is she able to experience her sexuality. She also suffers from physical disturbances, such as rapid heartbeat, vertigo, fear of fainting suddenly and a feeling of "heaviness" which prevents her from doing almost anything.

Lorenza dresses in a severe style, which looks almost masculine; her light-colored eyes cast glances of disarming harshness. What most strongly presented during our first encounters, is her voice, thin and monotonous, with a slightly nasal tonality, like a soft infantile moan.

Her communications are monosyllabic and brief, at times interrupted by hints of humiliated and enraged weeping. It is evident that she lives the decision to begin analysis as a defeat that embarrassed her. At the same time she bears a suffering, which is dense and not very penetrable, like a concrete object.

The beginning of the analysis

The first phase of analysis, consisting of four weekly sessions and the use of the couch, is characterized by an enraged modality, that seems clearly tied to the necessity and the extreme difficulty of renouncing a sort of self sufficient or autarchic omnipotence, which until now has allowed Lorenza to move ahead. Often, with her provocative and definitive style, she engages me in verbal run ins like brusque calls to order, but as I soon recognize, they are in reality attempts to annul the boundaries between us, to then regain them and lose them once again. It is her way to be the master of the relationship. Lorenza cannot stand feeling at the mercy of anyone or anything.

"How does this work?" she asks. She presents a double movement: on the one hand she tries to keep her distance from me, expresses an extreme hardness, and shows me to be a pseudo adult; and on the other hand, I prematurely perceive her extreme need to have absolute control over me. Already in this phase of the analysis, I feel a dulling of my thoughts, an unnatural torpor, which I am able to decode as Lorenza's attempt to establish in her transference a unity which permits her to lose sight of boundaries, *not* to feel the labors of her own thinking process, and, we might say, of her own existence.

She describes two dreams:

O. graduates, I am very annoyed and angry about this. Someone says that O. is graduating to favor herself – to get an advantage over everyone else. First I go away, then I return late for the graduation. I already knew I would arrive late.

O. and I must take the same exam. O. uses symbols taken from a book and tells me I must use different ones. I ask myself: why do I have to do all this work if O. just copies from the book?

In associations with these dreams Lorenza believes that in this period everything is going cross-wise; even her clothes don't fit her. O. is Lorenza's best friend, with whom she often studies, and she is about to graduate. She is a sort of idealized alter ego. I say to Lorenza that she seems to have placed all the good in this unreachable O./Lorenza, while "this" Lorenza is the unfortunate one and remains ill-fated. I actually begin to introduce what is evidenced always more clearly in Lorenza: the gap between herself and an ideal self that she keeps constantly in check, animated by the fantasy that there exists an absolute dimension, perfect, already given (like the symbols in the second dream), and that all one has to do is find it, and in some way come to possess it. This gap, apart from generating an angry frustration, has kept Lorenza substantially distanced from the possibility of meeting others and experiencing herself in the world. However, this massive, idealized fantasy, in fact, devalues and invalidates that which could be lived or achieved in reality, because, by definition, it will never be provided for in the characteristics of the ideal object.

Another dream seems to allow for the emergence of the dimension of the "continuous":

> I seem to have lost one of the rings that I wear, the prettiest. Then I realize that there are still four, but the light blue one is missing.... Maybe I lost it.

She likes these rings very much, she always wears them, she bought them a long time ago, they seemed appropriate, even though rings in general don't go well. But these go well together, they are complete, like a series in sequence, and if one is missing, they would no longer have any meaning.

The rings are a "continuous" sequence; they make sense only together and not singularly, since the series annuls distinctions and differences. There are four members in her family, maybe the light blue one, the most precious, is her brother, which gives sense to everyone, to the entire sequence. It seems in the dream she asks if she can let something go, "lose it", something that, until now, has made her feel complete, meaningful.

It is very important to have control of oneself, says Lorenza, almost angrily, like knowing what you need to do in your life, unlike her mother who was not able construct anything of her own in her life. It was terrible for her to go out knowing her mother remained at home. Lorenza cries without trying to hold it back, and it is the first time she has such a potent and immediate feeling.

After some days, she brings two dreams from the same night:

I am in the bathroom in front of the mirror with my mother and I am looking at my underarm hairs.

I am in the garden of the house in B., I look beyond the hedge, I see a lake with two rivers that flow in and out. I see Aunt R. and F., the oldest of my aunts and the youngest of my cousins, who are having a swim. So, everyone knew. I say to myself. I am very surprised and perplexed. The hedge circled the house, so we couldn't see outside, nor did we want to, since inside it was so intense...beautiful, like the house in Rome or in Sicily in the summer.

With distressing, painful accents of nostalgia, Lorenza talks about the house in B. and the other two, where for a long period of time, from infancy to late adolescence, she shared her life with her many cousins, children of her mother's siblings. She passed as much time as possible with them. On the weekends she packed her bags and took the subway to go where her cousins all lived together in the same building. She slept there, at times in one house, other times in another, and Sunday evening she returned to her home. All week she couldn't wait to return there; she didn't like school and all the rest. She knows that this prevented her from having other experiences, but this is what she had.

This long period of Lorenza's life provides recurring paradigms and grammar of our shared language, as the dream of the house in B. becomes the central element during the course of her analysis. The perfection of that garden, of that *claustrum* that welcomed and didn't ask anything but to be oneself, must have allowed Lorenza to protect herself from fantasies and probably from experiences very different in character. Now, as the dream seems to indicate, she is beginning to look "beyond the hedge", beyond that blissful paradise where she lived for a long time the intense cohabitation-confusion among her cousins-siblings, united as if they were one body. And she becomes aware of "what one has always known", that everyone from the youngest to the oldest and herself, after all, have always known, and that Lorenza knows that it is no longer the time to avoid. There OUTSIDE is the world – the waters of life – there is a reality that calls, and it is not possible to get away with or *to* keep it at bay with previous means. But it is a reality which Lorenza still feels the lack of adequate means to confront, as she recounts in the other dream: what can she do with these hairs, with her sexuality, with this body that calls, that demands, that desires? And where to find these means? Will her mother-analyst be able to furnish them or will she remain defenceless like her, in front of the mirror, double of a baby in the body of a woman? After all, the image of double satisfies Lorenza's fantasy to remain in a continuous and infinite mirror-image duality.

This particular use of idealization – which implies a dimension of completeness, of "continuity", and has the purpose of avoiding the encounter with reality – is nearly constant and declined in all its most varied forms. The incessant search for the perfect object which, once found will guarantee absolute wellness and stability, leads her to turn outside herself and display violent sentiments of frustration. Lorenza is reluctant to complete the psychic work necessary to face the reality that still appears like a dismaying void and gives her vertigo, a reality separated from a painful division, from a censure, from the "garden of B.". It has to do with a refusal to experience the void understood as a defect, that is as an inescapable human dimension that nevertheless requires her to differentiate herself, "lose the ring", give up the illusion and face death. Or perhaps it has to do with another void, a mute void, not able to be symbolized, tied to problem that have to do with identity and narcissism at its base?

Anguish and anger are often evident in beginning of the transference, along with experimenting with a relationship, which is other in respect to the dimension of the continuous.

She brings me a dream:

> I come here, but a woman arrives who is not you. She is also dark-haired and young but it is not you. She stands in front of me and tells me what I have already been thinking, that is, sometimes it is you and other times it is somebody else. I tell myself that all this happened because we are not looking at each other.

This is a disturbing and bothersome dream, because of the fact that the analysis turns up even in her dreams. She is weighed down by everything and doesn't want to think too much. Lorenza's tone is dry and doesn't allow replies. Her attempt seems to be to maintain a bond with me dictated by concreteness, of by what she can "see and touch", as if, by just thinking of it, the tie and the object itself would fade and allow the emergence of the traumatic aspect of what is the same but also in a disturbing way, (the) other.

The impossibility, the refusal to symbolize, at least to the degree required to make possible a differentiation between self and non-self, to create the void necessary to circulate thoughts and desires, originates then from the unnerving, or rather, uncanny element of the other. In the case of Lorenza, this element seems to me to be made up of unpredictable aspects of the primary object that make it "insane", in the sense not only of her feeling at this object's mercy, but also in the sense that the object is at mercy of itself, in need of surveillance and salvation. Lorenza pays the price for not being able to let herself go, to have to constantly keep watch and watch out for herself.

Another dream seems to clarify the register that characterizes Lorenza's tie with the primary object:

> I am at home at night. I hear a scream and think that someone may have been hurt and is calling for help. I feel like someone who is about to faint, as if everything is not real. I go to my parents' bathroom and see my mother with a razor in her hand. I think she is wounded, I look for the blood but I don't see any. Then, in a bathtub full of water, I see that there

is a piece of my mother that is floating, I don't know which piece. I think
that she can put it all back together. I feel anguish.

Strangely, in her dream she was like her mother and her mother
was like her daughter, Lorenza says; it is more logical that a
mother helps the daughter rather than the contrary. At times she
puts herself in bed with her mother as she did in her childhood,
and feels good, secure. Now that she is leaving home she asks
herself how her room will be put to use. Lorenza's tone, slightly
embarrassed, communicates to me the all-consuming, unfillable
desire and the nostalgia for something that has been lost and will
not return, not in the same way. In fact, Lorenza has recently decided
to go and live with a girlfriend. This imminent event seems to elicit
anguish tied to a separation lived like a razor cut, like a surgical
amputation (and therefore in some way also necessary) of herself-
shapeless-indefinite-piece-of-the-body-of-her-mother, left to float,
thrown away, lacking sense and any life of its own.

At the same time, I feel that the atmosphere of the sittings has
changed. It is less studded by the brutal breakdowns of the times
before, as if, by not having to always begin at the beginning, she
has earned access to a dimension different than one of a space-time
reduced to fragments held together moment by moment, like an
eternal present.

IV The second year of analysis

At the resumption, after the summer interruption, Lorenza talks
about the difficulties encountered during a trip with her friend,
culminating in what from now on will be "the scene in the tunnel".

Her friend was very authoritarian, always reprimanding her,
criticizing her, and she felt always worse. The fear of fainting became
stronger, and her physical ailments, her rapid heartbeat, the vertigo,
the sensation of suffocating increased. The oppressive heat and the
beautiful but strange panorama contributed to her malaise and
disorientation. During the trip back, her friend compelled her to drive
on the highway, Lorenza continues to tell me angrily. At a certain

point, in a tunnel, she felt very ill and felt she would faint and lose her senses at the wheel. She wanted to escape but couldn't, there was all that darkness... so she musters up her strength enough to be able to make it to the end of the tunnel... she doesn't know how. There was light at last, even too much, and finally she could stop.

The power of the scenario that Lorenza evoked, her trip in the tunnel, the extreme darkness and the sudden lights, were strong enough to solicit not only one image in my mind but a complex experience, of strong sensorial resonance, as if, for a moment – how long does a moment like that last? – I/we were actually there – here? – at the scene together. It seemed to be a birth scene – or a non-birth scene – in which Lorenza was forced, in which she was herself aborted. An unlimited terror lived in her, literally without boundaries, to be sent off, catapulted out into the blinding light, and at the same time to remain closed, entrapped in a *claustrum* inside of which any hope of an autonomous and differentiated life was lost forever. I had the impression that an aspect of the trauma of Lorenza was powerfully evoked and "lived" in the occasion of the session, more than "told".

During the following period of analysis, I have the impression that I'm following Lorenza almost in real time. She seems to have given up any harshness towards me but an anxious form of expectation prevails. I get the hint of an implicit but clear request for continuous contact in the liquid look in her eyes as they probe me when we say hello and goodbye, during the dense, permeated atmosphere of our sessions.

When she tells me she has lost her rings, as she did in her dream (but this time for real), Lorenza mentions Lorenzo, the boy she's been going out with for some time. If he were to leave her, she would feel the world fall apart around her, and she would feel annihilated; she wants to talk about it often, she wants to feel ready. Lorenza's eyes are more liquid than usual, more wandering, as we say goodbye. I feel that opaqueness, that oppression again towards the end of the session; a vague sensation of lethargy and apathy that make thinking such a strained effort at the very moment I do it. I feel her proximity and her pressing request, her movement towards merging with me as she does with Lorenzo. This is the period when the confusion of the boundaries overflows, becoming real at every distancing move I make, and I am increasingly committed in my areas of undifferentiated identity. What's Lorenza afraid of? What holds her back from the path towards "losing the rings"? That loss fatally awaits her at the end? The concrete absence of the other (that she still perceives as unbearable) which leaves her in a state of helplessness, annihilation and non-existence?

In the following session, she points out that I haven't greeted her in the usual way: She has perfectly recognized the fact that I was keeping a necessary and sufficient distance from her effort to merge with me. But the atmosphere of the session is completely different; intense but fluid, with no fogginess.

Lorenza discovers and is beginning to make room for the other in her life. She is paying a very high price for relinquishing her allocation in a dimension which is that of

> the loving calm of your arms, [when] the amorous embrace repeats the motionless clinging to the mother, everything is suspended: time, law, prohibition, all desires are abolished for they seem definitively fulfilled (Barthes, 1978).

She enters a dimension where risk is represented not only by the mere existence of the other, but also by this other's characteristics and movements. The discontinuity of the concrete physical presence of the other, who is me or Lorenzo, constantly risks generating in her feelings of annihilation and non-existence.

It is in this period that Lorenza asks me if she can sometimes phone me, especially at home alone during the long afternoons she devotes to her dissertation. During telephone calls, which are not frequent, and during sessions which are often devoted to the former, I have the clear perception that in these long lonely afternoons Lorenza experiences a practically constant sensation of an incipient loss of spatial and temporal coordinates, of an internal and external order that has to be reestablished by a real presence, such as my voice or the arrival of the girl with whom she lives, to restore her to corporeity, to existence. In solitude she feels she is not animating things but that someone else must do it. I have the impression that in her huge derealization, Lorenza experiences simultaneously the temptation and the threat of abolishing the flow of time, so that, by eliminating the category that historicized, she may come into contact with the primary object, similar to that described in the tunnel episode: one that is absolute, limitless, not allowing any hope of differentiation nor a life of her own – a hope that Lorenza also pursues, as when she sits at her drawing table, picks up her pencils, erasers, sharpeners etc., not as normal actions, but as an exhausting act; seeing the blank page at the start is terrible, she often thinks she'll never be able to start drawing, but gradually...

It seems that, at this moment, any form of relationship with the world sets, for Lorenza, on a ridge: from one side of this she can see the possibility of emancipation, from the other side the possibility of remaining in the tunnel, in the *claustrum*. Sessions now are mainly devoted to accounts of everyday life, to the many strategies she conjures up to pass the time, "to get out of the jam": music, her mobile phone, the two alarm clocks she uses at the same time, which sometimes work and sometimes don't. Lorenza often hints at our analysis, especially at the beginning of sessions, the ones on Monday in particular. It's as if she wishes to re-establish our contract, but certainly with different modes than earlier sessions. She has now been coming to sessions "without even thinking about it" for some time. Sometimes she feels she can't remember anything we talk about and thinks it was all a waste of time, but also that so much has changed in her life. At other times she does think about what we said together and sees things differently. It seems that by saying this Lorenza wants to signal the growing possibility of conserving the relationship beyond the concrete presence of the other and an initial elaboration.

However, Lorenza is perplexed and troubled. What if she hasn't understood anything about what is happening in the sessions? What if things aren't as they seem? After all, it has happened other times, for example in the me-not-me dream of many months ago, when the uncanny feeling dominated the scene; from the moment she looked me in the face, Lorenza made the distressful unsettling discovery that it wasn't me.

What generates the anguish in Lorenza? Is it only because I now offer myself and reality now offers itself as other object and which she cannot control omnipotently? Or does this feeling of the uncanny emerging from the relationship allude to past experiences, to the traces left by these experiences and from contact with a primary object with specific characteristics?

V From the third to the fifth year of analysis: toward a possible subjectivation

The date to hand in her dissertation is approaching and Lorenza switches from moments when she is obstinately certain she wants to hand it in on time, whatever the cost, to periods of total dejection when she seems to want to let everything go adrift. She seems to be reserving something similar for her relationship with Lorenzo and with myself. With difficulty, holding her anger back, Lorenza tells me in more detail about the topics of her dissertation. She never liked projects and doesn't know where to begin. The "project" Lorenza feels anger and reluctance towards is the one that concerns herself in the world "beyond the hedge". This project implies giving up forever the illusion that the other will do things for her and with her, canceling boundaries and distance and finally soothing the tiredness, fears, hunger and painful awareness of herself. She defends herself by transferring everything on*to* a concrete and emblematic plain.

After a few attempts at equivocating and gaining time, Lorenza approaches her dissertation and project once more and all the problems this causes her. She doesn't know where to begin when she starts revising, and she sees that she doesn't really understand what her professor is saying to her. This is how Lorenza gets across to me her reluctance to retain something she would rather reject and that she now identifies in this professor/father's demand that's pressing her, that's asking her to define herself, something that also fascinates and excites her very much. In the time preceding her graduation con-fusion phenomena start taking place in sessions once again. During these I feel dazed, confused and impotent once more. I often think about Lorenza outside sessions.

In the thirtieth month she tells me a dream:

> Someone, a woman, accompanies swimmers to a platform from where they dive in high seas. The woman tells me to wait. I'm annoyed and disappointed at this, but then I think it's for the best, that I'm still too afraid to dive into deep waters, however much I would like to.

Lorenza still cautiously keeps this motherly body at a safe distance, although it is still both threatening and attractive. Now she seems to be in a very different condition, in analysis and in life, from when she let herself be swallowed up and then expelled from the tunnel, as she experienced in real life. But now that she seems set gradually to give up con-fusion with the other, problems concerning survival achieved by her own means are getting in the way.

She has been to see her cousin who has just had a baby girl. As she watched her, she noticed what an effort it was for the baby to breathe, and the same follows for her, common practice is an effort. This metaphor refers to a work on herself she feels is necessary in order to gain something that is not just given, is not guaranteed, and that is just as essential, just as basic as breathing. To what extent is it just metaphor we're dealing with?

I'm changeable, she says, sometimes I'm one way and at other times I'm another way, like when I have to make an effort to make time go by. When I point out that this is very similar to the effort the baby seemed to make just to breathe, Lorenza admits that indeed she does feel that way, as someone who has to make an abnormal effort. When she feels "normal" she isn't happy, only normal, and that's something different. But when she's the other way it seems to her that something is coming from outside, and she has to wait for it to go away. But she needs something to hold on to in order to get out of it, that's why she's afraid of being alone. Yet again, it becomes clear just how intolerable it must be for Lorenza to experience this distressing void. I wonder if there is a point beyond which lacking becomes a void, no longer symbolized but merely mute, and if so where. At the same time, I get the impression that the repetition of all this, both in the form of a narration and in the here and now of the session, is of great help to her, acing like a sort of "procedural construction" which, as far as possible, has the job of replacing the void.

The counter-altar to those moments that are earned with great effort is when Lorenza describes her home, how beautiful it some-times is to hear its reassuring sounds, the voices, the scent of coffee in the morning. At night, on the other hand, everything is more difficult, as if people no longer existed, and she doesn't feel seen, as if she no longer existed either. Indeed, to sleep alone seems impossible. The loss of consciousness necessary for sleep to occur, the abandonment, requires someone else to keep watch, for the entrance into the *claustrum*, the tunnel, not to turn into a trap and to guarantee exit from it. Lorenza is very tempted to remain in her condition of depending on the other, of "sisterhood", like in the B. house.

It is clear that, with great difficulty, Lorenza is trying to come to terms with a dimension of her relationship that is not absolute, a mutual absorbing, an expectation of everything, a panacea capable of healing, anaesthetizing, of suspending every single tension and need: all in the painful attempt to enter a new dimension of greater integration and definition of the self, an inevitably greyer, more realistic one.

Lorenzo is sad lately, she tries to cheer him up. Otherwise it seems to her he is forgetting her. This, together with other elements, make me think of a relation to a primary object that is not only moody and unpredictable, but above all, as I have pointed out before, explicitly or implicitly demanding to be looked after, watched over, saved, thus using all the resources the other has, in a labor that always needs to start over. Saving the other determines one's own existence.

She brings a dream which seems to signal a decisive pass toward her own subjectivation:

I'm in bed with two boyfriends, I talk to one then to the other. I think it's not very nice of me, but that the thing would soon be over and that I had to pig out on it.

She associates Lorenzo's resemblance to her brother: both are elusive, both feel well when they are alone. As kids she and her brother would always talk about how, when they grew up, they would live together or as neighbors, eat together and so on. At home their beds are separated only by a fitted sidewall. Once Lorenzo slept there too, as in the dream. In her life with all the cousins too, her brother was always present. This dream seems to be an attempt to begin to consider the transition from the "fraternal couple" (a variant of the "sisterly" mentioned before) to the full exogamous couple, in spite of the hesitation and the temptation not to give anything up (to "pig out"), to keep both men, who together form a "double" (Rank, 1914).

Nevertheless, I still have to do a lot of work for her, and it's still me who has to take upon myself the burden of elaboration. Some of her dreams stress this element: a house she lives in, with rooms laid out in a C (the first letter of both my name and surname) shape; a double study, hers and mine, connected via an underground passage, a sort of anthropomorphic cavern, "beautiful, charming".

She has the following dreams:

I was at a kind of exhibition but I couldn't get in. Someone was inside who had something very important for me and I had to get in at all costs. G. (her boss where she works) lets me in but says I have to leave. I'm disappointed, I think I might have stayed.

I'm with Lorenzo (through the associations we will see that he is the analyst) on a boat in the open sea. The water is very blue, too deep, there's no anchor. I can control it, but I'm scared.

I'm on a boat on a lake, perhaps with M. (a girlfriend) and with others. It's beautiful, like stolen time, a strong intense sensation. At one point we see a dead body, M. sees it too and so does everyone else.

To the first dream she associates the fact that she may not be hired in this office. All her life is in anticipation. She doesn't see how one can even think of getting married, as her friends are doing. She would like to get married one day, but in three... ten years. She can't think of anything else apart from her family. With Lorenzo, it's as if she were alone. To the third dream she associates the fact that everything is so beautiful, limitless.

It is obvious from the first dream that Lorenza still feels that something fundamental is not in her hands, but rather in the hands of the primary object, and with that she seems to be hanging in the balance, unable to decide whether she can separate. A separating father who controls relationships appears: she may come in and collect what's hers, but then she must leave. She can't continue lying comfortably in the *claustrum*, in the confusion of borders between self and the other. In the same way she cannot stay in analysis forever, "hired". Her feeling constantly in waiting is just this ridge, this indecision between the inside, which ultimately is a trap, and the outside, which makes her feel alone, exiled, different, "unanchored". As the third dream suggests, it seems that she feels a part of her has to die for her to find emancipation from her own limitlessness, which is connected to a limitless bond to the other.

Phenomena that Fachinelli (1983) calls co-identity date back to the fifth year of analysis, appearing in a dream:

> I come to analysis but she (the analyst) is in another place, somewhere else. The hall is like this one, but then she takes me to another part of the apartment to do the session. It is a space on two floors connected by a staircase, like a 70's apartment. Everything is connected, each area is specialized. It's a very beautiful bright space, and there are lots of books. It's more like a house than a consulting room. There are people sitting on a sofa, friends of hers, they speak German and she can understand them, me not too well, I ask them to speak more slowly. By the end of the session she has turned into a man.

Lorenza seems to have caught an existential moment of mine, which somehow makes me "be somewhere else". The different consulting room, this "somewhere else", is incredibly similar to my house of the time. It is as if, perceiving my relative distance, Lorenza tries to reestablish with the phenomenon of co-identity expressed in the dream, a proximity to me, in a mode that seems to be very different from the moments *of* numbness I experienced during some sessions, fearing that thought and presence itself might fail. German, after all, is the "foreign language", the non-maternal language she was forced to learn at school and that she had loathed in the days when she was oscillating between the community of brothers and the foreignness of the rest of the world. In the dream she makes the effort to speak this different language – which is also the original language of psychoanalysis – as if she *were*, with difficulty, accepting access to a new code, that of the differentiated.

While I'm on a trip to the desert, Lorenza has the following dream:

A line of people are walking on the background of a boundless and very strange landscape, like a huge plateau of sand and rocks.

It's the perfect description of one of my travel episodes, which of course Lorenza knew nothing about.

During a serious period of bereavement for me, Lorenza brings me a dream identical to that of another patient, also a woman:

I'm holding a boy by the hand (but one understands that he is the analyst). The atmosphere is one of great intimacy, and I feel very happy, at one point we begin to fly.

Another patient has an identical dream, with the same atmosphere, the same experiences, in which I explicitly appear. I think of a twin double that manically denies death. The transience of borders is even higher here. On all these occasions, Lorenza is able to capture the moments when my own feeling of definiteness is fluctuating. My therapeutic choice was to use these dreams only as indicators of Lorenza's interior movement, without interpreting them, rather like a "silent interpretation" (Spotnitz, 1969) that can eventually be proposed over a long period of time and "diluted" within the rest of the analytic material.

The appearance of co-identity phenomena, which signals a progressive movement towards the ability to symbolize, goes hand in hand with the fading of other phenomena of the continuous: numbness, the feeling of fluctuating or fainting, which Lorenza can now talk about as they occur, without having to communicate them to me through projective identification.[2]

VI Toward the conclusion

Towards the end of the seventh year of analysis, when we begin to talk about a conclusion, Lorenza discovers she is pregnant. A significant recrudescence of her symptoms occurs: vague troublesome indispositions, hints of phobias, as well as nausea and the evident intolerance for her condition, experienced for the first three or four months of pregnancy as a sort of colonization, a tiresome impediment. Lorenza appears frankly lost, in part because of an evident and, in many aspects, surprising lack of knowledge of her body. Much of analysis revolve around her nausea and the almost total impossibility to eat anything without being disturbed by it.

Two dreams from this period:

I'm walking in the water, I find a stool with some food, I eat a mini pizza, but I'm going down and I risk drowning. My father takes me out.

I have to go to analysis but I'm going around in circles. I turn into a boy. I tell myself that I'm so late, that there's no point going.

She associates it to the fact that she has to find tasteless food to avoid nausea. Yesterday she called on a friend who made her some broth. Now that she's pregnant, will the analysis go on? It would seem that Lorenza's condition has overbearingly awakened her ambivalence towards maternal nourishment, which, however wished for, is also rejected and feared as something that makes her sink into

---

[2] I have already discussed the communicational function of projective identification: Cimino & Correale (2005).

waters it now seems not too easy to resurface from (but is this her own greedy desire?).

A father is needed to help out. Passive desires, in what seems to be a regressive identification with the baby who is about to be born, or oral enjoyment, must really scare her. So it's best to keep well away, at least in dreams, from the mother-analyst, and try rather to manage alone, through this sister-friend double. The extreme remedy is to become a boy, root out the chance of being inserted in this feminine line.

For a certain period some recurrence of projective identifications phenomena is present, though these are less intense compared to the beginning of analysis. Sometimes it becomes necessary to give her technical explanations about the body and its changes. Lorenza seems to be very reassured by the fact that the analyst is also a doctor. However, her tone is once more reproachful and recriminatory. Why is she reproaching me? I get the impression that Lorenza now realizes that her time as daughter is really over, though this pregnancy must have induced the regressive fantasy of a further extension of the analysis. This interpretation induces protests, it solicits the activation of regressive defenses and a relative aversion for the tiny stranger who is about to usurp her place. It slowly seems more possible to identify with the child in a non-narcissistic way, and she even asks: "How must she (it's a baby girl) feel inside of here"?

She brings a dream:

I dive from a high rock. I find myself in murky waters, I can't see a thing, I wish I knew where I was going.

It is evident how the dream (which is even a dream of birth) concerns the imminent conclusion of the analysis, which hasn't been prolonged precisely to allow Lorenza "to be born" before her daughter. The dream announces that such a passage is laborious, but not unfeasible. Lorenza begins to brighten up a little, even experiencing periods of happiness that she seems most self-conscious, even ashamed about. She dreams of lots of houses, from her past and her fantasies:

small cozy houses, some harmoniously separated, some with long corridors, which make me think of the birth canal.

In April we conclude analysis. At our last session it's difficult for me to hold back the tears, which respond to Lorenza's. In June she phones me triumphant, happy: Giulia is born.

VIII Conclusion

I believe that in Lorenza, the urge to merge with the other, fully unfolded in transference during the course of the analysis in a form that tends toward, as I have already said, not only an actual fall of the boundaries and a con-fusion of identity between patient and analyst, but also, as in the form described by Fachinelli, the phenomena of co-identity. I think that both forms have a potent communicative valence that signal, with different modalities, (a) the zones of undifferentiated identity of the subject, that in turn solicit and commit to analytic work, and (b) the zones of undifferentiated identity of the therapist, who must be able to receive the communication. In fact, I believe that fundamentally this is the importance of these phenomena, in their individualization and decodification (through the already cited "silent interpretation"), although an eventual interpretation could, but not necessarily, be proposed during the course of a long period of time.

What seems central to Lorenza's case is a fantasy related to a primary object that can be well represented by the doll Olympia in Hoffmann's "The Sandman". According to acute observations by Jentsch (1919), the essential thing in producing the uncanny effect is the aspect of intellectual uncertainty, i.e. doubt over what Freud calls "orientation", the possibility of distinguishing between what is animated and what is not and vice versa. According to Freud, Olympia is not the central element causing the "uncanny" feeling, but rather the Sandman, who carries the threat of paternal castration, is. If we try to read the paper at another level, however, it is the doll Olympia that becomes essential, being the bearer and generatrix of a radical impossibility to access castration. In other words, Olympia is the emblem of an "automaton mother", not alive and not dead, who must constantly be questioned about her true nature. She is remote, sidereal and "sidereant" – not the dead mother described by Green (1983), inaccessible because closed in her bereavement: she is not alive and not dead, a sort of "mother-revenant", incapable of actually generating because she herself isn't wholly generated, excluded from symbolic castration, which in turn ties the subject down to a sort of incomplete birth, a non-birth. Here lies, substantially, the excess of the Real of Lorenza and hence her trauma. This does not consist, in this case, of having experienced a specific event, but of having been exposed to the relationship with a primary object with the characteristics, which I tried to describe, matched to the modality Lorenza experienced. In all intents and purposes, we can speak of trauma only on the basis of its psychic effects and not in an "objective" way. I believe that the traumatic event becomes "splitting of consciousness" in the sense utilized by Freud (1894) and not in the sense of specific defense of "splitting" (Kernberg, 1966). In other words, it becomes as "encysted" and "dissociated" from the rest of the psyche (Putnam, 1992; Bromberg, 1998, Van Der Kolk, Van Der Hart, 1991; Van der Kolk, Fisler, 1995; Van Der Kolk et al., 1996; Varvin, 2003). The trauma is therefore excluded from the possibility of being symbolized and represented: it can arrive only repetitively – "acted out".

In the case of Lorenza, working with the trauma was manifest in the sessions by the urge to merge with me. At the same time, during the course of her treatment the urge to merge with me assumed different modalities of declination that also signaled the progressive integration of the identity of Lorenza.

I cannot be grasped in the here and now
For I live just as well with the dead
As with the unborn
Somewhat closer to the heart
Of creation than usual
But far from close enough.

This epitaph on Paul Klee's gravestone, talks to us about a precocious knowledge, not only of death, of "the dead", but also of the "unborn", and of a radical, unconceivable alieness that signals an equally precocious encounter with a brutal, untamed and untamable Real.

The Real, as it is for Kant (Benvenuto, 2006, pp. 39-40), is something substantially unattainable, and it radically avoids our grasp and any demand for subjectivization. The encounter with this naked Real is thoroughly different from the *Heim* (home), from familiar objects, to the point that, rather, it is their opposite and is for some subjects a very common experience, paradoxically a familiar one, ever ready to emerge, to reveal itself with all its uncanny power. In Lorenza, the traumatic alternation of living and dead, or rather of not living and not dead, prevents in Lorenza the building of the *Heim*, of whatever is homely, domesticated, essentially the building of relationship and so of the other. The automaticity of the primary object is not so much simply related to aspects of coldness or "non-empathy", but to an imperfection in its ability to impose its own limits upon its passions, to express self-control over its symptom, i.e. over its own pleasure. Lorenza's primary object seems, in turn, bound to its own primary object by a dual relationship characterized by the primary pleasure it was unable to renounce. It is in this sense that castration is, in the Lacanian sense, precluded. The object has to be constantly watched over for its moves to be prevented. Its intermittent presence is characterized by presences/absences as vertiginous as chasms during which automatism manifests itself in full power. Discontinuity, unpredictability, the alternation of moments of contact and moments of loss, the sudden and unpredictable entrance into and exit from different states generate an impression of automaticity, of appropriation by anything alien, "non-human", not living and not dead. At the same time, these alterations don't allow the necessary domestication of the object itself.

The need, the urgency to control in order to survive gives rise to the practice of "malignant omnipotence", a sort of evil variant of what Winnicott (1971, 1984) described as necessary to every child so that it may experience the necessary illusion of creating the world. I actually have the impression that the function of omnipotence, for which perhaps we must think of another name, constitutes a structural and structuring moment (that prevails upon the defensive aspect, even if it is understood) necessary to the constitutive experience of the human being's defencelessness, that is, of its "bare life". I understand defencelessness (in which the nucleus resides only in part in the Freudian *Hilflosigkeit*) to be a primary experience of total exposure to events which generates the feeling of being under threat and uncertain of one's very existence, at the complete mercy of the other upon whom salvation depends. With respect to borderlines there has been talk of a tragic search for an ungraspable truth (Racalbuto, 2001). My impression is that in some subjects, definitely in Lorenza, the truth request becomes, at least in certain moments, even more radical and concerns their very being alive, their very state of existence. It's a short step from this exposure to a constant waiting for a "sentence" by the other, who is omnipotent.

In the last century we have witnessed tragic events through which helplessness, exposure to the naked life, the absolute power of the other, has become political or social fact, normal or mad anomaly, such as in racial persecutions and, above all, the concentration camps. Giorgio Agamben (1995) defines, in judicial and political terms, "sacred life" as the life subject to the sovereign power over life and death. Sacred life is then "naked life", not just natural life, but life exposed to death, which he considers to be the original political element. The prerequisite of sovereignty resides here, and therefore harbors unavoidable violence. Agamben's modern prototype of naked life is the Jew under Nazism within the concentration camp as the space where power exerts its sovereignty and turns the natural life (*zoé*) or the political life (*bios*) into killable, naked life. My impression is that this legal-political phenomenon, primal according to Agamben, has its psychic equivalent in the experience of helplessness that opens life, which is thus marked at its very beginning by a constitutive violence. The impossibility to domesticate the other, in itself tragically and constitutively human, under certain conditions translates into an experience of brutal, inaccessible, mute reality. As I've argued before (Cimino, 2002), such a background reaches its peak in psychosis, the other side of which is represented by the continuous.

It is from this extreme experience that the condition of being helpless arises, exposed naked life, completely at the mercy of the other. In spite of the preservation of vast functioning zones, this dimension repeatedly emerged in Lorenza during analysis and in transference in various modes. I believe, with Winnicott, that the only possible antidote is to experience, in the early phases of life, a sufficient condition of omnipotence, or perhaps I should say illusion, to make the denial of the primal traumatic condition possible enough. The cure itself ought to go in the same direction, at least in the areas where this is called for, i.e. towards the creation of a true "transitional space" within which that illusion of omnipotence capable of domesticating the other can exert its influence. This seems to me the only possible place, the only third way. It is half way between establishing oneself in pain, which often has no access to the psyche and is linked to the condition of being exposed, helpless, constantly awaiting a sentence, and the attempt to manage through scission, idealization and above all, as in Lorenza's case, by confusing oneself into the other in the manifold modes of the continuous. To achieve this it became mandatory and useful to leave Lorenza a quota of the continuous itself, which once cleansed of its more symptomatic aspects contributed to her settling in a middle place. In this place, Lorenza would say, one isn't happy, but only "normal", and therefore, perhaps, it is a practicable place for a frail human happiness.

Edited by Janet Thormann

Bibliography

Agamben, G., *Homo Sacer. Sovereign Power and Bare Life* [1995], Palo Alto, CA: Stanford University Press, 2001

Barthes, R., *A lover's discourse: Fragments* [1978], London: Vintage, 2002

Benvenuto, S.:
- "Introduzione", in S. Žižek, G. Daly, *Psicoanalisi e mondo contemporaneo*, Bari: Edizioni Dedalo, 2006
- "The Drive towards the Real. Philosophy in the Epoch of Bio-Technologies and Bio-Politics", 2008, Web-site "Biopolìtica", http://www.biopolitica.cl/docs/Benvenuto_THE_DRIVE_THE_REAL.pdf (accessed 16 January 2009)
- Benvenuto, S., Molino, A., *In Freud's Tracks*, New York: Jason Aronson, 2008
Bromberg, P.M., *Standing in the Spaces, Essays on Clinical Process, Trauma and Dissociation*, London: The Analytic Press, Inc., 1998
Cimino, C., "La psicosi e il continuo", *Rivista di Psicoanalisi*, XLIX, 1, pp. 59-72, 2002
Cimino, C., Correale, A., "Projective identification and consciousness alteration: a bridge between psychoanalysis and neuroscience?", *Int. J. Psychoanalysis*, 86, pp. 51-60, 2005
Fachinelli, E.:
- *Claustrofilia*, Milan: Adelphi, 1983
- "Freud's Clock. On time on psychoanalysis", *Journal of European Psychoanalysis*, 12-13, 2001, pp. 137-150
Freud, S.:
- *The neuro-psychoses of defence* [1894], *GW*, 1; *SE*, 3, pp. 45-57
- *The Uncanny* [1919], *GW*, 12; *SE* 17, pp. 219-249
- *Analysis terminable and interminable* [1937], *GW*, 16; *SE*, 23, pp. 216-252
Green, A., *Life Narcissism, Death Narcissism* [1983], London: Free Association Books, 2001
Lacan, J., *Écrits* [1966], *The first complete edition in English by Jaques Lacan*, transl. by Bruce Fink, New York : W.W. Norton, 2006
Racalbuto, A., "Vivendo lungo il border", *Rivista di Psicoanalisi*, XLVII, 1, 29-49, 2001
Rank, O., *The Double: A Psychoanalytical Study* [1914], London: Karnac, 1989
Spotnitz, H., *Modern Psychoanalysis of Schizophrenic Patient*, New York: Grune and Stratton, 1969

Van Der Kolk, B. A., Van Der Hart, O., "The intrusive past: The flexibility of memory and the engraving of trauma", *American Imago*, 48, 1991

Van Der Kolk, Fisler, R., "Dissociation and the fragmentary nature of traumatic memories: review and experimental confirmation", *Journal of Traumatic Stress*, 8, 1995

Van Der Kolk, B. A. et al., "Dissociation, somatization and affect disregulation: The complexity of adaptation to trauma", *American Journal of Psychiatry*, 153(7), 1996

Winnicott, D. W.:
- *Playing and Reality*, London: Tavistock Publication, 1971
- "Fear of breakdown" [1963], *Int. Rev. of Psychoanalysis*, 1974
- *Deprivation and Delinquency*, London: The Winnicott Trust, 1984

Disidentity Shock in Transference and Counter-Transference

Giampaolo Lai, Pierrette Lavanchy

Key Words: Disidentity – Transference – Counter-transference – Temporal Logic – Logic

Summary: *Transference is the therapist's hypothesis that the patient perceives, imagines, knows him, – the analyst, – not as he is in the actual psychoanalytic situation, but as other fictional persons were in the patient's past history. Conversely, counter-transference is the therapist's hypothesis that his own feelings, perceptions, imaginations do not belong to his actual self, but are derivatives of the experiences of his past elicited by the patient. The two hypotheses construct a possible world inhabited by disidentical persons, such as a therapist who is not what he is and is what he is not, while seeing a patient who is also not what he is and is what he is not. The phenomenon of disidentity shock is characterized by a set of feelings of surprise, uncertainty, confusion, bewilderment, which can arise anywhere, every time you open the door expecting a known person and see an unknown one. From this point of view, psychoanalysis is not the endeavor to transform disidentity into identity, but the ability to tolerate the uncertainty of disidentity. The authors distinguish two types of disidentity, diachronic disidentity, as in the example of saint Paul, and synchronic disidentity, as in the example of Dorian Gray. In the paper, two clinical vignettes illustrate these concepts, also in the light of tense logic and of modal figures.*

I Ouverture

When someone comes across an actual situation that is different, i.e. non-identical, therefore dis-identical, compared to how they had imagined it or to how they believed they knew it, they suffer a disidentity shock. Finding the world to be different from how they had prefigured it, they verify the disidentity of the world compared to their representations of it. At the same time, having to verify that they are different from how they prefigured themselves, they have to deal with their own disidentity. For example, it would be appropriate to talk of disidentity shock in the actual situation where Othello, who had always imagined he had a faithful wife, perceives, through the handkerchief, that he is a wretched victim betrayed by an unfaithful wife. But we may also talk of disidentity shock for the analyst who, two years after their last encounter, sees a young patient who reveals she is pregnant. Disidentity shock is therefore the disruption of the imaginative and cognitive representations of oneself and of the world, brought about by the sudden emergence in the actual situation of unexpected perceptive representations, which force one to redesign one's previous perceptive, imaginative and cognitive structures. Though disidentity shock is ubiquitous, we shall limit ourselves to studying it within the conversational analytical situation and using its tools.

I.a Object of research

The object of our study will be the phenomenon of disidentity shock, investigated through the filters of transference, counter-transference and of temporal interval logic, in two conversation fragments, one with Viola and the other with Alessia. We shall present the two text fragments, recorded and transcribed, in the tradition of Conversationalism. Preliminarily, however, as transference and counter-transference are controversial concepts, it is a good idea to define them.

II Definition 1. Transference

By the term transference we mean the therapist's hypothesis that the patient brings to the current psycho-analytical situation a set made up of perception, imagination and knowledge in relation to the therapist, but that this set is not original, it is rather a repetition, in the current situation, of perception, imagination and knowledge contents the patient had in past situations with regards to other persons in his personal history. As can immediately be seen, this definition is not in terms of absolute transference, but rather of the patient's transference in relation to the point of view of the therapist who will work on the transference ingredient.[1]

I Corollary. When the therapist forwards the hypothesis that the patient perceives, imagines, is acquainted with, the actual sensorial persona represented by the therapist (which is in any case the current sensorial object that triggers off the patient's triad: perception, imagination, intellection) in the same way as in the past he (or she) had perceived, imagined, been acquainted with, other persons in his personal history, then it is as if the therapist were making the patient live in a possible world where the therapist is the person he is and yet is another person from the patient's point of view. In this same possible world the patient too is what he is, for example in the faculty of perceiving the therapist in the way he is in actuality, while he is another person, in the faculty of imagining and knowing the therapist as if he were another person from the past. In other words, the therapist is not always identical when moving between one world and the other: he is different. In a world where he goes to live, he becomes the counterpart of what he was in the world he left. In the same way, the patient does not preserve his identity in moving between one world and the other. In each world he becomes different from himself. In the terminology of Conversationalism, the therapist is disidentical, i.e. at once identical to himself and different. On the basis of corollary 1, the patient's transference hypothesized by the therapist is produced through the precondition of the patient's and the therapist's disidentity.

ⅢⅢ Definition 2. Counter-Transference

By the term counter-transference, from the therapist's point of view, we mean the set of perception, imagination and knowledge

---

[1] Benvenuto, 2004.

the therapist has in relation to the patient in the psychoanalytical or conversational situation. As we can see, in the definition the two concepts of transference and counter-transference are not symmetrical, as they are when presented in absolute terms, but are two descriptions of two different fields of investigation in the therapist's domain. However, the clause valid for the patient's transference is also valid for the therapist's counter-transference: i.e. that the set of things the therapist perceives, imagines, knows, the triad of the therapist's counter-transference, is not so original or primal as the repetition, in the actual situation, of perception, imagination and knowledge contents the therapist already had in previous situations with regard to other persons in his personal history.[2]

II Corollary. We do not have enough space here to argue the fact that the therapist too, when producing counter-transference, assumes both himself and the patient to be living both in the actual world and in possible worlds, in a to and fro of counterparts made possible by the disidentity of both.

III.a Note

Let us here supply brief definitions of these two notions of disidentity and possible worlds.

IV Definition 3. Disidentity

A person's disidentity in general, in this case of patient and therapist, is the thesis according to which a person, patient or analyst existing in the space and time of a four-dimensional universe is not always and anywhere identical to himself, i.e. not unique. Instead the person in question, the patient/respectively the analyst, is multiple, in the sense that the patient/respectively the analyst living in a world, is disidentical from the patient/analyst living with the same name as a replicant android in one of the many worlds he happens to frequent

[2] Bassi, 2004.

either simultaneously (*synchronic disidentity*) or subsequently (*diachronic disidentity*).[3] We find examples of *diachronic disidentity* in saint Paul, persecutor of Christians before his fall from a horse and persecuted as a Christian thereafter. We find examples of *synchronic disidentity* in Dorian Gray: young, handsome and damned in his actual world and wrinkled, aged and repulsive in his other world, the painting in the attic. A poetic example of *synchronic disidentity* can be found in this song by Johannes Ockeghem (circa 1450):

Ma bouche rit et ma pensée pleur,
Mon oeil s'esjoye et mon coeur maudit l'eure.

V Definition 4. Possible Worlds

Disidentity theory is based on the theory of possible worlds, which assumes the existence, alongside the actual world, of multiple other possible worlds. So, next to the actual individual called Dorian the theory assumes the existence of multiple other individuals, inhabiting other possible worlds, disidentical "replicants" of the actual Dorian, perhaps bearing the same name. For example, the mouth of the laughing maiden inhabits the actual world, while the thoughts that cry in the maiden with the same name, disidentical replicants of the laughing mouth, live at the same time in another possible world.[4] In our argument, while the actual patient, perceiving the therapist as he is, inhabits the world of the actual psychoanalytical situation, the patient with the same name, perceiving the analyst in the form of a person far away in personal history inhabits another world different from the actual. The same can be said of the therapist, who also has a disidentical replicant inhabiting a parallel disidentical world, different from but similar to the actual world.

---

[3] See Lai G., 1988; Lai G. et al., 2005.
[4] Lewis D., 1968; Lewis D., 1986.

VI The logics of identity and difference

After supplying definitions for the terms transference, counter-transference, disidentity and possible worlds, there remains one other concept to define: identity. Of no great use to us is the concept of absolute identity of a thing or person either with itself or with another thing or person, as expressed by formulae (1) and (2)

(1) $a = a$;

(2) $a = b$.

More useful is the concept of relative identity, relative to one or another property of a particular thing or person. For example, it is possible for a thing, 'a', called Antonio, to be identical to another thing, 'b', called Giorgio, from the aspect of particular property, W, let's say 'being white', but different from the aspect of another identification property, let's say G = 'Genoese' for 'a' and M = 'Milanese' for 'b'. Hence, in formula (3), 'a' and 'b' are identical [Antonio and Giorgio are identical insofar as they are both white]; in formula (4) 'a' and 'b' are different [Antonio and Giorgio are different insofar as one is from Genoa and one from Milan]; in formula (5) 'a' and 'b' are both identical and different.

(3) $W(a) = W(b)$

(4) $G(a) \neq M(b)$ [the symbol $\neq$ stands for 'not equal to']

(5) $W(a) = W(b) \ \& \ G(a) \neq (M)b$

The contradiction of these formulae and the possible bizarre quality of (5) can be solved using the concepts of possible worlds and disidentity. If we accept the concept of relative identity – i.e. of disidentity, synchronic disidentity and diachronic disidentity – we can say, without contradicting ourselves, that the two passengers are identical, insofar as they are both white and carry an Italian passport, even though they are different, because one is from Genoa and the other from Milan. Along with synchronic disidentity, expressed in formula (3), it is also important to consider diachronic disidentity, i.e. the persistence or non-persistence of identity with the passing of time. If the arguments put forward so far have helped us understand a synchronic disidentity, when a person lives simultaneously, t^1, in multiple worlds, as in the Johannes Ockeghem example expressed in formula (6):

(6) $M(a)t^1 = T(a)t^1$

where M stands for the mouth of the maiden 'a' and T for her thoughts; it becomes easier to accede intuitively to the idea of a person's diachronic disidentity with the passing of time, from t^1 to t^2. For example, formulae 7 and 8 express respectively the fact that at one time, t^1, in 1980, Mary is a very young child, being born in 1975, and the fact that the same Mary, at another time, t^2, in 2005, is a grown woman: this leads us to conclude that Mary is diachronically disidentical.

(7) $C(a)t^1 =$ 'Mary is a very young child at time t^1, 1980, being born in 1975'

(8) $G(a)t^2 =$ 'Mary is a grown woman at time t^2, 2004'.

Or let's take the example of Mr. Stephen, 'a' = 'industrialist, heterosexual with wife and kids, in the time interval until 2002'= E(a), and again Mr. Stephen, 'a' = 'industrialist, homosexual who has abandoned his family and become part of a gay community in the time interval starting from 2002' = G(a). Is the Mr. Stephen of the time interval before 2002 identical to or different from the Mr. Stephen of the time interval after 2002?

If in order to solve the problems raised by the above examples we simply need to draw on the concept of relative identity and, even better, of disidentity, the examples have, however, helped us to see how an individual's identity does not remain unique with the passing of time, but instead diffracts into the possible worlds of disidentities, inhabited by disidentical replicants of an original identity.[5] ["Here I add that the conception of change, and with it the conception of motion, as change of place, is possible only through and in the representation of time; that if this representation were not an intuition (internal) *a priori*, no conception of any kind could render comprehensible the possibility of change, in other words, of a conjunction of contradictorily opposed predicates in one and the same object; for example, the presence of a thing in a place and the non-presence of the same thing in the same place. It is only in time that it is possible to meet with two contradictorily opposed determinations in one thing, that is, after each other."[6]]

VIII Definition of the term *identity* (and the correlated term *difference*)

We are now in the condition to give a simpler definition of identity, on the basis of our arguments so far. We shall not refer to the identity of non-living entities such as, let's say, a manuscript, or, in relation to our field of work, conversation turns, objects that do not change with the passing of time. We shall refer only to living beings, to speaking persons, all of whom keep an identical name with the passing of time, while some of their other properties change. For these subjects, speaking persons, it is of little use to refer to the concept of identity, to the absolute person, one should instead refer to the person in relation to his properties at a specific time. One shouldn't therefore say: 'a', i.e.: Giorgio, but should specify those properties of Giorgio's relevant to our discourse, for example:

(9) (W, M, P, t) a

in other words, 'Giorgio, White, Milanese, Protestant, in 2004'. The definition of identity arises from all this quite naturally.

---

[5] See Varzi, 2001, 2003.
[6] Kant, 1781.

VIII Definition 5. Identity

By the term identity we mean a person's set of relevant properties. It is necessary to understand what each of us means in different situations when using the qualification 'relevant'[7] applied to the noun 'property'. For example, to establish the identity of saint Paul before and after falling off his horse, from the Christian perspective the properties of "lack of faith" or "presence of faith" in the subject Paul (§ IV) are absolutely relevant, whatever is meant by these expressions. However, the same properties may have been irrelevant to the tax collector, for whom it would have been enough, in his function as a tax collector, to establish whether the Paul in question was identical or not to the citizen owner of five horses, two houses and three vessels.

IX The relevant properties in the conversational situation to calculate transference and counter-transference

Returning to the thread of our discussion, we should now ask: what are the relevant properties of patient and therapist for the objects of transference, counter-transference and disidentity shock in transference and counter-transference? In fact the choice of the domain for these relevant properties will inevitably orient the calculation of transference and counter-transference. First of all one must be aware that both clinically, when the therapist converses with the patient ['at the time of the material live conversation'], and during successive meta-clinical reflection ['at the time of the deferred immaterial conversation'], we do not have access to all of an individual's properties, neither ours, nor the patient's, but only to a few partial, fragmented, often uncertain properties. In terms of the *logic of relevance*, all that is available to us is a set of limited objects accessible only in the concrete situation of material conversation and a set of limited objects accessible in the abstract situation of immaterial conversation, and it is within these boundaries that we are

[7] Mares, 2004.

forced to work. Furthermore, when one tries to translate the elements of a concrete system, peculiar to material conversation, into an abstract situation, peculiar to immaterial conversation, one needs to choose the scheme for the abstract situation that seems more suitable to account for the concrete elements that interest us.

X Transition

But now, after having supplied the preliminary conceptual elements, we can begin to present, at paragraph 10, the concrete situation of the material conversation with Viola. At paragraph 17 we shall present the concrete situation of the material conversation with Alessia. We shall then justify the use made of the abstract schemes of conversationalism in translating the concrete objects of material conversation into the abstract objects of immaterial conversation.

XI Conversation with Viola

Example 1. Conversation recorded by Giuliana Andò on October 1st 2004, with Viola, a patient in analytic treatment since approximately a year earlier.

1 VIOLA (*shortly after the beginning of the conversation*): I'm a surgeon! (*She says something about her job, which we do not reproduce for privacy reasons.*) On my way home on Saturday, while buttoning my blouse, I felt a lump. It was about two centimeters in size and that's impossible for someone who does a mammography regularly every year, (*she dwells on the procedures for histological tests*). A two-centimeter tumor, a case of one in a hundred, even positive lymph nodes in the axillary folds, which reduces the chances of recovery. Something that never occurs in someone who does a mammography every year. The problem is I'm really angry about these things.
1 GIULIANA: Really angry.
2 VIOLA: Because it's not fair. (*She cries.*) It really brings me back to my job, which is really important, which gives enormous gratifications (*she talks about her relations with university professors and her conferences*). I like public relations, it's something I'm good at and I also like relief work with women. I would always understand what they felt and I was available ten, twelve hours a day, even at nine in the evening, I never

sent anyone away. I dedicated twenty-eight years of my work to this thing and now I feel ripped off. (*She cries*).

2 GIULIANA: Ripped off.

3 VIOLA: By life, in the sense that I don't feel I deserve this. If at least I'd had one of those tumors that we try to contain with mammographies every two years. We usually find them small. Once a year I did screenings, perhaps they did it wrong. I'm really mad now, I don't know with who or what, and I find myself being afraid of losing my job. Looking at the clinical records of a woman who's had a relapse I'll feel, I'll be afraid. I owe it to women, for years I've been saying that you shouldn't be afraid of breast cancer, that it's curable. If I'm the one who's going to sit at home crying, I'm ripping all of them off. I have to regain my credibility, about everything I've told them. It's difficult, because I know all these things, the probabilities of recovery do exist.

3 GIULIANA: They do exist.

XI.a Viola's transference in the current situation of material conversation

Viola immediately starts off the conversation with her shock at discovering a lump on her breast. It is a dramatic account, full of anger, desperation, consternation, resentment, dismay. But it is, before anything else, an account Viola gives Giuliana, establishing, in the actual situation of material conversation, a specific triangle:

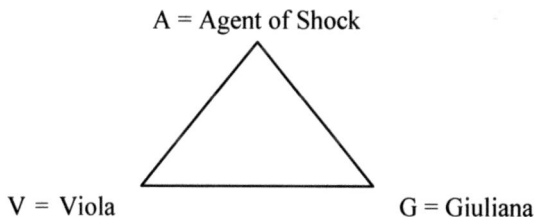

A = Agent of Shock

V = Viola   G = Giuliana

Fig. 1 Triangle of the actual situation of material conversation

In the triangle at fig. 1 we see Viola, V, at the vertex at the lower left of the triangle. At the vertex, at the lower right, we find Giuliana, G and at the vertex at the top of the triangle we find the agent of shock, A, that Viola tried to indicate with the terms: 'life', 'an unfair being', 'a being that rips you off'. This is the object of Viola's account, what Viola talks about, the propositional content, the 'p' of our logical formulae.

Then the question arises: why does Viola give Giuliana her account? More particularly: what does Viola expect from Giuliana with her account? We are in the midst of the transference perspective in the concrete situation of material conversation, i.e. Viola's transference, insofar as it can be accessible to Giuliana in listening to Viola's words. And here we are moving in the category of Giuliana's perception, in the more or less objective perception on behalf of the therapist of what the patient Viola is saying (cf. § III). At this point the category of Giuliana's imagination can come into play (cf. § III again), i.e. the construction by Giuliana of images detached from but set in motion by perception. Giuliana can imagine Viola coming to her and telling her in tears how she has been the victim of an extreme act of violence perpetrated by a being she would never have expected such an aggression from, a being that has been unfair to her, has betrayed her and fooled her. But such a being, because of the law of retaliation, is a being Viola expected fairness, kindness and welcome from: therefore a well-known being, a familiar one. At this point, in Giuliana, mixed in with the previous categories, the cognitive category comes into play (cf. § III again), which introduces the schema of possibilities: whether Viola says all this to Giuliana in order to be protected by her against this vile treacherous being, or whether she is accusing Giuliana of being herself, the therapist, from whom she expected protection and help, the one who has betrayed her and struck her hard. In both versions Giuliana is holding in her hands the construction of Viola's transference in the concrete situation of material conversation.

XLb Giuliana's counter-transference in the current situation of material conversation

Giuliana is holding in her hands the representation of Viola's transference, such as she, Giuliana, infers from the perception of what Viola has said (in verbal turns 1, 2 and 3), through the mediation of her imaginations and intellections. But, if perception, insofar as it belongs to the sensorial object produced by Viola, can, without too much quibbling, be attributed to Viola, (identifying the fact that Giuliana has heard such and such words with the fact that Viola has said so and so), the mediation of Giuliana's images and intellect is undoubtedly also indebted to Giuliana's personal and professional history: they belong, in other words, according to definition 2 of § III, to Giuliana's counter-transference. Giuliana's counter-transference is shaped starting from the shock produced in her by the perception of Viola's dramatic account, and which continues in the images and concepts that can lead to a representation of the type in proposition (10):

(10) Viola tells me she was the victim of the deadly shock inflicted by her illness and desperately asks me to help her. But what can I do? I just do not have the instruments to rescue her from her fate as the victim of a sly, evil and possibly mortal aggression.

If things had gone thus in the actual situation of material conversation, as the words fictionally attributed to Giuliana in proposition (10) suggest, then this proposition would contain Giuliana's counter-transference, tuned into the desperation of Viola's words. But, according to definitions 1 and 2 of § II and III, in order to talk of transference and counter-transference, it is necessary for the set of perceptions, imaginations, intellections that the patient, respectively the therapist, have of the therapist, respectively of the patient, to be not so much original and primal, but rather to be the repetition in the actual situation of material conversation of representations occurred in a distant past of the patient's, the therapist's, history. According to this stipulation, we can complete the partial representation of the counter-transference shown by formula (10) with formula (11):

(11) Viola tells me she was the victim of the deadly shock inflicted by her illness and desperately asks me to help her. But what can I do? I just do not have the instruments to rescue her from her fate as the victim of a sly, evil and possibly mortal aggression. And so, Viola now finds herself with me in the same situation in which, a long time ago, after being her father's victim, she asked, to no avail, her mother for protection, who was stultified and also just did not know what to do. (And I, Giuliana,

could it be I was a victim of the father, noticing that the stultified mother was unable to protect me?)

XI.c The trans-universal transition from concrete material situation to abstract immaterial situation

We hope to have given a relatively adequate account of the construction of the therapist's counter-transference in the actual situation of material conversation. The next step is to move on from material conversation to immaterial conversation, in other words, to translate the concrete objects of material conversation, perceptions, imaginations, knowledge, into the abstract schemes of some simple and precise figures adopted by conversationalism, i.e.: a) the figures of modal logic [cf. § XII] and b) the figures of the logic of time intervals [cf. § XIV].

XII The translation of Viola's concrete objects of material conversation into the subset of modal logic figures: alethic, deontic, axiologic, epistemic

Canonically, the modal logic figures usually employed in conversational practice are the following:

FL1. Alethic modal logic figures (from *aletheia* 'the true')		
Possible	Mp	'it is possible that p'
Impossible	~Mp	'it is not possible that p'
Necessary	Np = ~M~p	'it is necessary that p'
FL2. Deontic modal logic figures (from *déon* 'duty')		
Permitted	Pp	'it is permitted that p'
Forbidden	~Pp	'it is not permitted that p, it is forbidden that p'
Obligatory	Op = ~P~p	'it is obligatory that p', it is not permitted that p do not'
FL3. Axiologic modal logic (from *axios* 'value')		
Good	Gp	'it is good that p'
Bad	~Gp	'it is not good, it is bad, that p'
Indifferent	Gp = ~Gp	'it is neither good nor bad that p'

FL4. Epistemic modal logic figures (from *episteme* 'knowledge')		
Knowledge	Kp	'knows that p'
Non-knowledge	~Kp	'does not know that p'
Belief	Bp = ~Kp & Kp	'believes that p', 'neither knows nor does not know that p'

Table 2. The 4 modal logic figures and corresponding operators are indicated with capital letters. The propositional content, in respect to which each operator revels the propositional attitude of the sentence, is indicated with the symbol *p*. The symbol ~ stands for the negation 'not'.

In practice, for the calculation of the modal logic figures, one proceeds to make an inventory of the modal logic figures that the words of the text conform to – in the same way as the stars in the sky conform to the geometrical figures of the triangle or the mythological figures of Sagittarius – by listing all the simple sentences in a column on the left and initialing in a column on the right the corresponding modal logic values, as in table 3.

No.	Propositions	Time	Modal logic figures
1	I am a surgeon!		
2	Saturday, while buttoning by blouse, I felt a lump, about two centimeters in size [*'On my way home'* = interval; *'I felt etc'* = Punctual time]	Punctual time and interval	~Kp; ~Gp
3	that's impossible for [*'impossible'* = ~Mp]		~Mp
4	someone who does a mammography regularly [*in the sense of 'according to the rules?' Then* = Op],		Op
5	A two-centimeter tumor, a case of one in a hundred, even positive lymph nodes in the axillary folds		~Gp
6	which reduces the chances of recovery.		~Gp; ~Mp
7	never occurs [*in the sense of propositions 3 and 4 = impossible* = ~Mp]		~Mp; Op

8	in someone who does a mammography every year		Op
9	The problem is [*in the sense of 'issue', 'interrogative'? Then ~Kp*]		~Kp
10	I'm really angry about these things		~Gp; ~Pp
11	Because it's not fair. [*in the sense of 'not permitted'? Then ~Pp*]		~Pp
12	It really brings me back to my job,		
13	which is really important,		Gp
14	which gives enormous gratifications		Gp
15	I like public relations.		Gp
16	It's something I'm good at		Gp
17	and I also like relief work with women,		Gp
18	I would always understand what they felt [*perhaps also in the sense of "I was permitted to'? then= Pp*],		Gp; Pp
19	I was available ten, twelve hours a day [*perhaps also in the sense of 'duty', thus an 'obligation'? Then = Op*],		Gp; Op
20	even at nine in the evening [*as for proposition 19: Op*],		Op
21	I never sent anyone away		Op
22	I dedicated twenty-eight years of my work to this thing		Op
23	and now I feel ripped off [by life] [*in the sense of 'necessity', 'fate'? Then Np*].		~Gp; Np
24	By life, in the sense that I don't feel I deserve this. [in the sense of 'it wasn't necessary'?; or 'it wasn't obligatory'?]		Np; Op
25	If at least I'd had one of those tumors		Mp
26	that we try to contain with mammographies every two years		Gp; Op
27	We find them small		Gp
28	Once a year [*incredulity, impossibility: Bp; ~Mp*],		Bp; ~Mp

29	perhaps they did it wrong		Mp
30	they did it wrong		~Gp
31	I'm really mad now		~Gp
32	I find myself being afraid of losing my job.		~Gp
33	Looking at the clinical records of a woman [hypothesis of a possible world = Mp]		Mp
34	who's had a relapse		~Gp
35	I'll feel...		Mp
36	I'll be afraid.		Mp; ~Gp
37	I owe it to women		Op
38	for years I've been saying	time	
39	that you shouldn't be afraid of breast cancer		Op
40	that it's curable		Gp
41	If I'm the one [possible world = Mp]		Mp
42	who's going to sit at home crying		~Gp
43	I'm ripping all of them off		~Gp
44	I have to regain my credibility		Op
45	about everything I've told them		
46	It's difficult [in the sense of 'not impossible' = Mp]		Mp
47	because I know all these things,		Kp
48	the probabilities of recovery do exist		Gp

Table 3. Inventory of modal logic figures in the 48 simple sentences
of Viola's verbal turns.

Next the distribution in percentages of the respective values of the
modal logic figures is expressed in numbers (box 4) or images (hist. 5).

Categories	No.	%	Categories	No.	%
~Gp	12	25%	Mp	6	12%
Gp	11	22%	~Mp	4	8%
Kp	1	2%	~Pp	2	4%
~Kp	2	4%	Op	12	25%
Bp	1	2%			

Box 4. Distribution of modal logic figures of the 48 sentences of Viola's turns

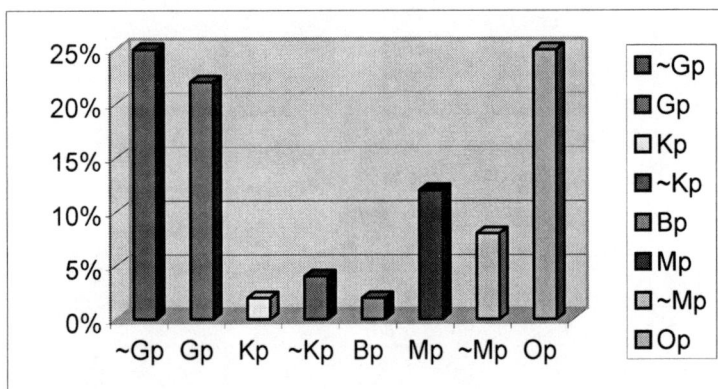

Histogram 5. Distribution of modal logic figures.

XIII Discussion

From the distribution of modal logic figures in box 4, and in histogram 5, we see that the majority of Viola's 48 sentences conforms to axiologic modal logic figures by 47%, with 22% for Good, Gp, and 25% for Bad, ~Gp. The sentences conform to the other figures, which add up to a total of 28%, with much lower percentages, between 4% and 2%. The deontic figure of Obligatory, Op, which reaches 25%, like the figure of Bad, ~Gp, occupies a separate and extremely important position. The result is a conversational profile, in logical-modal terms, of the following type: 'the concrete objects of the material situation, i.e. Viola's sentences, markedly fit in the following scalar succession: Bad, ~Gp, 25%,

Good, Gp, 22%, Obligatory, Op, 25%'. These three dominant modal figures could then merge into a multimodal figure of the type:

(12) 'the Bad of the Obligatory' = ~G(Op),

which recalls, with a trans-universal jump, the diagnosis of obsessional neurosis; or, in a more interesting way, in the multi-modal figure

(13) 'The Obligatory of the Bad' = O(~Gp),

which recalls again, with a trans-universal jump, the diagnosis of the borderline, with the endless repetition of the death instinct or primary masochism. In any case, this is neither the place nor time to delve further into these aspects of research pertaining to the calculus of the modal logic figures, however fascinating. Let us instead move on to a second translation of the words of the material conversation, again in the abstract situation, but now mediated by the figures of time.

XIV Point-based and interval-based temporal logics

The figures of temporal logic orient the account of actions and events in terms of a 'before' and an 'after', established by a deictic 'now': for the speaker, from whose point of view the things of time are oriented, the future is after 'now' and the past is before 'now'. The point, in the logics of temporal points, is a place with no extension, as in the sentence: 'while traveling on the road to Damascus, Paul was struck by a bolt of light'.

Before / Now / After

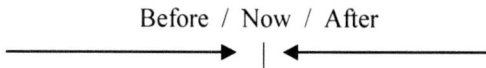

Figure 6. The deictic 'now' is a point with no extension in respect to the temporal extensions of the before and after.

The event 'was struck' is considered a point with no extension; but the event 'traveling on the road' is treated as a temporal extension including the 'before' and 'after' of figure 6, and which therefore also includes the 'now' of the punctiform event of the bolt of light striking. Point-based temporal logics have the advantage of allowing a visualization of graphical representations (see fig. 7). Given two distinct points on a line, t^1 and t^2, the first may come before or after the second: '$t^1 < t^2$' means that t^1 comes before t^2; '$t^2 < t^1$' means that t^2 comes before t^1. The operator '$<$' therefore means 'before'. As for the logics of temporal intervals, the interval is a particularly interesting temporal operator in conversations.

Figure 7. Punctiform event t^1 comes before punctiform event $t^2 = ($'$t^1 < t^2$'$)$ on the timeline terminating with two arrows on the left and right.

An interval, as a period of time intervening between two facts, recalls the idea of a limit on the left side, let's call it A, and one on the right side, let's call it B, as well as the space between A and B, the actual interval, which we shall call I, the symbol of the interval itself. With things standing thus, as in box 8, we talk of a closed interval:

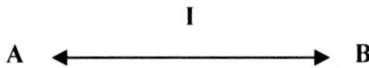

Box 8. A closed interval, on the left side towards the past and, on the right side, towards the future.

We indicate it with a line terminating with two arrows (box 8, figure 7). Sometimes the interval may be an open one, at the time of the uttering, ('now'), or in a succession of events, either on both sides or not, with the open side indicated by deleting the arrow (box 9).

Interval open on the left, on the past		I ———————→
Interval open on the right, on the future		←——— I ———
Interval open on the future and on the past		——— I ———

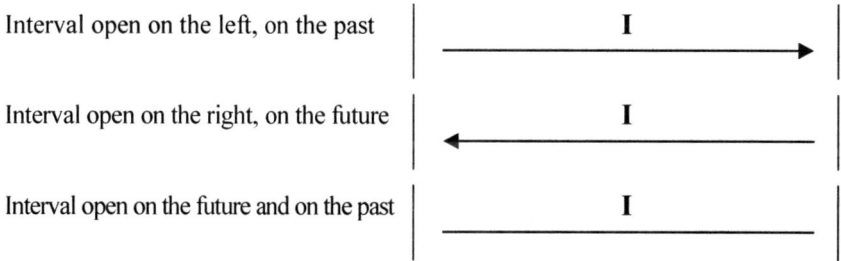

Box 9. An interval open on the left (top line with arrow on the right); open on the right, (middle line, arrow on the left); open on both sides, no arrows.

In the same way as temporal points can come one before the other (as in fig. 6) but also meet, i.e. lie one next to the other, intervals can also establish various other relations, at least 13, as formalized in figure 10, defined by adverbial operators: 'before'; 'after', 'during', 'meets' and by 'overlapping'. Before A, before the limit of the interval on the left, before the interval comes into question, after B, when the interval is closed, after the limit on the right; during I, while the time of the interval is taking place.[8]

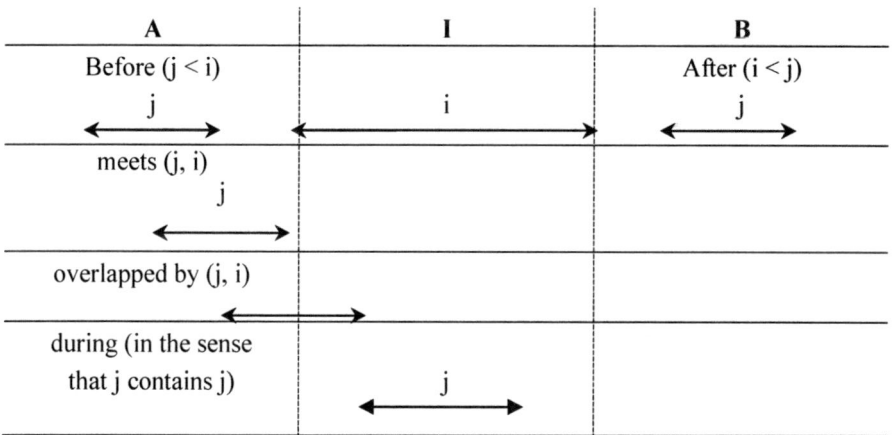

A	I	B
Before $(j < i)$		After $(i < j)$
j ←——→	i ←————→	j ←——→
meets (j, i) j ←———→		
overlapped by (j, i) ←——→		
during (in the sense that j contains j)	j ←———→	

Box 10. The relations between intervals according to the adverbial operators *before, after, during* and '*immediately before*' = meets (j, i)

[8] Allen, 1983; Allen, Ferguson, 1994; Endriss, Gabbay, 2003; Hirsch, 1994; Ohlbach, 2004.

But let us return to Viola's conversation and isolate the first sentence of verbal turn 1:

(14) On my way home on Saturday, while buttoning my blouse, I felt a lump. It was about two centimeters in size.

So, if in the concrete situation of material conversation Giuliana could have been the victim of the same shock Viola had originally been a victim of at the time of the event she is describing, now, in the abstract situation of immaterial conversation, it is possible for the therapist to detach herself from emotional participation and concentrate on conceptual elaboration. We can thus formalize the proposition (14) with box 11. Visually box 11 shows us that point 'p' takes place instantaneously inside interval 'b', which lasts in time and which in turn takes place inside interval 'a'. We need not take into account the possible semantic incongruities of the sentence: literally, interval 'b' begins after the end of interval 'a', in the sense that, rationally, Viola starts unbuttoning her blouse after interval 'a', her going home, is over. But we shall instead choose to remain in the possible world of Viola's grammar, which, moreover, has the advantage, rhetorically, of showing us the busy overlapping of events leading to Viola's shock: 'I felt a lump two centimeters in size'.

	I	
	a	
On my way home	⟵——————⟶	a = interval, durative
	b	
While undoing my blouse	⟵————⟶	b = interval, durative
I felt a lump	*	p = point, instantaneous
	p	

Box 11. The interval b is included in interval a and point p is included in interval b; i.e. the punctual event p included in the extended time of b and a.

Box 12 takes us half way between point-based temporal logics and interval-based temporal logics. But it is punctiform temporal logics we most need in order to translate into abstract formulae the concrete situation of Viola who suddenly, surprisingly and unexpectedly receives her shock concentrated in one point, which lays in between the intervals of the 'before' and 'after' the point of shock. The discovery of the lump, in the temporal logics, is a punctiform temporal event.

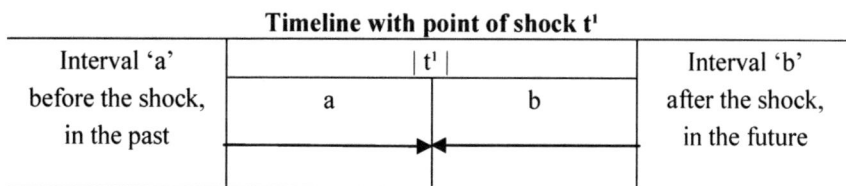

Timeline with point of shock t¹

Interval 'a' before the shock, in the past		t¹		Interval 'b' after the shock, in the future
	a	b	

Box 12. The two temporal intervals, past and future, cut by point t¹

XV Viola summary

The shock of discovering a two-centimeter lump on her breast is for Viola a punctiform event that suddenly, surprisingly and unexpectedly separates the timeline into two unsalable sections: before and after. Before the shock Viola is sure of herself, passionate about her job, she believes that with regular check-ups cancer can be avoided. After the shock Viola is furious, but above all she is dismayed: she no longer believes in what was once one of her most steadfast beliefs. She is another person, at least in what is an absolutely relevant property for a person's identity, believing or not believing in an object of the world. For this transformation it seems pertinent to talk of disidentity shock in the conversational analytic situation, and possibly in transference.

XVI The text of the conversation with Alessia

After having examined, in Viola's text, disidentity shock in relation to an event situated in a temporal point, Alessia's text now gives us the opportunity to study disidentity shock in events situated in the duration of temporal intervals.

Example 2, from the conversation with Alessia recorded by Giampaolo Lai on December 15th 2004.

1 ALESSIA (*from approximately 35 minutes into the conversation*): Yes, there is this attempt to try and understand how things went, and in fact in this period a lot of things about my childhood come into my mind, the things I never remembered. I don't know, I see again this relationship I had with my grandfather's house in B – my paternal grandfather – where they'd basically segregated me, there in the country, at the time it was, it came into my mind that I'd go out to look at the *Gamb de Legn, Wooden Leg,* which was the tram, the tramway that passed there and was the only link with the centre of the city, because this was plain suburbs, we were so isolated, and what also came to my mind was my relationship with animals, because the only living presences, apart from my grandfather's second wife, who, I don't know why, I was never fond of, but she was present, she cured me, and I remember the animals, I remember the peacocks, I remember the turkeys. Once a turkey pecked me, I remember this early childhood I'd never remembered before, I mean this early childhood never came to my mind, but I also remember that perhaps I was, this coming and going, right? Saturday and Sunday, dad and mum's house and then exiling me again, I remember this composition on exile a teacher gave me when I was nine, entitled *Nostalgia, Homesickness,* and my composition was so good that they read it out on the radio and I remember I made everyone cry with this composition and when they sent me to sleep, down there, in that hovel, on my own, and if I came down my granddad would also pester me, and I, and in the photos that my mother later threw away I have a gloomy expression, I look very sad.

1 CONVERSAZIONALIST: Aged nine, at elementary school.

2 ALESSIA: Yes, in third grade, and then this wanting to appear good for my mother, then it came into my mind that putting me with these nuns, right? With these *Pious Ladies,* right? where the environment wasn't so rural, but more middle class, and I also met some very refined nuns, a more refined environment, for example, I never spoke the dialect, I know it, I know it perfectly, because at home everyone, including my brother, the one nearest to my age, everyone spoke in dialect, I never, never spoke my mother's language.

2 CONVERSAZIONALIST: So, you didn't speak the dialect, they accepted the fact you spoke Italian.

3 ALESSIA: Yes, and they spoke in Italian with me. Because I was a foreigner, I lived away from home, obviously my grandfather spoke to me in Italian, the little Italian he knew, right? My grandmother was from Parma, she didn't know the B. dialect, so I never spoke my mother's language, never, it, it, and with me, but only with me, they all spoke in Italian, just think how strange.

3 CONVERSAZIONALIST: Yes, yes.

4 ALESSIA: And not to my brother, I'd never thought of that. It's incredible. And I learnt it at school with the nuns, with the *Pious Ladies*.

4 CONVERSAZIONALIST: And without an accent.

5 ALESSIA: And without an accent, because I never spoke the dialect. It's incredible. I never spoke my mother's language. And once my mother, by chance... She would send us to summer camp, I knew that already and I never forgave her, she didn't want me at home, who knows why? And look, I was a cute girl, in those photos I was a little doll, but she didn't want me at home, so when I was five, not yet six, she'd sent me to summer camp, before, when I was younger, they sent me to sun treatment summer camp, so they sent me to C., I remember it as a kind of hell, just think that in '45, my birthday was in '46, in August, I wasn't even six yet, so they sent me to this summer camp in a valley of the Bergamo province and I have terrible memories of it, I even caught head lice and they put petrol and vinegar on my head, and then the separation between those who had head lice and those who didn't. And I fell ill and never spoke. And the principal, who was really strict, a really strict mistress, at first even put me in charge, she saw how cute I was, of keeping the hallway of the summer camp building clean, which was an arcade, but I didn't manage to keep it clean, because I was five years old, I didn't know how to keep a hallway clean, right? So she punished me in front of everyone, saying I was incapable of doing anything and then I caught head lice and fell really ill, I'd caught something in my throat. So they called the doctor, because I wouldn't speak, I was silent and the doctor examined my throat and, I remember this clearly, it took place in a space under the staircase, he said: "this girl has a throat infection" and he gave me some, and then they asked me some questions, but I didn't talk, I never answered them, I was mute, so the principal, I remember this clearly, said: "but this girl's a bit retarded", right? "She's a bit retarded". This I experienced as a great pain, something terrible.

5 CONVERSAZIONALIST: Yes.

6 ALESSIA: And just think that, one of life's little ironies, when I was at elementary school, this lady, who was a school inspector, came to visit my school too and my teacher introduced me as the best girl in my class, right? She didn't recognize me, or pretended not to, I recognized her, but she pretended not to recognize me. All these kind of tragic things came to my mind.

6 CONVERSAZIONALIST: Lots of things having to do with words. Talking, muteness, Italian. Rejection of the maternal dialect.

7 ALESSIA: Yes. But they would speak to me in Italian, I don't know why. My mother, with my brother who was only a couple of years older than me, my mother would speak to him in dialect.

7 CONVERSAZIONALIST: And did your brother speak to you in Italian?

8 ALESSIA: My brother too. My brother too: "give me this, do this for me", he gave me orders in Italian, like a foreigner. I was a foreigner. I was a foreigner in my own home: "You have to speak her language with her, she doesn't understand ours". And at the same time I was the little lady. Because I knew Italian, then when I started being smart at school, probably due to the fact that I'd learnt Italian, right? And so I'd learnt Italian and asked the nun for the difference: "tell me what blessed is the fruit of thy womb Jesus means", and so I beat my brother, with whom there was a lot of competition, obviously, because he was much more loved than me, he'd always stayed at home, not me, I beat him in school things. I beat him in what my mother was really concerned about, because she'd never had the opportunity to get an education, she was always saying that. And so, basically, I was really good until about the first two grades of senior high, then I had some bad emotional crises with my mother, with my best friend, with everyone and my grades started dropping, and at my finals, at the time you could do them in September if you weren't admitted before, as I fell in love with a guy from the male class, I'd lost my head, I didn't study, I couldn't study anymore, instead of studying I'd dream, I didn't revise, I couldn't do anything at the exams. I had a sort of trauma. Then he left me, he became a personality, a TV director. He left me and I turned the thing into a tragedy, as always. Then after two years he came back and I didn't want him anymore. Yes, I had a very difficult emotional life, always, very very much so.

XVI.a Alessia's transference in the concrete situation of material conversation

The opening of Alessia's account is very different from Viola's under several aspects. Viola's account, as we saw, (§ XI and XII.a), begins with the shock she had been a victim of in a very recent past. Alessia too talks of a shock she underwent, also situated in the past, but decades earlier. And yet both shocks are conveyed as equally present by the actuality of the account. From this perspective they are both coetaneous to the 'now' of the enunciation. The form of the shock seems different in the two patients. Viola's shock is punctiform, in the sense that it occurs in the instant of a temporal point. In Alessia's case we actually have more than one shock, at least two or three, and in the form of events that last in time, that take place in the space of various more or less extended intervals. From the point of view of perception in the current situation of material conversation, Viola's shock is easy to capture in its simplicity: the tactile detection of a lump in her breast of approximately two centimeters. From the same point of view, Alessia's shocks are more complex and articulated. The agent of the first is her mother, who exiles her first to the grandparents and then to the nuns; the second, the principal who humiliates her before the other girls at the summer camp; the third, a subset of the second, the head lice that cause her to be segregated in isolated places. Beyond these differences, however, these three shocks, these three *tokens* of shock, come together in a single shock-*type* fitting the interchangeable names of 'exile', 'segregation', 'separation', 'removal'. Now, here too, as with Viola (§ XI.a), it is fair to ask: why does Alessia give this account – centered on exile, abandonment, segregation and set in a remote past – to her therapist Giampaolo? In particular, what does Alessia expect from Giampaolo by giving him this particular account structured around the contents of exile? With these questions we take the path of transference in the concrete situation of material conversation: Alessia's transference, as it can make itself accessible to the conversationalist Giampaolo through the perception of Alessia's words. Indeed, by moving from the perception phase to the imagination phase, the conversationalist can imagine Alessia, a lively, intelligent, particularly cute child whose mother, however, won't hear of – 'she didn't want me with her, who knows why?' – and actually repeatedly exiles her. Perhaps her mother did not wish to marry, but was forced to because pregnant with an unwanted child, Alessia. Perhaps she was passionate for her studies or for a particular job and had to give it all up to look after the newly born Alessia. Perhaps the pregnancy had caused the mother an infirmity of some sort, for which Alessia was held responsible. Perhaps at Alessia's birth her father had distanced himself from his wife to pursue a lover. Ultimately, perhaps, Alessia had contributed to making her father distance himself from her mother.

If the conversationalist then moves on to the register of intellection, prepared by his studies and readings, he may reflect on the following: if Alessia is repeatedly abandoned and exiled, and the people who do this to her are always different, it may become necessary to consider the possibility that Alessia is also somehow the cause of these abandonments, that the people she comes across are not only cruel torturers, but that something in the way Alessia relates to others, former or future torturers, sooner or later contributes to the scene of abandonment. At the end of this path the therapist, after perceiving Alessia's words, imagining Alessia's possible relations, reasoned over and become acquainted with her schemes, has at his disposal Alessia's transference, translatable in the following formula (15):

(15) Alessia has always and repeatedly been sent away and exiled by everyone: by her mother, by the principal, by the head lice. And Alessia tells me about her shock as an exile, a refugee, a stateless woman, asking to repeat even with me her destiny as a perpetual wanderer, if even I send her away, or asking to rest her feet in a safe land if I decide to welcome her.

XVI.b The conversationalist's counter-transference in the concrete situation of material conversation

But in this formula (15) something is unconvincing, something is lacking: the property of Alessia's ill-treated beauty. "She [my mother] didn't want me at home, who knows why, and look, I was a cute girl, in those photos I was a little doll, but she didn't want me at home"; "the principal, […] at first even put me in charge, she saw how cute I was, of keeping the hallway of the summer camp building clean". Alessia is mistreated and exiled in connection to her beauty, in spite of it or because of it. The conversationalist is reminded of the tale and film *Girl with a Pearl Earring*, and the scene where the young housemaid is sent away by the mistress because she is beautiful to her husband's eyes. This representation, a figment of the therapist's imagination and then of his intellection, linked to the pervasiveness of the oedipal triangle, shows us the direction of the conversationalist's counter-transference. But it doesn't make the formula (15) more convincing. However, that transference is a question of repeating in the current situation the picture of being thrown out once more, or of being welcomed, is stressed by a trait of the therapist's counter-transference (not of formula 15, but towards the end of § XVI.a), when the therapist starts thinking that perhaps Alessia is acting in collusion with her torturers to be thrown out: in following the pattern of some diagnosis that makes Alessia responsible for, or even guilty of her being thrown out, is the therapist not perhaps rejecting Alessia like everyone else who has thrown her out? [As can be seen, in this phase of the development, the therapist's counter-transference moves on the triangular oedipal horizon rather than on that of the diagnosis of borderline personality disorder.]

XVI.c A trans-universal leap from material conversation to immaterial conversation

Let us now try to translate the results of our survey, carried out in the concrete domain of material conversation, where transference and counter-transference dwell, into the abstract objects of immaterial conversation, where both modal and temporal logic figures dwell. For reasons partly of space, we shall limit ourselves to translating the concrete objects of Alessia's text into the logical figures of time intervals (cfr § XIV and boxes 6 to 12).

XVII The logics of the temporal interval

Within the perspective of temporal intervals, Alessia's verbal turns allow to spot without difficulty at least three intervals. Let us begin with the most easily datable, with a limit on the right, A, and on the left, B, with Alessia aged between six and eleven, corresponding to elementary school with the *Pious Ladies*: we shall indicate it with 'i' in box 13.

	A		B	
Before the *Pious Ladies*		←——————————————→		After the *Pious Ladies*
A = 6 y o				B = 11 y o

i = duration of elementary school with the *Pious Ladies*

Box 13. A closed interval, on the left, towards the past, before six years of age, and, on the right, towards the future, after eleven years of age.

Before this interval two more intervals can be located, which we are forced to reconstruct somewhat approximately in box 14, there being a lack of precise information on Alessia's behalf. The first can be reasonably set between Alessia's birth and when she is four or five years old: her 'early childhood'. We shall indicate it with 'b'. Overlapping, towards the end of interval 'b', we can place a very brief, but crucial, interval, we shall call it 'c', consisting of Alessia's stay in a mountain summer camp and the muteness episode. Still to come is interval 'd', Alessia's exile with her grandparents, from ages 4/5 to 11 (see box 14).

At her mother's	Muteness	Grandparents/Pious Ladies		
←————————→ mother 'b'				
	←————→ muteness 'c'			
head lice 'c²'	←→			
grandparents 'd'		——————————————————→		
pious ladies 'i'		←————————————→		
~maternal language			←———————————————————————	
4/5	6		11	

Box 14. The succession of intervals with the years of age indication in the bottom line.

Each of the three intervals, 'd', 'c', and the head lice sub-interval, 'c²', included in 'c', is marked by a shock suffered by Alessia and exerted respectively by the mother exiling Alessia to her grandparents' house; by the principal, who punishes Alessia before the other girls; by the head lice, which segregate Alessia yet again. To make the argument simpler let us take interval 'd' as a model, the one where Alessia's mother repeatedly exiles her daughter to her grandparents' house from the age of five onwards, isolating from box 14 the 4th line and completing interval 'd' with the interval before it, 's¹', Alessia before age 5.

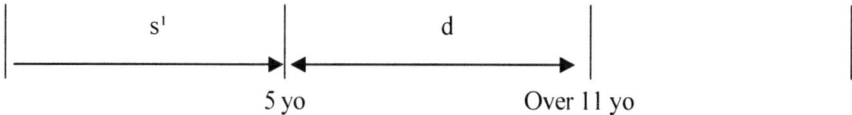

Box 15. The shock at five years of age, when Alessia is exiled to her grandparents' house by her mother.

What is special about the shock suffered by Alessia at five? At first sight one may say, as we have done, that the shock is identified in the painful fact of being exiled, in the condition of refugee, of statelessness [in interval 'd'] with the consequent home-sickness, the melancholy desire to return [*nostos*] to the condition of the irrecoverable past [interval 's¹']. But there is something more. Alessia says so herself: 'she [her mother] didn't want me at home, who knows why, look, I was a cute girl, in those photos I was a little doll, but she didn't want me at home.' And again: 'the principal, […] at first even put me in charge, she saw how cute I was, of keeping the hallway of the summer camp building clean, which was an arcade, but I didn't manage to keep it clean, because I was five years old, I didn't know how to keep a hallway clean, right? So she punished me in front of everyone.' To convey the affair with the principal graphically, from the point of view of interval logic, from box 14 we shall reconsider interval 'c', muteness, from the ages of 4 to 5, and detail it in box 16. Here we have a first interval, 's²', where the principal treats Alessia kindly, because she is a pretty girl: 'she saw how cute I was'.

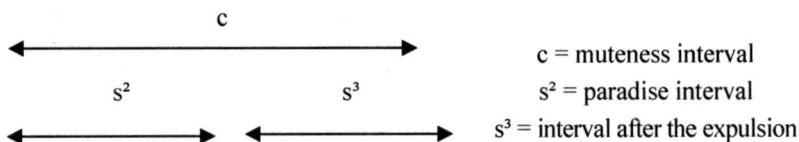

$$c = \text{muteness interval}$$
$$s^2 = \text{paradise interval}$$
$$s^3 = \text{interval after the expulsion}$$

Box 16. The expulsion from Paradise because of one's beauty.

In the second interval, 's^3', Alessia has been punished and exiled by the principal who starts being mean to her. As with her mother, so with the principal too Alessia couples exile and her beauty. To account for the dramatic and shocking representation, with its somatic and psychological effects ('and I fell really ill, I'd caught something in my throat, and then they asked me some questions, but I didn't talk, I never answered them, I was mute'), we need to immediately examine the property of Alessia's beauty and the property of not understanding why her mother had sent her away not just once, but twice. It is not so much, or not only, the pain of being sent away that can account for the trauma: it is rather this not understanding, this being confronted with a universe that is different from the one she had represented to herself. More precisely, if Alessia's identity, and that of everyone else, is based on the values-beliefs-norms triad, the blow received by the mother who sends her away ('who knows why?') shakes Alessia's epistemic identity [Kp, ~Kp, Bp, cfr § XII and box 1]. The category of causality collapses with the collapse of the quasi-syllogism that formerly allowed her to find her bearings in the world:

(16) 'all cute girls are loved,
    I'm a cute girl,
    therefore I am loved'

If she is not loved, if she's even cruelly mistreated, it means that she is not a cute girl; but she knows she's cute; then that means that not all cute girls are loved; and yet this was the belief that allowed her to find her way in the world. Hence her disorientation, her dismay, her not knowing what to think of the world: with the consequence of the shock, in the forms of muteness on the one hand and the refusal of her mother's language, the dialect, on the other.

XVIIII Disidentity shock

Before this long tour around the logic of temporal intervals, the formula reached by the therapist to account for transference and counter-transference was No. (15) of § XVI.a. Now we can modify this formula (15) as in formula (17):

> (17) Alessia has always been sent away and exiled, despite her cuteness and the fact that she founded her identity on the belief that her beauty would necessarily make her immune from the violence of the world. And Alessia tells me about her pain, of course, but most of all about her dismay at the collapse of her identity under the impact of the shock inflicted on her by the world that abuses and exiles her, either because it does not recognize her beauty or because the world is also capable of abusing beauty. Alessia tells me all this in the hope that I will recognize her and so help her talk to me speaking my language, and still terrified that I too will fail to recognize her beauty, because this shortcoming would perpetuate her mutism, or lead her to speak a language foreign to me, in which she would tell me incomprehensible things.

XIX Transference and counter-transference production by the therapist

A. The patient's transference is produced by the therapist through the inferences obtained from three main sources:

a. *the perception* of the words spoken by the patient;
b. *the imagining* scenarios containing the narrative motifs of a story made available by human culture: in Alessia's case the motif of the expulsion from the Garden of Eden, of the little girl sent away from home by her wicked mother; in Viola's case the motif of a cruel Mother Nature treacherously striking her children with haphazard deadly diseases;
c. *the knowledge of the conceptual patterns* of the therapist's school of thought, which first reduces the narrative motifs to the

representation of an affair with two main actors on the stage, patient and therapist, and then distributes between them the two roles so as either to allow the presence of a third character, as in the triangle for Viola, or to exclude the presence of further characters other than patient and therapist, as in the face-to-face discussion with Alessia. In the former case we speak of oedipal transference, to which Viola's account seems to conform more; in the latter we are more prone to speak of pre-oedipal or narcissistic transference, which seems to better describe the conversation with Alessia.

Phase a) of the process, *the perception of words*, entirely situates itself in material conversation; phase c), *the knowledge of conceptual patterns*, belongs to immaterial conversation; phase b) of the process, *imagining possible worlds*, is a transition between the sensorial concreteness of material conversation and the logical abstraction of immaterial conversation. After all, it is in this phase b) of imagination that the search of narrative motifs finds expression, an important procedure in conversational practice, which we can only mention here in passing and refer the reader to other works on the subject.[9]

B. We have partially seen the therapist's counter-transference as filigree while looking at the production of the patient's transference. We can safely say, however, that what sets in motion the therapist's counter-transference are the words spoken by the patient, *the perception* of the words of the conversation. But it is then the therapist, with his *faculty of imagination*, who accommodates the words of the patient's text to the narrative motifs shared among all the members of a community, though perhaps not accessible to all, or not accessible to all in the same way. So, already in capturing the narrative motifs, for the production of patients' transference, it is reasonable to talk of counter-transference by the therapist, at least in the sense of seeing in it a more or less decisive contribution of the therapist's counter-transference. For this very reason it is in phase

[9] Lai, 1993; Lai and Lavanchy, 2003.

b), *imagining*, that the patient's transference and the therapist's counter-transference have the greatest chances of mixing inextricably. Finally, it is in phase c), *knowledge of conceptual and theoretical patterns,* that the therapist's counter-transference mainly unfolds, through the employment of abstract schemes in which he tries to accommodate the words captured in perception together with the narrative motifs produced in the imagination.

After all, it is the therapist's conceptual patterns that, perhaps more than perception or imagination, are liable to guide the conversation on paths leading away from the road indicated by the patients words – in the past one would have said: 'which preclude an understanding of the patient; which prevent the patient from being understood'. For example, at a certain point in his production of Alessia's transference, the conversationalist, guided by his conceptual schemes, leant towards the idea that Alessia was asking to repeat a sort of triangular drama where she was attacking the bond between the mother [the analyst] with the father to the point of forcing the mother to send her away, and that, therefore, Alessia was responsible or jointly responsible for her exiles (§ XVI.a). On the other hand, when used with cautious relativism and fair common sense, the same conceptual schemes sometimes allow to re-direct the therapist's digressions, diversions and confusions, like when the conversationalist, thanks to the logics of temporal intervals, recovers the property of Alessia's beauty, a recovery that allows him to capture the drama in two, face-to-face, without other interlocutors, between himself and Alessia (§ XVII and proposition 17).

Bibliography

Allen, J. F., "Maintaining knowledge about temporal intervals", Communications of the ACM, 26(11), pp. 832-843, 1983

Allen, J. F., Ferguson, G., "Action and Events in Interval Temporal Logics", *Journal of Logic and Computation*, 4(5), pp. 531-579, 1994

Bassi, F., "Progressi nell'impiego clinico del controtransfert", *Tecniche conversazionali*, 32, pp. 5-12, 2004

Benvenuto, S., "Che cosa vuole l'analista? Transfert e desiderio dell'analista in Lacan", *Tecniche conversazionali*, 32, pp. 13-24, 2004

Endriss, U., Gabbay, D., "Halfway between Points and Intervals: A temporal Logic Based on Ordered Trees", www.doc.ic.ac.uk /~ue/pubs/file/EndrissGabbayESSLL12003.pdf, 2003 (accessed 15 February 2009)

Hirsch, R., "From points to intervals", *Journal of Applied Non-Classical Logics*, 4(1): 7-27, 1994

Kant, I., *Critique of Pure Reason* [1781], English translation by J. M. D. Meiklejohn, § 6, "Transcendental Exposition of the Conception of Time", p. 57, Sioux Falls, SD: NuVision Pub., 2005

Lai, G.:
- *Disidentità*, Milan: Feltrinelli, 1988
- *Conversazionalismo*, Turin: Bollati Boringhieri, 1993

Lai, G., Lavanchy, P., "The predictions of the text", presented at the study day "Psicoterapie: analisi dei trascritti di seduta", Bologna University, 22nd November 2003

Lai, G., Mazzetti, M., Merini, A., (2005) "Culture shock and disidentities shock", *Rivista Italiana di Gruppoanalisi*, 2, pp. 33-49

Lewis, D.:
- "Counterpart Theory and Quantified Modal Logic", *Journal of Philosophy*, 65, pp. 113-126, 1968
- *On the Plurality of Worlds*, Blackwell, Oxford, 1986

Mares, E., *Relevant Logic: A Philosophical Interpretation*, Cambridge: Cambridge University Press, 2004

Ohlbach, H. J., "Fuzzy time intervals and relations", the FuTIRe Library, Techincal Report PMS-2004-4, München: Inst. F. Informatik, LMU, 2004. See also: http://pms.informatik. unimuenchen.d/mitarbeiter/ohlbach/systems/FuTIRe.

Varzi, A.C. :
- "Parts, Counterparts, and Model Occurrents", *Travaux de Logique*, 14, pp. 151-171, 2001
- "Entia Successiva", *Rivista di estetica*, 22(1), pp. 139-158, 2003

Transference: A No Man's Land

Antonio Maiolino

Keywords: Psychoanalisis – Transference – Setting – Preliminary conversations – Dream – Individual psychotherapy – Family psychotherapy – Private studio – Rehabilitation center

Summary: *'Preliminary conversations' are very important, both in private and in public settings, for in these conversations we wait for the emergence of the question that will enable us to begin therapy. My argument proceeds from this consideration. I shall describe a case, which I regard as representative of what is done in a public institution when we activate the psychoanalitic device and its functionality. I found this case interesting because it shows how one can speak of psychoanalisis (performance wise) in an institution and not only in a private studio. It also shows how, all in all, the difference between the two settings is irrelevant for the functioning and destiny of analysis, because if there is a difference, this is due to the listener and not to the place where one listens. Finally, in the case I describe, I shall focus my attention on the possible passage, in the analytic discourse, from a public to a private setting, making the preliminary remark that one sets to psychoanalytical listening upon receiving a demand.*

Introduction

I met the Rossi family in a Rehabilitation Center (RC) belonging to the "Azienda Sanitaria Locale (ASL)" of an Italian city where I carry out psychotherapeutic consultations. This RC provides therapies such as speech therapy, movement therapy, physiotherapy, psychotherapy, hippotherapy, occupational therapy, etc.

The users of psychotherapy are very different. Clinical cases include children, adults, individuals, groups, and range from individual to family psychotherapies.

These multidisciplinary interventions are inserted, as is the case in many of the Italian territorial centres, in a framework called "maternal-infantile". That is to say, the intervention begins when an ASL sends us a child (usually it is infantile neuro-psychiatrists who decide this). For instance, an adult is almost never sent to us without a background concerning a child.

These considerations are important in the light of the "question": "who asks what?" Which is also "who asks to whom?" The question never comes to us directly, as it could, for instance, emerge in a private setting. Instead, different persons and institutions filter it. In doing so, we end up creating further defensive layers in the patient. As far as I am concerned, I believe it is important to work on the preliminary conversations, in order to let the question emerge. The emergence of the question – even if it is not the true one – forms a virtual, but fundamental (therapy-wise) "moment zero". Let us take for instance the initial diagnosis. When the RC assigns me a therapy, they give me a consignment letter with the child's name (if it is an individual therapy) and the relevant diagnosis made by the infantile neuropsychiatrist of the child's ASL. The same stands for a family therapy, that is to say, on the consignment letter there is written the couple's son/daughter diagnosis. This explains why I stated that intervention begins with an infantile matter. In this way, the child's parents are authorized to ask the usual questions, such as "what do we have to do with this?", or "we didn't ask for anything!" The majority of us know that we should not overlook such questions and we can – and must – begin from these. Starting right from what I called "moment zero", in the case of couple therapy – we should let the parents understand that if they are here, there has be a reason. Obviously, this is the case also for an individual therapy. In this scenario we encounter another typical question. For instance, if we ask the child why is he here, ninety-nine times out of one hundred he answers "boh? (I don't know)".

The "question" is crucial in order to begin a therapeutic work on the psychic discomfort broadly speaking. Regardless of the setting, often nature and destiny of the psychic discomfort depend on the involved subjects. With "regardless of the setting", I mean that –

despite the differences between a private and a public studio – the setting is more important for the patient than it is for the therapist, as his listening remains the same (or at least it should) in both cases.

Needless to say, every therapist has his own (ethical) rules, but to these we must add those imposed by the institution to which he belongs. Often, these institutional rules hinder the functioning of therapy, or, better still, the beginning of a therapy. It is for this reason that preliminary conversations must be kept into the highest account. In a private studio it can be quite different, as there is more freedom, though this does not mean it is less difficult.

One must always keep into account what the preliminary conversations are, even when acting inside the institution, in order to understand our orientation and the direction we are taking.

This being the case, "preliminary conversations" are very important, both in private studios and public services, for it is during these that we wait for the initial question from which therapy begins. It is from this point that this article begins. I will define a clinical case, chosen from the many I am in charge of weekly, as a sample of a job carried out activating the psychoanalytic device and its functioning in a – so to speak – public institution. I found this case interesting because it shows how you can perform psycho-analysis inside institutional and not only private conditions. This case also shows that the difference between the two settings is, all in all, irrelevant for the functioning and destiny of therapy. If there is a difference, this is attributable to the listener and not to the space where the listening takes place.

II The public case

I receive the Rossi family for the first time at the RC where I work. On the first meeting I am introduced to the whole family, a married couple (Giacomo and Caterina) and two siblings (Cristiana and Roberto). They explain me why they are there. The eldest child, Cristiana – four years old – is excessively attached to the mother. Consequently, first they consulted a pediatrician, then an infantile psychotherapist, who decided that the child indeed needed therapy. Six months later he advised a family psychotherapy.

Before this meeting, Cristiana was already coming weekly to the RC, where she was seeing a behavioral therapist: the initial diagnosis was that of "separation anxiety disorder". On the occasion of our first meeting, the mother says: "My daughter is morbidly attached to me!" As I stand up to dismiss them, I answer: "Why do you allow it?" Later, she told me that precisely this answer "hooked" her to the therapy, because it was the first time she felt directly involved in the situation: "It's not about her that we will talk but about me."

In the following weekly meetings, the parents describe their daily activities. They knew each other since she was thirteen and he was seventeen. The married nine years later. Mr. Rossi co-owns with his brother-in-law and his brother a clothing factory and his wife is employed there as a seamstress. Also, occasionally she acts as a model for their production items. Mrs. Rossi works only in the morning, while in the afternoon she takes care of their children at home. She describes her daughter as very similar to herself, timid and reserved. On the contrary, concerning her son, she comments: "I can't seem to hear him."

Though she loves her children, she finds it very tiring for her to look after them. Even playing with them seems to be very costly, though this does not happen often. She is bothered when they ask for attention, as they distract her from her own thoughts. In particular, she says that when she is far from the children she feels a strong sense of guilt for having left them alone. Conversely, when she is with them, the guilt is associated with a sense of bursting.

She never misses an appointment, while her husband sometimes is late or absent. On one of the occasions when he is very late (he almost misses the session), his wife brings me her first dream:

I am standing at the entrance of a church because I have to get married. While I wait for my husband to arrive, his mother approaches me and tells me not to worry because her son would arrive, sooner or later. When Giacomo arrives, I am surprised because he is young and small. During the walk from the entrance to the altar, he grows, reaching his actual age. Halfway through the walk, I look at the ceiling and notice an enormous cockroach on the lamp. I feel a strong sense of disgust and I move closer to my husband to seek protection. The dream ends right when I arrive at the altar.

During another meeting, the Rossis show up with their children. They claim that they have been unable to leave them with someone and they ask if it is possible to do the session anyway, with them present in the room. I agree they can take sits as they prefer, on four chairs I place in front of the desk. The children sit in the middle, Cristiana next to the mother and Roberto next to the father. I give paper and colored pencils to the children, telling them to draw whatever they want while I speak to their parents. Roberto does not hesitate; he grabs the materials immediately and begins to draw. Cristiana gets closer to her mother as to protect herself, but after a while, she also begins to draw.

During our meetings, Mr. Rossi shows a tendency to alienate himself from therapy. In his opinion, this therapy concerns more his wife and daughter than him. This happens until he brings me a dream:

> I see a helicopter fall in a valley in a point where my family members and friends live and I run to see if anyone is still alive. When I woke I felt anxiety and I still feel disturbed by the "turning blades."

Immediately before, he had told me that he was tired to "repeat always the same things" during our meetings, accompanying his words with the eloquent gesture of rotating his fingers in the air. From this meeting on, Mr. Rossi does not return to therapy.

During the first meeting without her husband, Mrs. Rossi brings me a dream:

> I am with my husband and I am walking in a long hallway full of doors; it's as if we are getting married. At the end of this hallway we enter in a room where there is a priest that, while celebrating Mass, turns to my husband and says: "Do you renounce Satan?" At this, he answers with a witty remark.

Caterina then adds "As usual!" As I see it, symbolically this dream represents the ritual in which the family is participating. At the end of her story, I ask what she means with: "as usual!" She answers that her husband tends not to take things seriously, especially what regards her.

Mrs. Rossi used to come to the RC every another day to take her daughter to a behavioral therapist. On one of such occasions, I ran into her in the hallway and noticed that, when she entered my colleague's room with her daughter, she remained inside. Later, she told me that at the beginning her daughter was not able "to leave her", even if with difficulty. She immediately corrected herself, "to remain with the colleague of yours", she said. I answered that, by doing so, her daughter was telling her something that she already knew, as her slip of the tongue demonstrated. I ended there our meeting.

In the following meeting, Mrs. Rossi continues to show commitment in that she is punctual. Yet, after a few moments of silence, she expresses her fear concerning our previous meeting. After that, she says: "It's not my daughter who is morbidly attached to me, but me to her!"

From this meeting onward, Mrs. Rossi's journey begins: she begins to talk more about herself and less about her daughter.

When she begins to speak she recalls two dreams:

> I find myself in a dark room where there is a strange, transparent piece of furniture with internal shelves, which are also transparent. I try insistently and with great effort to place this piece of furniture between two other. I am very tired, but finally I achieve to do it.

It seems to me that in this dream it took a lot to squeeze a third element in between the couple.

> I find myself at the RC, leaning out of a window from where I can see a room without a roof, and I see you working. Your patient is a very pretty girl but I cannot see her face. I am extremely bothered by her as she keeps speaking of herself and does not listen to you. All of a sudden, the girl says: "Do you know that I have a mother?" And you answer: "Oh yes! And where is she?" And the girl says: "Outside". The dream ends when the door suddenly opens, a woman appears, and you ask her: "Is this your mother?"

It seems evident to me that this is a transference dream.

At the end of the recount, she borrows the question from the girl in the dream. She asks: "Do you know I have a mother?" I ask Mrs. Rossi: "and your mother?" She answers that she thinks that her mother is very different from her. During her childhood – and still today – she does not accept her mother's unhidden platonic love for man who is not Mrs. Rossi's father. She remembers that she never saw her parents showing affection. Often, her mother showed her dissatisfaction through frequent provocations and complaints towards her husband, sometimes also trying, without avail, to stimulate his jealousy by speaking about the other man. She sees her mother as a fundamentally egoistic person. When Mrs. Rossi's father died, her mother led a tranquil life without showing any sign of suffering. Furthermore, her mother did not show affection to her. They do not see each other much and sometimes Mrs. Rossi wishes they could have a more friendly relationship.

She speaks also about her five siblings (in order: the eldest, her sister, a brother, a sister, herself and a younger brother). The younger brother is the only one who is single and still lives with their mother. The eldest sister always acted in a very maternal way with her siblings; her eldest brother, who has my same name (Antonio), works and lives out of town and gives her "a sense of fear", as all males do. With her third sister, three years older than her, she has the most confidential relationship; on the other hand, she affirms that her youngest brother Giacomo is the only man with whom she does not feel out of place.

She speaks very little about her father. She tells me that he passed away when she was twenty years old, about two years before her wedding. Her memories of him are blurry; she describes him as a taciturn person, fundamentally absent for what concerns affection. She remembers that she desired but was also bothered by the little contact and the little caresses she received. She is pleased to remember that he was gifted with a certain irony and sense of humor.

Though Mrs. Rossi takes the over-attachment of her daughter upon herself, the fact remains that Cristiana continues therapy with my colleague.

During a conversation, Mrs. Rossi tells me that Cristiana comes to the RC each time with less desire. I ask her if she continues to be present at her daughter's sessions and with a tone of auto-reproach she responds affirmatively, adding that in this way she can have two weekly sessions. She remarks that she feels more at ease with this colleague of mine, because she is a woman. She feels eager to tell her things that she does not think she could tell me. At this point, I propose to ask the secretaries for a change, so that she could continue individually with my colleague, while I would take care of her daughter. With a flat and resolute tone she answers: "That is not possible, my daughter would never come here with you." I reply: "If you say so?!", and I end the meeting.

During the following session she feels mortified and apologises for the comments she made during our previous meeting. She says that they "slipped". She remembers when the RC called her to begin her daughter's psychotherapy. She had hoped that she was not assigned to a man, as if that were the case, she would have not taken her to the RC.

At this point, I remark that, during our previous meeting, when I proposed she and her daughter could switch therapists, she told me that her daughter would never agree. I remark that, in what she has just said, something new and different emerged. Mrs. Rossi remains a few minutes in silence, then she breaks it by telling me an episode that occurred a long time ago. She was with her daughter in a bookstore where she met a male teacher of Cristiana. This man made a comment about the child, caressed her hair, and said that she was an angel. This episode upset the patient who – leaving the bookstore – felt a strong nausea. After the story she exclaimed: "It's me right? Everything depends on me!" Later, she told me that, when the teacher put his hands on her daughter's head, it had been like if he had put them on her own head.

During the next meeting, she brings me a dream:

I find myself in a small room in the neighbor's house, my mother's best friend. There are some pieces of blue furniture covered by a transparent bag. On a ladder there is a painter who is painting the ceiling. In the corner of this room there is an old man with little hair, naked and without genitals. I observe the room from the outside. All of a sudden, I find myself in a dark road near a car, driven by my brother-in-law. From the car, the old naked man comes out. I help him because he has to urinate, though I ask myself how he can do it without genitals. Then, I see my mother with a plastic cup filled with the old man's urine. She goes near the sewer and throws the urine. I am wondering how she could have got it. My mother is strangely dressed. Specifically, I am impressed by the scarf she has on her head. Behind her there is Cristiana from whom I try to hide the scene.

This dream brings out the matter of sexual differences, even though in the imaginary and not in the symbolic register. In other words, the problem of this dream can be summarised by the following question: how is it done without a phallus?

At this point, we are facing a fact: the patient's therapy seems to be a family psychotherapy in name only. Mrs. Rossi faces a personal and individual work inside a family setting. This is the only one allowed by the psychotherapeutic program assigned to her daughter, at least bureaucratically.

In the following meetings, the patient tries to put an end to this incongruence. Once, she says that her daughter was basically there for her, and this seemed to be an "exploitation"; she adds that, since she had discovered it, her daughter was getting better. This is the point when Caterina took her decision: having her daughter discharged and sacrificing her own psychotherapy. She does so, and my colleague gives her a ninety days extension. During this period, Caterina's meeting with me become more productive; during one session she reveals that at the age of four she was abused sexually, something that she had never told my colleague during her daughter's sessions. Each time she talks about the abuser, she refers to him as "that man".

During the first meeting after the summer break, Mrs. Rossi brings me a dream:

I find myself in my house; my mother is cracking the ceiling down. She tells me that when she is finished, she will go to the lady upstairs to tell her she had to air the house. Going into the bedroom, I see my father and my brother Antonio on the matrimonial bed. Antonio is talking with my father and I ask him to tell my mother to stop, or else I would go in the room and throw her down.

During the last meetings, Mrs. Rossi did not seem upset at all concerning the termination of our encounters. She told me that she intended to continue her work and I answered that at the end of our meetings I would give her some telephone numbers. On the last meeting, the patient told me that she intended to continue her journey with me. After a few days, she called me to take an appointment that same week, at my private studio.

III The private case

Mrs. Rossi comes to her first encounter at my office, punctual as usual. Her dark clothes and the sad look on her face are also the same, and they contrast with her beauty.

She does not speak right away, a characteristic she still maintains. She remains silent for a few minutes until she tells me about a dream she had the night before:

> I am going to the RC when I run into a dead end. Frightened, I turn back, but the road is blocked by an enormous wall. Then, I realise that I am crouched inside a hole. Dangling above me, I see a rope and I try to grasp it, but I do not succeed. I know that outside the hole there is a man who is holding the rope. I cannot see him but I hear him telling me not to worry because sooner or later he will pull me out of there.

This dream emphasises her perspective on her entrance in analysis, where the analyst is represented as the one who can pull her out of the pit of her problems.

From this dream, a fantasy – or conscious phantasm – takes shape. In this, both the patient and I are in the hole. At first, she sees herself as small, naked, and sitting on a rock. Then, she becomes an adult, dressed in black, and crouched.

During the following session, she announces that in the preceding week she had been sick and vomited. I ask about this sickness and she answers that she felt sick after dinner and forced herself to vomit. She vomits when she eats a lot, while she manages to control herself when she eats moderately. I ask her if this happened on other occasions and in a low voice she answers affirmatively. As an example, she relates when she met a man who looked at her insistently, and this man made her vomit. She relates another accident. While she was watching on TV a couple having a relation in bed, she devoured two packs of biscuits and afterwards she vomited. Interestingly enough, when she speaks about sex she almost always uses the word relation, or intimate relation, and hardly ever, except very later on and by means of her dreams, the word sex. She repeats that she wanted to feel something, which is why she used to stuff herself, it was an urge she was unable to resist: "I stuffed myself but I could not stand the feeling of being so full, which is why I forced myself to vomit. I do not eat a lot to vomit but to feel something, even though when I vomit it is awful. When I do this, I draw closer and closer to my anxiety. Is this what I want to feel? Why then am I afraid of it?" In my opinion, this compulsive behaviour indicates a sort of regression of the arousal from a genital to an oral drive, so that it comes to represent a form of oral masturbation.

Before therapy, she used to vomit sporadically. Ever since she began the treatment, it happens more often. This was especially true since she had the dream where she saw me working, and was jealous of the beautiful patient (see public case). Only during the private sessions she adds to the dream the detail that the patient was "dressed in black".

At a later stage, something happened, after which and for a certain time, the vomiting ceased, replaced by a frequent tachycardia. Cristiana drank a glass of cold water and her little brother told her that it was dangerous. As a consequence, the little girl could not sleep, and told her mother that she was afraid of dying. Caterina became obsessed with her daughter's words "I don't want to die" and made them her own. That is, she firmly asserted that thenceforth she would do all in her power not to vomit. If she did not want anything to happen to her (i.e. death) she had to assimilate what she ate. This brought about the withdrawal of the vomiting symptom.

A few days earlier, Mrs. Rossi had called me because she was worried about Cristiana for no apparent reason. We agreed that on the following day she could come to the RC with her, which she did. However, she brought both children. During the following session, she says that she particularly liked that encounter, especially since she saw her son converse with me naturally and without inhibitions. For the first time she said she "felt her son".

While she has several dreams in which she feels the presence of her son, without seeing or hearing him, she usually does not feel him, and fears this little contact might have repercussions (afterwards she will bring him to the RC for speech therapy because of a slight stutter). She says she has never been able to take her son into her arms, and for this reason she stopped breast-feeding him when he was three months old. She remembers that when he was born she sniffed him in order to feel him, and the gynaecologist told her: "You're not a dog, are you?" She answered that, like with food, it was the only way to feel him. She also adds that when she found out she was pregnant, she started crying, and the matter got worse when she found out it was a boy. Instead of gaining weight during her pregnancy, she lost it. She assumes that it is for this reason that he was born premature, after eight months.

Since Roberto was born, she has been living with the anxiety that when he grows up something may happen to him. In this respect, she remembers reading a quote, which said that when you love someone you inevitably live in fear of losing him. Since then, she believes she recovered her son.

During one of our sessions, she expresses her worry concerning the fact that Roberto still wears diapers at the age of six and often has the urge to go to the bathroom to urinate, especially when he has to eat. With regard to this, I once asked Roberto if he thought about his mother when he ate and he answered affirmatively. As a consequence, she asked again: "Doctor, is it me then?" Caterina tried to reassure the child, maintaining that she also wore diapers until she was six, and also she sucked her thumb until she was ten.

One day her son played a prank on his sister; Mrs. Rossi spanked him, and felt pleasure, something she could not stand. During a session, she declares resolutely: "This isn't normal". It disturbed her to perceive a glimpse of her own pleasure, all the more so as it was marked by a perverted gesture. However, her path towards recovery can be found precisely on the path of the subjectivation of what she feels.

She feels an unusual anxiety, "a lump in her throat", when she finds herself with her husband and Roberto at the same time. In this respect, she recalls an accident: one morning, she woke up between the two of them, and the first thing that came to her mind was: "I am between two men". This disturbed her. Once, her son asked her to wash him, something he usually did by himself. While she was rinsing him and touching his private parts, it appeared the picture of "that man" on top of her when she was little. Roberto noticed her expression and asked her why she was angry.

On the contrary, it arouses her to see her daughter naked. This troubles her a lot, because it makes her feel like a monster and consequently she is afraid. In this as in the previous case, we can see the emergence of a pleasure which is considered perverted.

In a dream:

I am in the house of one of Cristiana's friends' mother and I am waiting for her to come into the room in order to have a relation, but my mother comes in and we don't do anything. I wake up feeling an intense pleasure.

After the dream she tells me that she sees this girl outside school, when she picks up Cristiana. So she describes her: "What struck me was her beauty: but it was a masculine beauty, she has the features of a man with short hair". She added that often in her dreams she sees girls with short hair. She links it to the fact that when she was a child she used to wear short hair like a little boy, because her mother wanted it.

Talking about her children she relates the following dream:

It is August – she once specified that she could not stand this month – I am along the road with my children, Cristiana is in her underwear and undershirt – like herself when she was abused – Roberto is dressed, while I am naked. We are going to buy a bathing suit. While we are walking, I notice that people are looking at me, so I try to hurry up and put some clothes on. Instead of walking down the main road, I go down a secondary road where I run into an enormous obstacle. There is some stagnant water and in the middle a wooden board bound by four chains. On the other side of the water there is a very tall fence. I take Cristiana and put her on the board in order to bring her to the other side; she asks me what we would do about the fence. I tell her we would climb over it. In the meantime a crocodile appears and with three mouthfuls it eats up my daughter. In despair, I want to jump in too, but I see Roberto – who is now naked – crying desperately. I stay where I am, and I neither jump in, nor do I pick him up.

Later, Mrs. Rossi said that, while she was pregnant with Cristiana, she used to have panic attacks, connected with the fear of not being a good mother. In addition, her daughter had always been her "joint", but is no longer so. She would like to return to this condition. She says that she is looking for something, but she cannot understand what, and she adds that it is not possible for her to be both a woman and a mother: "It is as if I was dirtying them too, while before I wasn't dirtying anyone".

Her passage from the chair to the couch takes place in the following way: when the session begins she remains silent for a few minutes, then she says she cannot speak, she coughs a little while rubbing her hands (the rubbing of one's hands, as if to brush off the dust from oneself, is a frequent compulsive gesture, almost an apotropaic ritual, which she performs, along with the coughing, every time she touches subjects related to sexuality). Then she adds: "Do you know that when I was a little girl I loved to go to the bedroom to be by myself, lying down on my parents' bed and think?" At this point, I invite her to take a seat on the couch; without any resistance, she gets up, goes to the couch, and lies down. Right away I ask her to continue with her speech and she says: "I remember that when I was little I had fantasies, three in particular".

Her first fantasy emerged at the age of five. In this, she found herself in the woods where she noticed a baby who was tied up and sitting on a log, which she fed with "disgusting things" (*schifezze*) to eat, mud mixed with several dirty things. Once again, we see her imaginary identification with the aggressor, mediated by the expression "disgusting things" (*schifezze*), which in Neapolitan dialect has a clearly sexual meaning.

In her second fantasy, which she had at the age of seven/eight, she was in the woods, in a small house, where she had the pleasant feeling of being by herself. At the same time, she felt that this sensation could be dangerous, because of the presence of a male figure that lurked outside the window.

In the third fantasy, she was in a big, very bright room without a ceiling, where some doctors called three nuns, whom she had to undress.

Later on, it emerges that, sometimes, these fantasies appeared spontaneously, while in other cases she was the one to evoke them. In addition, they gave her at the same time both pleasant and very disturbing feelings. The number three is a constant in Caterina's life: in her dreams (not only in the contents of the dream, but because she almost always brings me three dreams at a time), in her fantasies, and even in her daily life, for instance she buys three things at a time, gives three bites if she happens to be eating a cake, etc.

For what concerns the relationship with her analyst, during a session she says she felt so sick that she had to stop the car. She associated this with an episode in which we were talking at the door. From this she takes the opportunity to add: "I chose you because of your pure gaze".

During a session, she relates that she was on holiday in a hotel room, resting: suddenly a fantasy emerged. At first she was alone and felt fine; then I appeared, and she felt so disturbed that she was forced to delete this picture. She adds that when I appear in her fantasies, she experiences anxiety. She also emphasises that she is fine with me until she sees me as a man; otherwise she tends to drive me away. She tells me about a fantasy that appeared to her in a parking lot, while she was watching a couple in a car. She imagined that she took the place of the girl, and I took the place of the man. Caterina then returned to reality, got into her car, and started eating avidly.

During an encounter, she relates the following dream:

I am with Cristiana in a garden and suddenly a dog comes to savage me (once she called 'that man' a thirsty dog). I pet him so he would not hurt me, but it bites my finger off. I call for help while I feel a terrible pain; then I notice a little boy who comes to take back his dog, but I can't see him; are you that little boy?

In this dream the reference to her castration is evident, as both a feared and desirable moment. With this question she asks me in a coded manner to be the boy who performs a symbolic castration on her, separating her from her distressing phantasms once and for all. She also believes that her husband should follow an analytical course because "it is as if I were changing my clothes, but underneath it is always dirty".

She relates the following dream:

I am going towards the garage of your office together with my husband. There are two men leaning on a car who want something from us. My husband grabs my arm and tells me to stop, but I proceed anyway, while he stays where he is. When I draw closer, one of the two men comes to me, and slaps me in the face, but I don't feel any pain. I see a young woman coming from behind this man, she pays him and he returns next to the other man.

In another dream:

There is a man in the woods who I don't know and he is holding an axe as if he was to chop down a tree, but I fantasise that instead of the tree there is another man. Next to the tree there is another tree on the ground.

After the dream she declares that the man/tree is her husband "even though she doesn't want to put him in that place." During the following session, she says that I was the man with the axe.

I rarely made changes to the rhythm of her sessions. Once I asked her to skip an encounter, she reacted anomalously, and phoned several people (her mother, her sister and some friends) because of a pressing need to communicate. During the following session, she tells me about this behaviour of hers, and brings me the following dream:

I call you because I don't feel well at all and you decide to let me come. Your room is very bright, full of school desks with overturned black chairs on top of them. Your chair is like a dentist's chair, it is black. Then a friend comes with some keys whose keychain is made of a paper that bears the lines of primary school notebooks and this written on one side: "I miss you, even though I pretend to be OK, but I miss you"; on the other side: a faded picture of a bride and groom.

At this point, I decide to intensify the sessions, by adding another weekly encounter to Mrs. Rossi's schedule.

Once I had to change the schedule of a meeting (morning instead of afternoon). She said that this was probably the reason why she did not feel well, since instead of going home she had to go to work: "When I go away from here, I need to go home and lie down on the sofa without anyone being at home because I have to think by myself".

The following session, Caterina relates a dream:

I am at home, I call you and you tell me you can't receive me and that you would come to my house. I am on the double bed, lying down on my side and you are sitting next to me, caressing my cheeks. I push your hands back, I go under the covers, while you place yourself at the foot of the bed and in an angry voice you say: "Don't you see how you reduced yourself, you have lost so much weight". Then you leave. Immediately afterwards I hear my husband telling me, with the same angry voice, to go and get the children because they are wet. I can see my children near the fountain, but no water is coming out.

She says that she dreams about the presence of water often, even though she does not actually see it in the dream. In this dream, the analyst is beginning to pass to the rapist's side. It also seems that the intervention of her other family members accentuates her feeling of guilt for the unfaithful fantasy.

I remark the coincidence between my angry voice and her husband's. She answers that, more than being angry, her husband was complaining, and worrying about how much weight she had lost – seemingly to attack her analytical treatment indirectly. She remembers that, when she came to the RC, she suggested him to join the sessions, while she would turn to someone else. Then she adds: "I gave him the chance, but when he refused I told him to step aside."

Later on, Caterina tells me about her relationship with her husband. She says she is angry with him because he acts of his own free will, he is ambitious, and for this reason she feels absent. His ambitions have always bothered her because he takes pleasure in them while she does not. When I ask her how he *should* be, she answers that he should think only about her and that she should always come first, even if this makes her feel like a little girl who has in her hands something to change. She calls this "something" *the truth*. The truth is that she feels absent and has to change.

She adds that long ago her husband was a recurring thought in her mind. According to her, this is what love means; it is the only condition that allows us not to feel emptiness and nothingness. Yet, since the first night it is no longer so, as if something had broken. I point out that something *had* indeed broken. While she is paying me, Mrs. Rossi thanks me for the first time.

She explains how she lives her conjugal relationship with the following words: "It is as if my husband, when he talks, is a hand that pushes me down. It gives me the same sensation I had when I was little. The feeling of something bigger that knocks me down. Something enormous that doesn't let me get out."

Also, she cannot stand to see her husband so attached to his own family of origin, which is made up mostly of female figures. This makes her feel neglected.

She tells me about this dream:

I must go to my gynaecologist and I let my sister come with me, but, on the way, there is another woman instead of my sister. Once we get there, I show the doctor my tooth and when he touches it, it falls out. Then he asks me what he has to do with the tooth, since I should go to a dentist for this. Then, I find myself outside, in a car, with my husband and his relatives and I ask myself: 'why should I be crammed here if I have my own car?

In particular she cannot stand her mother-in-law, since she fears that her husband thinks about his mother much more than about his wife. She considers her as a rival and she asks me: "If I feel nothing for Giacomo any longer, why does his relationship with his mother bother me so much?"

Once she saw a girl shaking Giacomo's hand and during all the time they were holding hands she felt a strong pleasure. With regard to this, she relates the following dream:

> I am going to the factory and there I see my husband kissing a girl. I feel a strong pleasure, and while I go away I think: "I got rid of him".

In an episode which took place at work, her husband touched a fabric. When she saw him she felt pleasure, but immediately afterwards disgust. Since she works in the clothing field, I ask her what is her favourite fabric, and she answers that it is silk because she loves its smell.

She describes Giacomo as a conceited and dominant person. She lets him take decisions and initiative, even if she does not agree with him. She feels inhibited when she wants to say something and adds "I can't feel him". Even with regard to their relationship, he is always the one to make the first move. She would like to have the desire to make love, in order to feel like a wife and a woman. Instead, there has never been a sexual desire, she has never felt pleasure, and she often feels used. However, she does not know if this depends on her husband or on the fact that he is a man. Later on, she asserts that she does not feel used in the man-woman relationship, but in the husband-wife one. In this respect, she describes a dream:

> I see a mobile phone with the word "used" on it. But I don't know if there is written used or abused.

Caterina says that, after having intercourse with her husband, she usually dreams to be by herself on the double bed, and feels intense pleasure.

Once, her sister told her that things were not going very well with her husband and that he slept "all alone like a dog". That sentence made such an impression on Caterina that, while she was having intercourse with Giacomo, "it crossed her mind" and disturbed her very much.

At times, during intercourse, she sees pictures of men who are about to die and disappear once dead. On other occasions, she sees herself as a little girl, leaning forward and sitting down. Sometimes, she sees "that man" with her children. Later on, she said that she also sees insects, animals, etc. Recently, she happened to see something that looks like a cockroach. Unlike the previous occurrences, she was convinced to have something in her eye, because she perceived the image true and real. She added that she attributes every slight noise she hears in the house to cockroaches.

Usually, she also has a strong desire to sleep, but after going to bed she cannot fall asleep, and feels the pressing need to eat something. Actually, she does not feel like eating, just as she does not feel like having intimate relations. According to her, this makes feel clean, perhaps because of what happened to her in the past. She claims that eating means gaining weight and gaining weight makes her feel dirty. Hence, she eats in order to feel something and "the more she does not feel, the more she eats." She goes back to bed without brushing her teeth intentionally; she does this to keep "the taste in her mouth."

Only once she woke up with the desire to have intercourse with her husband, but at that moment Roberto was present. Then she adds: "Plus I won't ask, given that like eating, I don't feel. Therefore why should I ask if I don't feel anything?"

During one of our encounters, she says: "Before eating, I have headaches, then I put the food in my mouth, and at the third mouthful I get dizzy. Then I imagine I am eating alone."

Caterina is particularly obsessed with cleaning; she has the habit of restlessly cleaning the house every day, dwelling in particular on the removal of dust, in which she takes a certain pleasure. Later on, she says that her way of overcoming this obsession is cleaning every other day in a deferred way, so as to form a thicker layer of dust, whose removal brings her even more pleasure. In addition, when she was in her parents' house, before going to the bathroom she used to clean it because others had been there, especially her brothers.

In the following dream:

> I am at my mother's house; I go into the bathroom to clean it. My mother talks to my older brother (Antonio), who comes into the bathroom and hugs me. I feel the same warmth I experienced in the past with that man. In the meantime I only see Antonio's image reflected in the mirror; I don't see myself, but I know that I was little.

When she does not do the cleaning she feels dirty. Lately, since she has been cleaning less, she feels a sense of dissatisfaction. Precisely because of her constant feeling of dirtiness, she tends to wash herself for a long time and clean the shower both before and after having used it. She always takes a shower after the others because she is the one who must dirty it.

In the following dream:

> I see you helping the maids with the cleaning, besides doing your job. Then, I find myself with you in my mother's bedroom (where as a little girl I slept for many years and had all the three of my fantasies). You help me clean, but then I ask you to leave it to me. My mother tells you to do the laundry and once in a while I come to check if you get wet, which doesn't happen. Then, I see you on the floor leafing through the newspaper, and next to you are my husband and my brother. You show them some pictures in the newspaper (a dog, an unkemptly dressed woman, and a man with patches of hair) and you all start laughing.

With regard to this dream, Caterina remarks: "Why didn't I want you to get wet?" And after a lengthy pause she adds: "When I used to get wet I felt even dirtier. I couldn't stand getting the lower part wet; it was a burden to me. The dog in this dream was the same dog that 'that man' had, while I was the unkempt woman, not completely dressed. Instead, the man without a face was very tall."

Mrs. Rossi says she always feels tired, especially on Saturdays and Sundays, even though she finishes whatever she starts doing. In the morning she is never able to get up easily, and in addition to the constant fatigue, she often feels a strong nausea.

She also maintains that, during a certain span of time, the vomiting was replaced by dizziness (she had the sensation of exploding, her head was heavy and she had difficulty breathing), as the result of a dream:

> Inside a room I notice a purple butterfly on the corner of a table and on the other side there are two men. One of the two beckons the butterfly to take flight, but it cannot do it; I see the other man first, but then he disappears. All of a sudden I spot a tube of glue on the table.

She adds that I was the man who beckoned the butterfly, the other man was her husband; and, "unfortunately" the butterfly's wings were stuck to the table, with the glue. She gets dizzy when she talks to strangers, especially men, including her husband, and also when she touches her son.

She relates an episode in which she was at the factory, and she had to assign a task to a worker. She was struggling to do it, and because of her dizziness she was afraid she was going to fall. I add – perhaps in a somewhat "savage" way, as Freud would have said – "into his arms?" Laughing, she says no. She then remains silent, and, putting her hands to her neck, she says she has a lump in her throat, as if she was suffocating. I suggest we stop here and she agrees, because she feels sick.

She begins one of the sessions by saying that she feels a greater sense of disorientation and dizziness since she stopped wearing blinkers. In her opinion, the only way to avoid this was to be by herself, without going out. When I add: "In short, put on your blinkers again", Mrs. Rossi smiles.

Caterina's most recurring dreams concern shoes and cockroaches, that is, two categories of objects extremely emblematic of two forms of pathological objectual relationship: the shoe is a classic fetishist object, while the cockroach is a classic phobic one. We can also consider them as two faces of the same "objectual coin" – two phases, positions, or logical periods of the same relationship to the object, as is represented in the phantasm: the idealised and lusted object; or the abhorred and avoided one. The course of the treatment obviously consists in trying to put together the good and the bad object.

She feels great pleasure when she puts shoes on and she feels a similar sensation when she sees little girls; she describes it as a pleasure so sweet that she would make one mouthful of it. Whereas she says she feels an erotic pleasure for little girls, for what concerns shoes her pleasure derives from seeing the tips of her shoes while she is walking.

She relates the following dream:

> I go to that man's house, I find myself on the stairs and I think: I must ask his daughters why their father is like this! Then I am on the road to buy some shoes and there are many people dressed in black whose faces I can't see'. After recounting this dream, she remarks: 'not only in my dreams, but even in reality I am very fussy about shoes. Why does a man feel pleasure on a little girl?

For what concerns cockroaches, she feels great disgust. She partially stops dreaming about them when we begin to face sexual themes during the sessions. She describes one of these dreams in the following way:

> My mother holds out her hand to me and on her hand there is an overturned cockroach and I wake up distressed.

In another dream:

> I am in this room and under the bed there is a pile of shoes. I bend down and take a black summer shoe, the one I like the most (and which I really have, I am very fussy with shoes, more than anything else). But then, thinking that it is a cockroach, it falls off my hand.

And another:

> I look at myself in the mirror and I see only the lower part of my body. There is blood coming out of my navel. The blood dries up and turns into many small cockroaches.

She points out that the cockroach is like a wall she does not want to climb, for the fear of losing something that belongs to her. There was a time when she used to lie down on the bed, close her eyes and see a pole in front of her face with a cockroach on top of it.

In this other dream:

I have a cockroach in my right hand which is closed tightly, when I open it, it is dead and falls.

She adds: "Perhaps it is where I felt myself dirtied by that man?"

When she talks about men she says that she looks at them, but she does not see them because this makes her "feel dirty." During a session in her early treatment, she said that the word "fear" made her think about men. At a later stage, she added "I'm glad that men approach me, but it is like two magnets of the same pole; there is a stronger force that repels us."

In this respect, she reports the following episode:

I am coming to see you, when I run into a car which gives me way. In the car there are three men. I feel pleasure in going away. I prefer the pleasure of chasing away rather than receiving, almost as if my enjoyment (*godimento*) – this is the first time she uses this word – lied in driving the pleasure away, then complaining about it and becoming sad.

In yet another dream:

My husband phones me and tells me to get ready because we have to go out for a dinner with some colleagues of his. Immediately afterwards I feel pleasure at the thought that I had to get ready in order to be desired, but "without belonging to anyone".

She stresses that it disturbs her to receive a compliment, but it is a short-lived feeling; instead, being considered becomes an obsession and destroys her. She tries to explain this to herself by advancing an interpretation. She advances that the desire of being considered by a man makes her see herself reflected in her mother who "made another man enter her head, even though platonically, leaving her father out." Caterina felt obsessed with this. Her imaginary identification with her mother, against whom she is desperately trying to fight, is evident in this.

For what concerns her father, Caterina relates the following dream:

I am at a town festival on the streets in the evening and a thief wants to steal something from me. My brother-in-law tries to defend me. My husband and a doctor are also present. Then, I hear a gunshot that strikes an elderly man who dies and a woman who doesn't die right away. Instead, she slowly bleeds to death. Although that elderly man is not my father, I saw in him my father dressed in black. My brother-in-law, who is at his side, argues with my husband, and the thief, who is next to my husband, argues with the doctor.

She emphasises that the old man is her dead father; the woman is herself, and the blood she loses is her anguish. Here, her aggressiveness towards the paternal figure appears evident; he is seen as the imaginary prototype of all violent men and rapists.

When she feels "considered" by a man, the more she drives him away, the more she becomes obsessed by his thought. I ask her what she meant by "feeling considered", and she specifies that it is the feeling of having being helped by someone.

During an encounter, Caterina says that she vomited again after that session, which took place during a particularly cold day. She was wearing a light dress and, at the end of the session, I asked her if she was cold. She says she felt considered, and she felt that a man was taking care of her. When I ask her for a further explanation of this "taking care of", she remembers an accident that happened when she was sixteen. She was keeping her first sister company, since her husband was out of town. In those days, Caterina's future husband told her that a young man, called Angelo, had told his fiancée that he would pick her up to take her home, because she was in the hospital. Thenceforth, Caterina, who took the place of that girl, created a fantasy that emerged and emerges every time she says she feels considered, that is, every time someone takes care of her.

Going back to her relationship with men, during another session she recounts when her husband introduced her to a salesman at the factory. The salesman said "Is this your wife?" a couple of times, and passed his hands through his hair. This set something in motion inside her. While she was there, Caterina had the feeling that he was putting his hands through her hair and this "obsession" (according to her definition) also returned once at home. In particular, when she went to bed, she saw him in the middle of her bed caressing her hair. This *obsession* disappeared suddenly, as soon as she remembered that her father used to say at the table: "I remember when you were little and I used to pass my hands through your hair". This episode explains not only the episode of the salesman, but also the one of the daughter's teacher. As described in the first part of this article, when Caterina's daughter's teacher caressed the girl's hair my patient was very disturbed.

Mrs. Rossi feels very uncomfortable when she believes men are considering her. It is just as difficult for her to talk about things pertaining to the sexual sphere. When this takes place, she feels that "she is destroyed as a person."

In a dream she relates:

> There are three women, an adult and two girls aged between fifteen and sixteen. They are sleeping in a kind of iron manger. Then, some soldiers in uniform appear in the room and they start to undress them, but I don't see them undressed and I start feeling pleasure.

The dreams in which her sexual identity is confused are rather recurrent:

> I am a little boy who goes to nursery school and I am at my desk. The teacher gives me fake male genitals and I refuse them because I don't want fake ones.

> With a car I pick up a little girl with long hair, and I am a man. We go into a room and we are about to have a relation, she goes onto the bed and falls asleep. I unbutton my trousers and notice I have female genitals. I wake up very disturbed.

> I am in a room in which there are an I-man and an I-woman. They argue because the I-man came to you, doctor, and the I-woman was jealous that something could arise from this. The I-man asks how two men could have feelings for each other, but the I-woman insists and the I-man gets some scissors and kills her. The I-man has a relation with the I-woman, and is able to obtain an excessive pleasure.

She had this dream after sexual intercourse with her husband.

I am in a room in which I see a man divided in two, half is you and half
is my husband. I masturbate him and when I finish you give me two
plush toys, a male one and a female one (I hate plush toys), but I perceive
both of them as males. First, I saw you and then I saw my husband and
my head was on the opposite side of what I was doing.

This dream emerged after having seen a similar scene on TV, in
which a masseuse was touching a man and the pleasure was not
seen in her but in the man.

I see myself inside my brother, the youngest one, I am in my bed and I am
feeling an intense pleasure touching my genitals, but they are those of a little
boy. I woke up right when the pleasure was increasing and I couldn't fall
asleep again.

She thinks she dreamed about her brother because a worker of
the firm had told her that she looks a lot like him. I ask her to tell
me something about her brother. She answers that when she was
little she used to play with him a lot. Right after this she adds that
when she said "used to play a lot", it made her sick. I ask her if her
children play together and she answers affirmatively, adding that
lately they had been asking her to take a bath together and, even
though she was not happy about this, she allowed them. She also
recounts when her son kissed her on the lips and for this reason she
scolded him. At this point, I remark that both the nausea that
occurred after she said "used to play a lot" and her son's current
games could have a connection on what she was trying to say.
After a brief pause, she answers: "Even though I don't see what I
was doing with my brother, I know that it bothers me." I concluded
the session maintaining that she had just said it, and she smiles.

I see myself inside a man with a towel around his waist: I am on the door,
and the room is very well-lit. Then I watch two children, a boy and a girl,
also with a towel around their waist, who go in and out of the room.

Some sessions later, she says that when she woke up from this dream she felt a strong pleasure, which was even more intense during the dream. This feeling disturbed her for a whole week.

She asks herself the reason why she sees herself as a man. She supposes that if she recognised her femininity she would have to love.

I see myself inside the children of the film *I'm Not Scared* (*Io Non Ho Paura*). At first, I am one of them, and then I am the other. There is a constant struggle between the two and precisely during that struggle I feel an erotic pleasure.

In this dream, the question of transference also refers to the childishness of her sexuality.

Once she finishes recounting the dream, she exclaims: "This isn't the first time I feel pleasure when I see myself inside a man, maybe because I am missing something". I add: "Something you don't have?" And she follows: "Yes, I don't have it, this is why I am unable to feel pleasure, because I am missing something." I tell her that it seemed to me that everything revolves around the couple "having it/not having it". She answers: "I think so."

She almost never spoke about "that man" and about the sexual abuse if not through her dreams:

My children have to go to a picnic, but even though I don't want them to, I allow them. The children are near your office and I see a car with "that man" inside. I don't remember dreaming about him ever. He is walking around the children. I am hiding and I refrain from intervening.

I hear noises, I get up to lock the door (I usually check that the door is locked at all times) and outside there is a man who is knocking, he wants to come in, it is "that man". I get a very long blade and I put it under the door, to make him go away.

I am on a very isolated road, at the end of which there is a horse that is looking at me, then he kicks me and when I get up and pet him, I see behind him a man who is holding out his hand for me'. After recounting the dream she adds: 'it isn't the horse in itself that scares me, but something about the horse reminds me of when I was little and which stands for the cockroach.

I am outside the main entrance of my mother's house building and I am waiting for Antonio the greengrocer to come, his name is the same as that man' – she makes a slip of the tongue, because, actually, that man's name is different. 'He brings me some crates of tomatoes which he weighs on those enormous scales. I ask him why there are eleven and not thirteen tomatoes. He answers that he would bring them to me later. Then, however, an elderly man brings the two crates and when I ask him why the greengrocer didn't come, he replies: he's coming no more!' (the person who abused her was old, and actually died).

I am on a bed and my husband says that he is a doctor. While he is talking, a very tall man with a pink jacket comes in and doesn't take his eyes off me. This puts me in a state of fear. My husband tells me not to worry because that man is full of sedatives and he adds that it is the man who disturbs my dreams.

After telling the dream, Caterina exclaims: "I keep on seeing that man in other men and this happens even with my husband, as if he appeared in each one of them." I add: "Did you say even in your husband?" And she answers: "Yes, maybe because he managed to have me."

She also tells about an accident that happened when she was little: "In the dining room, my mother kept a big pot where there were lots of papers gathered. Among them there was my medical report. On it there was written that I was ... and that I didn't immediately have ..." Caterina falls silent, then continues: "I used to secretly read that paper often, and I cried. I saw something of mine in it, which belonged to me."

In this respect, she recalls other, more recent, memories. In one of them, she was in her backyard and it was dark. She suddenly heard the lament of a little girl who was crying and she was so distressed that she ran away. She was the only one who heard that lament, but it was incredibly real. She adds that the dark part of the garden reminds her of *that man* (she says it with tears in her eyes). In another memory, she remembers that she was at her mother's house, who told her that the niece of *that man*'s daughter suffered of epilepsy. She saw that her mother was glad to tell this to her, while she felt sick. She refrained from telling her mother that *that man* took her because he was not able to take her mother. She claims that her mother knew that *that man* had sexual instincts, she should not have let her go playing, and she should have supervised her better as Caterina does with her own daughter. She adds that the worst thing, and perhaps the reason why she is angry at her, is that Caterina wanted to hush everything up while her mother made her repeat it constantly and exposed her.

In this respect she says: "Exposing myself too much is like stripping myself: I see myself as a naked little girl, and it is for this reason that running far away makes me feel strong, and I tend to cover and not expose myself."

Mrs Rossi acknowledges that in many of her dreams she is abused:

I bring my son to the dermatologist and he tries to abuse me. We have an incomplete relation because I run away. When I return there, I see Roberto asleep because the doctor gave him a sedative, then he takes me forcefully and I immediately feel pain.

Caterina really went to a dermatologist for Roberto, but it was a woman. In this dream:

I am in a men's clothing shop, three men come in, two hold me back and the other one abuses me.

Instead, in the following dream, she emphasises that there is no abuse and she adds: "Here it is me who want to touch anxiety with my own hands."

I am on the couch and you ask me to get up when you will be out of the room; but I jump to my feet as soon as you go to the desk and I go out. I realise I forgot my jacket (it often happens that when I go away form here I feel I have forgotten something), I knock and I see you holding it in your hands. I can't pull it because the door is ajar, but with an incredible effort I finally succeed and I go downstairs. You also come downstairs to call me and you bring me back inside, so we find ourselves in the elevator with two other women, who are colleagues of yours. One of them is wearing a flowered dress similar to mine, but the colour of her dress is much brighter, while mine is dull. She tells you that something is wrong with my breast; the woman with the flowered dress seeks and then shows you the problem, pointing at the breast. The elevator goes down, but we should have gone up, so we find ourselves in a room where we have a relation. I felt I was pulled into the room, as in the house, and I already felt annihilated as a person in the elevator. Then I see my husband's face behind you and it gets mixed up with yours. Someone knocks at the door, the girl with the flowered dress opens it and it is my husband. I go into the room to pay and I see you behind the desk. I ask you: "is it my problem the fact that I don't feel pleasure with a man? And now that it came out, should I stop coming?"

Afterwards, she emphasises her fear of overcoming the obstacle, because beyond it "there is love." She is afraid of the others and she does not know what could happen if she overcame the obstacle and was no longer afraid. When I point out that in this way something might change, she asks: "Perhaps I don't want to change?"

She tells me about a dream:

I am on some railroad tracks, and I am cleaning them always on the same spot. Next to me there is my first sister. Behind me there is a train that is moving, but it always remains in the same place.

Her interpretation is that she is unable to go forward, she feels paralysed; the train behind her is something that is watching her (she then says that it is me, always standing in the same place); she does not want to be like her sister, who dresses in black, and whom she sees as her mother. She adds that, after all, she is in treatment while her sister is off the track. She concludes saying that cleaning the tracks is sometimes useless, because they always remain dirty, no matter how much you clean them. I point out that a dirty track is not a dead track after all.

Later, she also says that she is happy about the treatment, because she is serene when she can give herself answers; it means she knows. But at the same time it makes her sad. When this happens she loses the feeling of her legs and cannot walk. She also has difficulty shaking hands.

She realises that, even though she finds out new things, there is always something else to discover.

She often says that her greatest moment of pleasure is when she is alone, since she feels free. During an encounter, she says: "If I could go back in time I would never get married, nor would I have children. This way I would be free and alone, which I like very much."

During the following session, Caterina begins with this dream:

> I am about to receive the news that my sister has died of a heart attack and while I think about it, I receive a phone call which confirms it. Then, I see hanging on the wall three short handbag umbrellas and three long ones, all black and arranged at different heights. I see the short umbrellas first, and then the long ones.

The day before, she spoke to her sister and saw a drawing made by her niece portraying an umbrella (the little girl is depicted under an open umbrella). But what strikes Mrs. Rossi most about the dream is the number three, which is constantly repeated. She associates these three 'insignificant' umbrellas with her three fantasies.

According to her, those fantasies were not licit. Yet, I point out that she used to lie down on the bed as if she wanted to turn them on, and she replies: "As if I were turning on the TV." They are *her* fantasies, she never spoke about them to anyone, and this is why she says they are not legitimate, "somewhat like a sin which can't be confessed." They used to come to her mind by themselves in an obsessive way, and afterwards she felt an enormous pleasure. When I ask her when they stopped, she replies that she does not remember precisely. After a few minutes of silence, she dates it back to the death of *that man,* that is, when she was twelve or thirteen. She adds that she finds it very strange that she can remember how old she was when the accident took place (she was four), while she cannot remember her age when *that man* died. I ask her if twelve-thirteen is about the age when she met her future husband; she confirms that it happened around two years later, then she got married, at the age of twenty-two. I also ask her when she lost her father and she answers that he died two years before she got married. Here, I point out that she got engaged after the death of *that man* and got married after the death of her father, and when I ask her if she thinks it is a coincidence, she declares "not at all!" We go back to her fantasies. Since when I asked her "Why the number three?", she answered "the three fantasies", I now ask her: "Why are there three fantasies, among which you said there was one you preferred (the second one)?" At this point, I see her completely absorbed and absent, it seems that she is in a trance and is by herself (as she seems to like it). In the utmost silence she whispers: "He called me three times." After a further gap of silence, I add "by your name?"; the woman comes to her senses, and asks me: "What does my name have to do with it?" I pick up on her words: she said he called her three times. She is surprised she said that, and after another long silence she says: "He had me three times." I remind her of the three "insignificant" umbrellas. Caterina says she must thank her sister, as she was the one who showed her daughter's drawing. I ask her how old her niece is and when she says she is four, I remark that it is an age she is familiar with. It is the age Caterina's daughter had when she took her to the RC, to begin her treatment. If she has to thank someone, she should also thank her daughter. It is correct to thank, but perhaps she should thank herself.

On leaving, she says goodbye at the door, shaking my hand for the first time.

ⅢⅢ Reflections on the case

We can see the mechanism we need to put into play (activate) to be able to listen to someone. From the very beginning of this case, we get the impression of a whirlpool where one does not quite exactly know who is asking for psychotherapy and who is requesting analysis: there is a clinical overlapping between mother and daughter and, first of all, one has to welcome the demand, but also understand where it lies.

What emerges in this case is the opportunity to begin a treatment for one of the persons involved in this set. At first, there is the clinical overlapping of the two cases. Afterward, the mother almost literally replaces the daughter. This is important, because we can think that it will affect not only the mother, but also the daughter in the second place: if the mother changes, her relationship with her daughter will also naturally change.

Now, in my opinion, the question that this case raised is the following: what to do with people looking for generic "psy" support? What can one listen to, what is one capable of doing? One must also bear in mind that a great difference exists between what happens in an institution and what happens in private practice. This is also true as far as preliminary conversations are concerned, which is a very important aspect. At least in name, inside an institution one is dealing with a family set and the first thing to do is to distinguish between children and parents, and separate them. There are therapists who receive both child and family as a matter of principle: but what should one do in such situations?

It is in the form of family therapy – and sometimes under this signifier – that the possibility of an analytical act can begin to take shape; the possibility to "therapeutise" (as we could say with a word that does not yet exist).

What should one do with a family group? Psychoanalysis as such has nothing to do with family therapy. In this perspective, the preliminary conversations are a fundamental aspect to decide in favor of one course of action or the other. It is true that inside the institution we find ourselves in a situation dictated by the institutional setting, and we are not as free as we are in our private practices, but this is only an initial datum that can be transformed. We can establish our stance as long as we take advantage of preliminary conversations also within institutions. This helps us find our stance and know the direction we are taking, both when we have contacts with entire families and when we have them with the individual members of a family.

Preliminary conversations represent an offer of the opportunity to enter analysis. In his technical writings Freud gives us some guidelines on how to handle this. Freud's rules, as he sets them out (attention to diagnosis; test sessions; selection of patients; clear definition of the therapeutic contract with regard to time and money), seem to be valid for the private sphere above all. However, it is possible to put the psycho-analytical discourse at work inside institutions as well, as long as one starts with the golden rule of psychoanalysis: allowing people to speak freely. There can be no rule other than freedom of speech: everything can be said through free association.

In the institutional sphere we can grasp some signs that show us if the road to enter the psychoanalytic discourse actually exists. For example, one of these signs is the level of the subject's resistance in following the golden rule, or the emergence of transference dreams.

Returning to our case, her dreams showed me that the woman had entered a transferential relationship. Thus, she could go on to ask something for herself, not just as a mother. Transference dreams are a first indicator, a signal that the subject can enter a psychoanalytical discourse: but these dreams must not be interpreted, so that the demand may unfold and develop.

What is the demand at the beginning of this meeting? How to capture it, how to seize it? At first, transference dreams carry a demand that has nothing to do with the subject's real symbolic question, insofar as this demand is focused on the therapist himself. The phantom – however stuffed with imaginary elements – has still allowed my patient to concretise her authentic analytic demand. On the other hand, this demand had remained blocked in her relation with the female therapist with a resistance – which is always also the therapist's resistance, as Lacan teaches. This resistance passed through the mutual identification between the one and the other. This sort of female complicity was reproducing an age-old situation of the patient's spanning three generations: between her and her mother and between her and her daughter.

This concatenation of identifications probably petrified and prevented the articulation of a therapeutic demand with a woman. A relationship with a male therapist, on the other hand, makes room for the fantasy of male desire, making a more typically analytic demand possible.

In my opinion, the question that made the patient's entrance into analysis possible was the following: why do you allow your daughter to do this? Why do you allow the child to remain attached to you in this way? The undoubtedly violent question was meant to adjust the mother's position with regard to her daughter and it was probably interpreted by the patient's unconscious as a sort of aggression. This, in turn, awakened and evoked the aggression she suffered at the age of four. This posed once more a fundamental question for her being and structure: who, what, made it possible for her to be abused at the age of four? A minimum amount of words uttered by the therapist opens up a huge space where those same words continue to work in silence, so to speak.

Returning to the general topic of how preliminary conversations work, the therapist's initial position makes the difference between what will either be a psychotherapy or a psychoanalysis (not the physical position but the therapist's position). Yet, the therapist's position leaves the person free to fight her own battles with her own words. If the therapist is too interventionist, then the direction taken can only be that of a psychotherapy, that is, a path between two barriers, where not only words but also behavior count (it is not a case that one often speaks of behaviorist therapies). In this case, even if one remains on the level of words, it is a level of a suggestive word, meaning a word that suggests something to the patient. Of course, there is room for suggestion also in the analytic work, but this space is opened only to make a proper analytic discourse possible.

In our case, the analytic discourse was made possible by referring to the tip of the real – the sexual abuse the subject suffered in her childhood – which was the centre of this woman who came with her four year old daughter. "Why do you allow her to do this?" These words – said by the therapist – allude to the interdiction, to the taboo – thus to the sexual sphere. Almost immediately afterwards we reached precisely the confession of sexual abuse.

This takes place within a very economical framework: few words, but well-targeted. Of course one does not just guess the good words, nor do they fall out of the sky. But in order to find one's way, and give the good words a chance to come out, one must have one fundamental thing in mind: words allow truth to speak but not to reveal itself in its entirety. It is impossible to tell the whole truth.

In the second part of the case, a set of imaginary formations of the unconscious comes to the foreground: lots of dreams, above all, but also daydreaming, which we could define as fantasies "to achieve *jouissance*" and fantasies "to avoid *jouissanc*". All these formations thematise, so to speak, transference and illustrate the various layers of the patient's relation to the Other: the desired Other and the feared Other, the fetish Other and the phobic Other. These two forms of the Other represent two sets of objectual relations as they are represented in the phantom: the coveted (and sometimes idealised) object and the loathed object (from which she escapes).

For the first time since she entered analysis, she manages to talk about her fantasies – the sexual ones above all – with a therapist she sees as the one who can get her out of her problems.

If her sexuality appears as "polymorphous-perverse" this is only because she is basically infantile, as her continuous regressions from the genital to the oral level show. The fact that she has become conscious of her phantoms, which have a perverse configuration like all phantoms, has obviously upset her. But it was just by bringing her perturbations out into the open that we were able to complete the cure.

Her apparently ambiguous relationship with femininity is related to her rejection of identification with her mother, who has trodden – also in the primal trauma – the same path of misrecognition as the patient. Hence, she seems to be almost blaming her mother for the pathological trans-generational repetition she has been caught in.

Besides, her father is included in the list of imaginary rapists – like all men, analyst included, from a certain point on. The analytic act I tried to accomplish was that of separating me from this list, pointing out the difference between symbolic, real and imaginary – between privation, frustration and castration – so as to help her measure her phantoms.

The therapy had three directions: the imaginary register, which amounted to the clarification of the fantasies and the attempt at finding the words to speak about those fantasies to the other; the symbolic register, with the attempt to interpret the fantasies, find their structural code, arrange the stratifications of the signifier; the register of the real, with the effort made to help her put together the good object and the bad one.

I shall now conclude my reflections with the account of the first dream Mrs. Rossi brought me, where, as I wrote, the whole analytic path of Caterina was being foreshadowed. From a Freudian perspective, what is better than a dream to get to know the functioning of the unconscious?

The narrated (manifest) dream is the following:

> I am standing at the entrance of a church because I have to get married. While I wait for my husband to arrive, his mother approaches me and tells me not to worry because her son would arrive, sooner or later. When Giacomo arrives, I am surprised because he is young and small. During the walk from the entrance to the altar, he grows, reaching his actual age. Halfway through the walk, I look at the ceiling and notice an enormous cockroach on the lamp. I feel a strong sense of disgust and I move closer to my husband to seek protection. The dream ends right when I arrive at the altar.

A posteriori, this is how we could interpret the *Wunsch*, the desire expressed in this dream:

> I would like (I am waiting for) the imaginary other, with his pleasant aspects (young and small) but also his disgusting ones (the cockroach), to turn it into a symbolic Other (my actual adult husband) capable of authentically operating on me (the marriage sacrament).

This is why I said, and here I stress it again, that this dream was the incipit of Mrs. Rossi's (ongoing) path. A path that has been re-written through the case, meaning that the case is what one can only write; it is what ceases not to write itself and becomes a possible that has been accomplished. On the other hand, the path of an analysis is already written down to a certain extent, as the subject's desire anticipates it. Mrs. Rossi is trying to read this path, understand it, and make it her own.

She originally addressed her written text, her letter, to a logical addressee – the therapist – with a fake sender – her daughter. But this often happens: in working with children one notices that parents often use their children to pursue their own issues, sometimes using their children as objects of their own phantoms. In this case, it is crucial to bring out the parents' issues so that they may find their logic addressee.

Finally, in the described case I wanted to focus on the possible passage, in the analytic discourse, from a public setting to a private one, with the premise (in the sense of preliminaries) that when one receives a demand, one should set oneself to psychoanalytical listening.

Edited by Alvise Sforza-Tarabochia

SGAI – Italian Group-Analytic Society. A Presentation

President: Franca Beatrice
Honorary President: Diego Napolitani
SGAI – 22, Via Vesio – I - 20148 Milan
Tel.: +39.02.392.7236 Fax: +39.02.392.55035 sgai.milano@tin.it

Group Analysis is a discipline, originating from psychoanalysis, founded by T. Burrow and later developed by S.H. Foulkes in its theoretical and methodological aspects.

In the 1960s Foulkes founded the Group Analytic Society of London, which became a model for other Group Analysis Associations later created around the world. In Milan the Associazione Milanese di Analisti di Gruppo (AMAG) was founded in 1974.

In 1982 the association changed its title-name to Società GruppoAnalitica Italiana (SGAI). The Rome-based Istituto di Gruppoanalisi (IGAR), founded in 1968 by Fabrizio Napolitani, joined the newly-named association in 1990.

SGAI qualifies in the group-analytic movement for the new developments it has given to group-analytic theory, the guidelines of which were presented for the first time in an international context by Diego Napolitani at the 7th World Group Psychotherapy Congress (Copenhagen 1980).

The historical roots of the Group-Analytic model, coherently elaborated by SGAI, lie in the "relational" current of psychoanalytic thought, already widely present in the non-deterministic part of Freud's works. Its most relevant representatives are S. Ferenczi (particularly for his elaboration of the introjective identification concept), W.R.D. Fairbairn (investment shifts from object to relation), D.W. Winnicott (creativity and transitional area), W. Bion (the concepts of protomentality, basic assumptions and transformation in relation to becoming).

The group-analytic model elaborated by SGAI is therefore founded on a selective combination of theoretical segments from relational psychoanalysis which finds a synthesis with the concepts of trans-personality and of dynamic matrix in Burrow and Foulkes.

These clinical and theoretical assumptions have been progressively structured by the perspectives opened up by the Complexity Paradigm, thanks to which it has been possible to integrate in a single model the epistemological foundations of an eco-systemic approach, hermeneutic phenomenology, the latest knowledge from the field of cognitive biology centered on Maturana's and Varela's concept of *autopoiesis* (self-making) and several contributions from genetic anthropology.

The clinical and theoretical axes characterizing the Group-Analytical model, as developed by SGAI, may be summarized with the following three points:

1. The "mind" is "relation", and mental processes, i.e. the complex of interactions between individual and environment, can be distinguished phenomenologically according to three basic types (the relational universes, known as Real, Imaginary and Symbolic). These interactions are structural (an individual unrelated to an environment is unimaginable, nor is it possible to imagine an environment not conceived by an individual), and their nature is characterized by recursivity (any modification circularly involves the very agent of the same modification). Individual identity, with the same structural and recursive characteristics, is a whole made up of the interactions between the internalized environment (the *idem*) and a self-organizing principle (the *autos*) of the same "internal environment".

2. Group Analysis is a hermeneutic practice aiming at the construction of consistent meaning hypotheses for internal/external relational experiences: this praxis, in its autopoietic originality on the symbolic level, contrasts with the tendency to repetitiveness ("repetition compulsion") of the consciousness and affection mechanisms learnt in the subject's original environment (the *family matrixes*).

3. The "group" in "Group Analysis" refers to the "*internal groupness*", which is pertinent to the group analysis concept of "matrix". This implies that such an analytical practice is not restricted to a group setting, because the analysis of internal groupness can be carried out both in a group and in a dual context.

Italian paths of culture

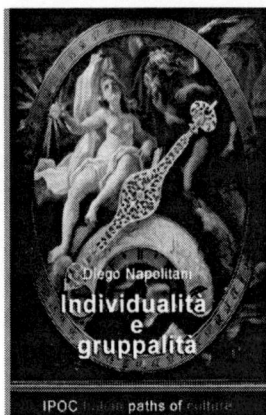

Diego Napolitani
Individualità e gruppalità

Book: ISBN 9788895145020 – pp. 256
e-Book: ISBN 9788895648 – pp. 142
Custom-made Book: chapter(s) – Keywords
and/or Loci Sections

Edi Gatti Pertegato,
Giorgio Orghe Pertegato
Trigant Burrow. Dalla
psicoanalisi alla fondazione
della gruppoanalisi

Book: ISBN 9788895145907 – pp. 284
e-Book: ISBN 9788895145938 – pp. 142
Custom-made Book: chapter(s) – Keywords
and/or Loci Sections

IPOC Italian paths of culture
159, V.le Martesana – I - 20090 Vimodrone MI Italy
Ph. +39-0236569954 – Fax. +39-0236569954
e-mail: ipoc@ipocpress.com
www.ipocpress.com

HISTORY OF PSYCHOANALYSIS

Bruce Fink,
Lacan on Personality from the 1930s to the 1950s

Matteo Vegetti,
Kojève and Lacan

Marta Csabai,
Development of Psychosomatics and the Therapeutic Relationship
The Impact of the Budapest School of Psychoanalysis

Lacan on Personality from the 1930s to the 1950s

Bruce Fink

Keywords: Lacan – Personality – Masks – Unity – Subjectivity

Summary: *The concept of personality plays an important polemical role in Lacan's early work, where he stresses the importance of psychological as opposed to biological determinants of mental illness. He defines personality at that point in time as a diachronic self-conception that evolves in tension with other people, it being a shorthand term in his vocabulary for the psyche. By the time he comments on Lagache's work (1958), he indicates that those who concern themselves with "personality" are taken in by the lure of wholeness, succumbing to the illusion that a person is or becomes a unified whole. Lacan instead emphasizes the mask-like quality of personality, relying on Lévi-Strauss's work to undermine the notion that a psychoanalytic topography could allow us to conceptualize a person as unitary. Lacan's work on Gide and Reich provide a number of other points regarding masks and so-called personality.*

In taking up the topic of personality in Lacan's early work, I will begin with a highly schematic account of his comments on personality in his doctoral dissertation originally published in 1932. In his dissertation, Lacan (1980, pp. 36-37) argues against a metaphysical conception of personality, including soul, form and/or substance, as well as against a psychological conception of personality, including "synthesis of our inner experience," "intentional reality," and "personal [i.e. ethical] responsibility" (pp. 32-33). He proposes instead a notion of personality based on the dialectical "development of the person" (p. 37). By "dialectical," I assume he simply means here that the person's development does not proceed in a fixed direction, but at times hesitates or vacillates between alternatives, changes tack, and so on.

> We thus find here a law of evolution [of the person] instead of a psychological synthesis [...] a regular and comprehensible development. (pp. 38-39)[1]

Lacan goes on to provide an "objective definition of personality phenomena" (p. 42), which stipulates that if we are to relate a human manifestation to personality, it must involve three things:

1. biographical development – that is, the affective ways the subject reads (i.e., understands) his or her own history;
2. a self-conception which includes dialectical progress (or movement);
3. a tension in social relations – that is, conflict between one's own autonomy and one's ethical links with other people.[2]

We can see here, already in the opening pages of his dissertation, that to Lacan personality is not based on a personal synthesis or some sort of psychological unity, which would be synchronic; rather, personality is *diachronic* in some important sense (p. 43). It is something that is not present all at once but is in fact defined by its very movement and progress, that is, by its meaningful – albeit not necessarily predictable – unfolding over time.

Lacan's concern with personality here seems to be part of a larger debate over the origins of psychosis (paranoia in particular): Is it biologically determined or psychologically determined? biogenic or psychogenic? constitutional or personality-based?

Personality seems to have often been discussed in the early 1900s in terms of character and Lacan addresses this question: Is paranoia characterological – that is, defined by a series of character traits – or is it, rather, based on life events, being related to the evolution of one's personality and having an impact on the latter?

---

[1] He seems to integrate the ideas of "intentionality" and "responsibility" into this development, intentionality being understood as the fruit of "education" and as based on "the whole of one's personal development."

[2] These three aspects (development, self-conception, and tension in social relations) are reiterated on page 56 and could, without much difficulty, be situated on the L schema, with $a–a'$ associated with self-conception and S–A with tension in social relations.

Lacan argues, firstly, that there is no unequivocal link between psychosis and a "definable characterological disposition." (p. 53)

> What we take at first to be an identity of character [among psychotics] may merely be a formal homology between similar appearances that in fact relate to entirely different structures. (p. 51)

Similar traits may, in different people, be the product of very different psychic structures, very different underlying personalities, if you will. *We can extend this argument: there is rarely an unequivocal link between a particular personality trait, or symptom even, and a particular psychoanalytic diagnostic structure.* The same behavior, character style, or symptom may express or represent something very different in neurosis and perversion or in obsession versus hysteria. (Constipation, for example, is not intrinsically linked to obsession and can be found in virtually every other structural category at one time or another. Narcissism is not inextricably linked to some particular structure – it is found across the diagnostic spectrum.)

Lacan argues, secondly, that

> a so-called constitutional characteristic [*propriété*], when it is a function whose development is linked to the history of the individual, the experiences that make up his history, and the education he undergoes, should only be *a priori* considered innate in the last resort." (p. 51)

In other words, if something in the subject's personality has meaning to the subject (i.e., he or she sees it as related to his or her history, life events, and/or language) it should first and foremost be considered psychogenic.

His overriding concern is to see *not* if there is some correlation between paranoia and "a definable characterological, constitutional predisposition," but rather to see what impact the evolution and semiology of paranoia have on the personality, *personality being defined as a diachronic self-conception that evolves in tension with other people.* In other words, his concern is to see what life experiences lead to paranoia and what happens to one's personality when paranoia is first triggered.

Lacan claims that

> right from the outset, German authors recognized a wide variety of character dispositions among those with delusions. (p. 82)

This was not so true of the French, who were fond of delineating specific character types. (This has a long tradition in French thought, going back at least as far as Charles Fourier's nineteenth century outline of 810 personality types). But the traits that defined this paranoid character type among the French were very different depending on which author one consulted! In other words, French psychiatrists could not agree among themselves on what characterized the paranoiac's character. In the 1950s, Lacan (1993, p. 4) reflects back on his early years in psychiatry and indicates that among the character traits of paranoiacs one found such vague items as nastiness, intolerance, pridefulness, distrustfulness, excessive sensitivity, and having an overblown sense of oneself.

At one point in his dissertation, Lacan (1980, p. 253) himself seems to drift toward providing a typology of personalities: he says that his patient, Aimée – the main patient discussed in the thesis – has "the salient features" of psychasthenics (Janet) and of sensitive types (Kretschmer). This sort of drift even leads him to talk about the "self-punishing personality" (p. 254). But one can nevertheless understand at the end of this discussion that Lacan is using the term "personality" above all to talk about the psyche as opposed to the organism:

> What my research has led to, and let me emphasize this, is a problem that has no meaning except as a function of the personality or, if one prefers to put it this way, as a psychogenic problem. (p. 254)

I would conclude here that Lacan's reason for adopting the term "personality" is not so much that he is a firm believer in the term, but that he is employing it polemically to combat the then prevalent belief in the biogenic nature of mental illness. *It is a shorthand term in his vocabulary for the psyche*, and it is quite clear at the end of his dissertation that he understands personality to be composed of the classical psychoanalytic agencies or instances: the id, ego, and superego. It is also quite clear that he does not consider the latter to operate in a harmonious, unified fashion, but rather views them as constituting a conflictual, evolving system.

Driving the last nails into the constitutional coffin, Lacan says that the so-called paranoiac constitution (the supposed set of personality traits of paranoiacs) is often not found in actual cases of paranoia, while other "constitutions" (such as psychasthenic and sensitive) are found instead (p. 346).

His general conclusion is that

> The key to the nosological, prognostic, and therapeutic problem of paranoid psychosis must be sought in a concrete psychological analysis that is applied to the entire development of the subject's personality – that is, to the events of his history, to the progress of his conscience, and to his reactions in the social milieu. (p. 346)

In other words, the key is something highly individual, akin to the kind of analysis involved in a psychoanalysis!

While he still allows that "organic processes" (biology) may play some role in the genesis of psychosis, and that "life-threatening conflicts" (trauma) may serve as the "efficient cause" (immediate trigger) of psychosis, a third "specific factor" must always be considered, and this may take the following forms (p. 347):

1. an anomaly of the personality (e.g., the subject's affective history);
2. an anomaly of the personality's development;
3. an anomaly of the personality's functions (infantile fixations at the oral and anal stages).

Overall, we can see that Lacan's major concern in adopting the term "personality" is to combat various tendencies prevalent at the time, including the tendency to attribute all mental illness to biological causes (specific illnesses or problems) or to certain constitutions present from birth, although perhaps evolving over time. His emphasis from the outset is on the importance of *development*, whether that development is smooth or proceeds by discontinuities; the importance of the subject's view of him- or herself in understanding that development (in other words, the way the subject reads his or her own history); and the subject's conflicts with other people. This conception seems to open the door to Lacan's later multilayered view of the psyche or personality in the L schema.

Lacan's dissertation was hailed by surrealists and others in the 1930s as a giant step in the direction of seeing psychotics as *human beings,* not as mutants or diseased patients suffering from a biogenic condition.[3]

Lacan on Lagache

Let us now fast forward twenty-five years and turn to Lacan's work in *Écrits* (1966/2006), in particular his paper entitled "Remarks on Daniel Lagache's Presentation: 'Psychoanalysis and Personality Structure.'" Daniel Lagache (1903-1972) was the father of clinical psychology in France. He studied philosophy at the École Normale Supérieure, became a physician, and then an analyst, being analyzed by Rudolf Loewenstein, who was also Lacan's analyst. Lagache became a professor of psychology at the Sorbonne after WW II, and supported the work of his students Laplanche and Pontalis in preparing their well-known dictionary of Freud's work: *The Language of Psychoanalysis* (1973).[4] The paper by Lagache that Lacan comments on here (entitled "Psychoanalysis and Personality Structure") was published in 1961 in *La Psychanalyse,* a journal directed by Lacan himself. Nevertheless, both Lagache's paper and Lacan's commentary on it date back to a conference held in 1958 in the town of Royaumont in France.

According to Lacan, Daniel Lagache's view of personality directly contradicts Freud's second topography, which Lacan claims

---

[3] In the English-speaking world, R. D. Laing is probably more widely believed to have taken this step first, but his *Divided Self* was first published only in 1960.

[4] In the "Geneva Lecture on the Symptom," Lacan (1989, p. 18) comments that "In *The Language of Psychoanalysis,* Lagache *a là gaché* [a play on words implying spoiled or ruined] all of psychoanalysis. Well, in fact, it isn't so bad, I shouldn't exaggerate. The only thing that probably interested him was to 'Lagachize' what I said" (translation modified).

is "not personalist," meaning that it does not form a harmonious state governed by a "higher synthesis" of some sort, as Lagache would have it.

Lacan (1966/2006, p. 671) reminds us that the root of the term "personality," *persona*, means mask; the Etruscan root of the Latin term *persona* means a theater mask, the kind of mask worn by actors on a stage. Such a mask might be understood to unify a character because it is fixed in expression; it disguises heterogeneity of feeling, ambivalence, and fragmentation, creating instead something singular and monolithic. *To talk about personality is thus a lure: it amounts to being taken in by the lure of wholeness*, to succumbing to the illusion that a person is or becomes a unified whole.[5] Lacan specifically indicates that two aspects of what Lagache calls personality, Freud's ideal ego and ego-ideal, do not fuse in any way or come to form a synthetic whole, for the first is an imaginary formation while the second is largely a symbolic formation (p. 672).

In his commentary on Lagache, Lacan presents optical schemas with which to depict the ideal ego and ego-ideal (1966/2006, pp. 673, 674, and 680). I will not go into all the complexities of these diagrams as they would take us very far afield; let me simply note here that in these optical schemas, he shifts the vase from the out-in-the-open position (in Figure 1) to the hidden position (in Figure 2), thereby perhaps suggesting that the container forms something of an illusion (he identifies the vase with the body *qua* container on page 676 and the flowers with part-objects or object-relations). When we think of the person as a whole or of personality as such, this is an illusion, and this particular illusion is based on our vision of the other, who we see as a whole, whereas we only see parts of ourselves, unless we can catch a glimpse of ourselves in a mirror – in which case we come to see ourselves as we see other people.[6]

---

[5] This illusion can be found, for example, in Erik Erikson's work on "integration" in *Childhood and Society* (1963); cf. his eighth stage of development in which the central conflict is "integrity versus despair."

[6] As Lacan (1966/2006, p. 675) indicates, according to the optical schema, in order to see $i'(a)$, his ideal ego, the subject must be situated in such a way as to see himself in the cone x′y′—that is, to see himself as $i'(a)$. In this sense he sees himself in the "other" ("form of the other") seen as a whole there. He only comes to think of himself as a whole

This brings about *the illusion of unity,* of ourselves as forming a harmonious unit of sorts.

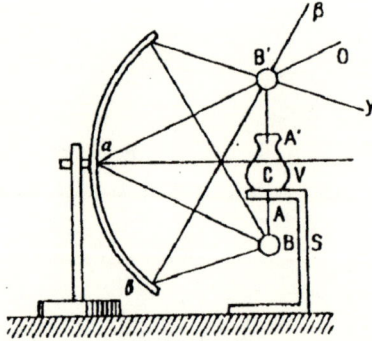

Figure 1. Bouasse's inverted bouquet illusion.

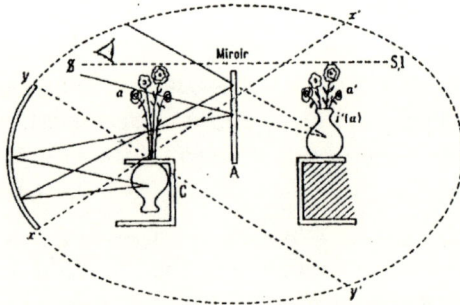

Figure 2. Lacan's first optical schema.

According to Lacan, Lagache "attempts to provide a personalist translation of Freud's second topography" (p. 678) – that is, Lagache tries to create unity from the diversity of the id, ideal ego, ego-ideal, and superego. Lagache considers the "medium of intersubjectivity" to be not speech, but rather the simple distance between the ideal ego and the ego-ideal.

Lacan suggests, however, that the ego-ideal is the constellation of the insignias of the (parental) Other's power, the Other's power "to

because he sees the other as a whole, as a body or container. Note here that $i(a)$ is the real image and that $i'(a)$ is the virtual image; a stands for the part-object, regarding which Lacan says: there is no "ideal totalization of this object" (p. 676).

turn [the subject's] cry into a call" (p. 679) – that is, to humanize it, to transform it into human language, into the symbolic.

> *per · sona*
>
> The person truly begins with the *per-sona* [*sona* referring to sound, in other words, the voice of the superego], but where does personality begin? (p. 684)

In saying this, Lacan is using "person" as a synonym for "subject," not as a synonym for "personality." He seems to be saying here, in other words, that the subject begins as a response to the Other's booming, resounding voice.[7] It is this voice that turns the subject's cry into a call, humanizing it. Hence the subject is quite heterogeneous, including as he or she does the Other's voice within him- or herself.

Let me back up momentarily and try to unpack something Lacan says earlier in his paper on Lagache (p. 671):

> To point out that the *persona* is a mask is not to indulge in a simple etymological game; it is to evoke the ambiguity of the process by which this notion has managed to assume the value of incarnating a unity that is supposedly affirmed in being.
>
> Now, the first datum of our experience shows us that the figure of the mask, being split, is not symmetrical. To express this in an image, the figure joins together two profiles whose unity is tenable only if the mask remains closed, its discordance nevertheless instructing us to open it. But what about being, if there is nothing behind it? And if there is only a face, what about the *persona*?

---

[7] In Seminar XXIV, he puts this a little differently, suggesting that the subject begins as a response to S_1, a first signifier, which comes from the Other.

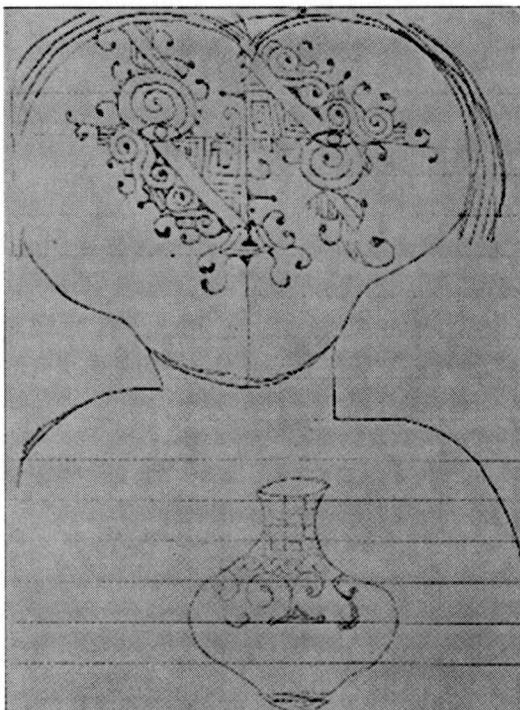

Figure 3. Plate VIII. Caduveo woman's drawing representing a figure
with painted face.

If one has not read Lévi-Strauss' article "Split Representation in
the Art of Asia and America" (1963), one is likely to be lost here,
for split masks are not necessarily something we come across
every day. Lévi-Strauss points out that Caduveo masks (see the
drawing of one such mask in Figure 3) are often split into four
quadrants, the symmetry being between the upper right and lower
left and lower right and upper left (reminiscent of Lacan's L and
even I schemas). The symmetry is far from perfect even then: in
certain cases the opposing quadrants are more complementary than
symmetrical. This is more visible in the two-dimensional drawing
presented here than in three-dimensional painted faces (see, for
example, Lévi-Strauss, 1963, Plates IV, V, and VI after page 251),
since in the latter one cannot see the two different profiles perfectly

at the same time.

In the Caduveo culture, one is considered "stupid" (an animal) prior to having one's face painted in such a way; face painting inscribes one in the social order in a particular place, a place based on one's genealogy and the social rank of one's family. Spiritual messages are included therein: "it is not just a design etched in the flesh, but all the traditions and philosophy of the race etched in the spirit" (Lévi-Strauss, 1963, p. 257, translation modified). As Lévi-Strauss puts it:

> In native thought ... the design is the face, or rather it creates the face. It is the design that confers upon the face its social being, its human dignity, its spiritual significance. Double representation of the face ... thus expresses a deeper, more essential splitting – namely, that between the "stupid" biological individual and the social person whom he must incarnate. (p. 259, translation modified)

Hence we see here the social face of the subject, which comprises her ideals and those of her family and group, contrasted with the raw, brute, "stupid" organism which has not yet been brought into and alienated in language. Perhaps we can now begin to understand what Lacan (1966/2006, p. 671) says:

> Our experience shows us that the figure of the mask, being split, is not symmetrical. To express this in an image, the figure joins together two profiles whose unity is tenable only if the mask remains closed, its discordance nevertheless instructing us to open it. But what about being, if there is nothing behind it? And if there is only a face, what about the *persona*?

The latter part of the quote still seems rather opaque, so let us look to another text to see if it can shed any light on this one.

Lacan on Gide

Here is a related passage from Lacan's article entitled "The Youth of Gide, or the Letter and Desire" (also written in 1958):

> Must I, in order to awaken their attention, show [analysts] how to handle a mask that unmasks the face it represents only by splitting in two and that represents this face only by remasking it? And then explain to them that it is when the mask is closed that it composes this face, and when it is open that it splits it? (Lacan, 1966/2006, p. 752)

The Caduveo mask "unmasks the face it represents only by splitting in two" (right and left profiles; area above the nose and area below) and it "represents this face only by remasking it" – the face can only be represented via a mask for there is no representation without a representational system that is something other than the living organism. The opening and closing of the mask might seem to refer to the laying flat of the two different profiles which can never be seen by a human being in the ordinary course of life (as in Figure 3); the closing might seem to refer to each profile as seen separately. But Lévi-Strauss (1963, p. 262) also mentions that there are certain kinds of

> masks with flaps (*volets*) which alternately present several aspects of the totemic ancestor: sometimes peaceful, sometimes angry, sometimes human, sometimes animal. Their role is to offer a series of intermediate forms that assure the transition from symbol to signification, from magic to normal, from supernatural to social. Their function is thus both to mask and unmask. But when it comes to unmasking, it is the mask that – through a sort of reverse split – opens up into two halves, whereas the actor himself splits, in the split representation that aims, as we have seen, to both display and lay flat [*faire étalage de*] the mask at the expense of its wearer. (Translation modified)

Having read that, I decided I had to find some images of such masks, since Lévi-Strauss did not provide any in that particular article. I came across Lévi-Strauss' preface to *La Voie des Masques*, translated as *The Way of the Masks,* where he cites at length his own 1943 article, "The Art of the Northwest Coast at the American Museum of Natural History," which Lacan most likely read. In it Lévi-Strauss explicitly mentions the extensive collection of masks made by American Indians of the northwest coast of North America on exhibit at the Museum of Natural History in New York; here is what he had said about those masks in 1943:

> For the spectators of the initiation ceremonies, these dance masks – which suddenly open into two flaps (or shutters), allowing one to perceive a second face and sometimes even a third face behind the second, all of which are mysterious and austere – attest to the omnipresence of the supernatural and the proliferation of myths (pp. 11-12).

I then finally managed to find some books that contained pictures of these dance masks. Figures 4 and 5 reproduce just one example from *A World of Faces* (1978) by Edward Malin.

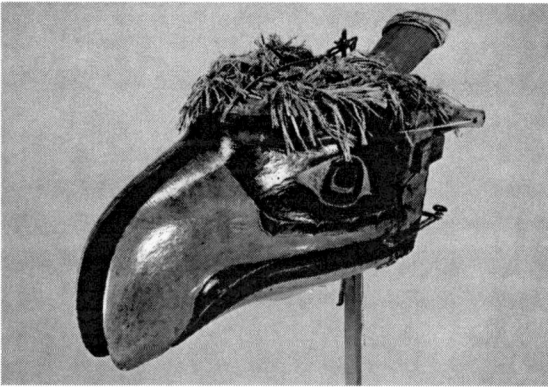

Figure 4. Family crest mask closed (Plate 27A)

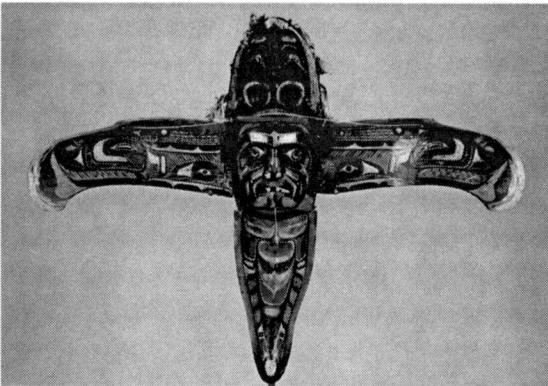

Figure 5. Family crest mask open (Plate 27B)

Two views (open and closed) of Transformation Mask by Herbert Johnson (Kwakwaka' wakw), Kingcome Inlet, BC. Before 1960. 42.8 X 47.1 X 104.3 cm. Photo: Bill McLennan.

As you can see from these figures, the outermost mask is often a stylized representation of an animal, fish, or bird, whereas the innermost mask is usually of a human being, ordinarily one's ancestor, but the innermost mask itself never opens up to reveal the face of the actor himself. Given the relationship between man and his totemic ancestor, we can perhaps now try to understand what Lacan (1966/2006, pp. 751-52) means when he discusses

> a mask that unmasks the face it represents only by splitting in two and that represents this face only by remasking it.

We can perhaps also grasp the notion that

> it is when the mask is closed that it composes this face, and when it is open that it splits it.

For when such a mask is open, we see quite clear images of the outer mask all around the inner one; we do not see one mask alone: we see the inner one and aspects of the outer mask simultaneously. Let us consider anew the above-cited passage:

> Our experience shows us that the figure of the mask, being split, is not symmetrical. To express this in an image, the figure joins together two profiles whose unity is tenable only if the mask remains closed, its discordance nevertheless instructing us to open it. But what about being, if there is nothing behind it? And if there is only a face, what about the *persona*? (p. 671)

We certainly never see the person or being behind the mask. We never see anything but a clash of totemic and human visages, and a transition from one to the other, but nevertheless a multiplicity including one's ancestors – the Other's thunderous voice that brought us into being – and certain familial identifications: hardly a harmonious whole!

Reich: Confusing the Imaginary and the Symbolic

Pursuing this discussion of Lacan on personality just one step further, I will take up Lacan's comments on Wilhelm Reich in "Variations on the Standard Treatment" (1966/2006), originally published in 1955. Here Lacan enunciates a sort of "deconstructive" method (*avant la lettre*), which he often uses:

> Let us follow the path of a kind of criticism that puts a text to the test of the very principles it defends. (p. 341)

In other words, we apply the principles laid out in the text to the text's own argument and see what we come up with.

What does Lacan have to say about Reich's notion of character and character armor? He seems to suggest that the latter is tied up with the imaginary – that is, with the narcissistic image. For he says that the notion of armor suggests a defense against something that is repressed (hence armor is structured like a symptom), whereas what we have here is, rather, an armorial or *coat of arms* (p. 342). An armorial is a configuration of heraldic signs (see Figure 6), and the latter are designed to visually impress people and display one's prestige; they are used to determine precedence in public ceremonies obeying a certain protocol, based on social rank. Lacan obviously associates this with display behavior (in reproduction rituals and aggressive territory determinations) in animals.

© 2001 Encyclopædia Britannica, Inc.

Figure 6. Coat of arms of the Duke of St. Albans.

Although Reich conceptualizes what he is doing in analytic treatment as breaking through the subject's defenses, Lacan seems to suggest here that at the end of such "treatment" the subject is still carrying around the weight of his defenses; it is simply that the almost symbolic mark which they formerly bore has been effaced. These defenses

> play only the role of a medium or material, since they persist after the resolution of the tensions that seemed to motivate them. This medium or material is, no doubt, ordered like the symbolic material of neurosis. (p. 342)

While Reich argues that these defenses disappear in the course of treatment, Lacan's claim is that they persist: it is simply their origin and lineage that have been effaced, leading Reich to assume that the subject has been freed of them (unbarred?); their mark has been effaced but their weight has not. It would seem to Lacan that the mark should, instead, be considered indelible: it is the mortal mark of death. A family coat of arms brings you into being within a certain tradition or family line, but it also seals your fate: you are destined to die in the service of x, y, or z. According to Lacan, Reich tries to exclude the mortal mark we bear when he refuses to accept Freud's notion of the death drive.

One might propose that Reich overlooks the fact that the neurotic's body is overwritten with signifiers. An exaggeratedly erect body posture may, for example, be understood as a phallic signifierness (*signifiance*); it may alternatively be the incarnation of "uprightness," suggesting a grafting onto the body of a parent's moral admonitions or an identification with a parent's rigid moral stance (see Fink, 2007, pp. 196-98). Reich, on the other hand, seems to take the body as if it were a natural thing (to sit hunched over is viewed by him as a protective phenomenon, as a sign of a self-defensive "character," as it might be in the animal kingdom, and as we might see it in most human beings who had just been punched in the stomach) or as pure resistance, instead of as manifesting unconscious identifications with one's ancestors, the taking on of their family crest (blazon, arms, armorial), and so on – in short, as something in which one's mortal fate has been etched.

What then is Lacan's "deconstructionist" reading here? Adopting Reich's principle of interpreting everything as a defensive move, Lacan interprets Reich's refusal of the death drive – which is a proxy for the symbolic in Lacanian theory – as itself a defense. Just as Reich constantly accuses the analysand of defending him- or herself against the analysis, Reich the analyst is accused by Lacan of defending against analytic theory. As is so often the case, Lacan does not really make the argument here – it is simply suggested ...

Subjectivity is Essentially Untotalizable

Beyond 1960, one would be hard-pressed to find Lacan use the term "personality" in anything but a pejorative way, ridiculing those who refer to the "total personality" or to personality as a unifying unity (or unit). He repeatedly asserts instead that "There is no unity to the subject" (see, for example, Lacan, 1983) and that the unconscious cannot be understood as some sort of second (evil or malicious) personality. He seems to view the term itself as almost ineluctably tending toward some totalizing view of the human condition, some totalizing view of subjectivity, and thereby over-looking our split subjectivity. The only occasion on which he takes up the word in his own name, he says that

> personality is the way in which someone subsists in the face of object *a* (Lacan, 1978),

object *a* being viewed by Lacan as precisely what makes us divided subjects.

Bibliography

Edward, M., *A World of Faces*, Portland, Oregon: Timber Press 1978

Erikson, E., *Childhood and Society* [1950], New York: W. W. Norton & Co., 1963

Fink, B., *Fundamentals of Psychoanalytic Technique: A Lacanian Approach for Practitioners,* New York: W. W. Norton & Co., 2007

Fourier, C., *The Passions of the Human Soul.* New York: Augustus M. Kelley Publishers, 1968

Lacan, J.:
- "Discours de Jacques Lacan à l'Université de Milan le 12 mai 1972," in *Lacan in Italia 1953-1978. En Italie Lacan,* Milan: La Salamandra, pp. 32-55, 1978
- *De la Psychose Paranoïaque dans ses rapports avec la personnalité* [1932], Paris: Seuil, 1980
- "Interview donnée par Jacques Lacan à François Wahl à propos de la parution des *Écrits,*" broadcast on the radio on February 8, 1967, and published in the *Bulletin de l'Association Freudienne,* 3, pp. 6-7, 1983
- "Geneva Lecture on the Symptom," in *Analysis* 1. (Lecture given in French in 1975), 1989
- *The Seminar of Jacques Lacan, Book III: The Psychoses (1955-1956)* [1981], ed. J.-A. Miller, translated by R. Grigg, New York-London: W. W. Norton & Co., 1993
- *Écrits: The First Complete Edition in English* [1966], translated by B. Fink, New York-London: W. W. Norton & Co., 2006 (Page numbers given to this work refer to the original pagination of the 1966 French edition provided in the margins of the new English edition.)

Laing, R. D., *The Divided Self,* London: Tavistock, 1960

Laplanche, J., J.-B. Pontalis, *The Language of Psychoanalysis.* New York: W.W. Norton & Co., 1973

Lévi-Strauss, C.:
- "The Art of the Northwest Coast at the American Museum of Natural History," *Gazette des Beaux-Arts,* 1943, pp. 175-82
- *Structural Anthropology* [1958], New York: Basic Books, 1963
- *The Way of the Masks* [1975], Translated by S. Modelski, Seattle, WA: University of Washington Press, 1982

Kojève and Lacan

Matteo Vegetti

Keywords: Desire – Need – Self-Consciousness – Otherness – End of History

Summary: *The paper traces the history of the intellectual relation between Kojève and Lacan and develops its theoretical implications. The analysis centers on the Hegelian notion of desire, one that Kojève redevelops with and against Hegel to found human self-consciousness within a relational framework in which otherness plays an essential and ambivalent role. Together with the Kojèvian theme of desire, this very ambivalence will become for Lacan the place of continuous critical confrontation: from the initial analyses devoted to the "mirror-phase" (1938) up to Seminar II (1954-55), this issue undergoes a range of theoretical mutations that reflect important phases of Lacanian thinking. Behind Lacan's complex hermeneutic debt towards Kojève what finally emerges is the knot of the Hegel-Freud relation with regard to the meaning and the limits of knowledge an human self-conscience.*

For example, I could easily have never met Kojève. If I had never met him, it is very likely that, like all Frenchmen educated in a certain period, I would never f suspected that the Phenomenology of Spirit *was something important.* Lacan, 1982

In the French cultural climate of the 30s, dominated by positivist and neo-Cartesian currents of thought, Hegel was either openly opposed or widely ignored. This silence was broken, and perhaps not incidentally, by the extraordinary teachings of a young Russian immigrant: Alexandre Kojèvnikov, better-known as Kojève.

The road that led him to Paris, pressed by the great historical events of the 20th century, was neither simple nor linear. Aged just 18, Kojève, nephew of the painter Kandinsky, illegally leaves his country to flee the dangers that threatened the Muscovite wealthy classes his family belonged after the events of the revolution. Kojève first ends up in Berlin, where he graduates with Karl Jaspers. But the political climate emerging in Germany in the 20s presses him to find refuge within the colony of Russian exiles in Paris. His encounter with Koyré, who was in his own right to become one of the great masters of contemporary epistemology, becomes of crucial value for the history of French culture. Indeed, when Koyré, lecturer at the *Ecole pratique de hautes etudes*, moves to Cairo to undertake his new studies in the field of philosophy of science, he appoints Kojève as his replacement for the course on Hegelian philosophy of religion. This substitution would last seven memorable years (from 1933 to 1939) during which Kojève was to comment, line by line, on Hegel's *Phenomenology of Spirit* with extraordinary intellectual acumen and an uninhibited hermeneutical vocation. Kojève's lecture room would attract a small but selected audience. Among these: Raymond Queneau (who then collected the lessons in the famous *Introduction à la lecture de Hegel*, Kojève, 1947), Éric Weil, Maurice Merlau-Ponty, Georges Bataille, Raymond Aron, André Breton, Roger Caillois, Jacques Lacan.

In *Séminare VIII, Le Transfert*, Lacan pays tribute to the Kojève who initiated him intowards Hegelian thought:

> someone whose importance for my training I would regret not having already told you about, and to whom, as I think some know, I owe having been introduced to Hegel, that is Kojève.[1]

With regard to this debt, another confession would be appropriate at this point. In a 1948 letter Kojève writes to the Marxist phenomenologist Tran-Duc-Thao:

> Finally, concerning my theory of "desire of desire", it is also not in Hegel and I am not sure that he saw the thing in the right way. I introduced this notion because I intended not to write a commentary to phenomenology, but an interpretation; in other words, I tried to find the deepest premises of Hegelian doctrine and to build it by logically deducing it from its premises. "Desire of desire" seems to me one of the fundamental premises in

[1] Lacan, 2001

question, and if Hegel himself did not stress it clearly I consider that, by formulating it expressly I have made some philosophical progress. It is perhaps the only philosophical progress I have made, being the rest all more or less philology, i.e. precisely an explanation of the texts (Kojève 1990, p. 133, my translation).

Kojève's hermeneutical style reflects a tactics of dissimulation that plays subtly between Hegel's words and their interpretation, between the form of the comment and the meta-theoretical construction of an independent argument. The former develops from Hegelian nuclei of thought from which Hegel himself would have been unable to draw all the possible consequences and implications. According to Mikkel Borsh-Jacobsen, Lacan took this stylistic mode from Kojève, suspending his own theory in the turns of Freudian dictate, in the dissimulative play on comment, where theoretical instances alien to the text intervene, producing controlled twisting effects. Now, one of these instances is that very *theory of desire* Kojève lays claim to as his true contribution to philosophical thinking. The stylistic analogy is not then, at this point, only external, but generates a problematic hermeneutic intersection: as in a sort of chiasmus, the Kojèvian notion of "desire of desire" ambiguously articulates the Hegel-Kojève relation as much as the Freud-Lacan relation, and does so in such a way as to hide behind the Hegel-Freud relation, engendered by this very chiasmus, the relation between the actors.[2]

---

[2] According to Elisabeth Roudinesco, "Not only would Lacan arrive at a reading of Hegel's works that will always be inspired to Kojève, but he would also acquire a way of transmitting knowledge orally that was to remain his model for the rest of his life. He too was to dominate an intellectual generation through speech dispensed as part of a seminar centered around the commentary of Freudian texts; he would benefit from the help of a transcriber of his verb and, finally, he would occupy a paradoxical place within French Universities: marginal and at the same time perfectly integrated" (Roudinesco 1997). To dispel any doubts about the direct derivation of Lacan's hermeneutical method from Kojève's, it is enough to quote the "confidence" given us by Queneau (1996) in his recently published diary: "So Lacan tells me the whole story of the schism within the Psychoanalytical Association and tells me how his seminar works. He comments, following Kojève's method, particular Freudian texts". According to John Forrester (1993): "One may also say that, for those seeking an introduction to the philosophical world of Lacan, the best suggestion would be to read the *Introduction to the Reading of Hegel* (1947) by Alexandre Kojève".

To draw closer to the question a good idea would be to get back onto the path of the Hegelian-Kojèvian notion of desire, stressing its positional value within *Phenomenology*. Hegelian self-consciousness emerges with the difference between the concept of need and desire. Need is the manifestation of life in the animal fundament of the living. The most primordial feeling of the self originates in living under the mark of a lack (hunger), for which the real (the object) appears as a potential source of nourishment and sustenance. But once the independence of the object is denied (once the appetite of need has been satisfied), life reabsorbs the difference, leaving it to disperse in its apparent accidentality. The cyclic nature of need keeps the living being chained to the rule of natural objects, which it denies so as to satisfy itself. The logics of need are thus not enough to explain the onset of human self-consciousness. Indeed, by definition, self-consciousness goes beyond the mere immediacy of natural objects. It transcends the natural sphere the living being generally belongs to and at the same time it transcends itself: it understands itself in relation to the object that reflects it and modifies itself via this same relation.

What is then the requirement for that lack of need that gives rise to both historical and relational self-conscious human reality to emerge? In Kojève's words, what is required is for desire engendered by the lack not to be directed towards a simple object (as in the case of need) but rather towards another desire: the desire that turns towards another desire, that desires to be desired (or recognized) by the other (by another self-consciousness) is truly human. This famous formula gives rise to several other important consequences: First of all, Hegelian self-consciousness is constituently dependent on the other, precisely insofar as it is a self-consciousness. Human existence is structurally dependent on the other, because it is from the other that it receives the certainty of self, deriving from the fact that it is objectified through recognition. An exchange relation is thus established that functions via a double link, in the sense that "each one of us" is himself only in virtue of the other, in a circular dynamics of mutual co-dependence. This is where we begin to catch a glimpse of the paradoxical essence of the Hegelian subject: self-consciousness aspires to establishing itself as an autonomous and independent reality, but at the same time this doesn't happen without the fundamental mediation of the other. With this ambivalence Kojève triggers several crucial consequences. First of all the roots of human violence (fighting) are of an essentially symbolic order: consciousness cannot affirm itself as an "Ego", an autonomous reality, without a fight to deny the symbolic cause of its alienation. The latter, therefore, depends not on an extrinsic imposition of force, but on the very ambivalence of recognition, which is at the same time what constitutes and removes the self-assertion of the subject. Now, even if we leave aside this aspect for a moment, together with the phenomenology of the figures engendered by the dialectics of fighting, these implications already allow us to capture Lacan's primary debt with Kojève.

In fact, as early as 1936 he and Lacan planned to jointly write a paper entitled *Hegel et Freud: essai d'une confrontation interprétative*[3]. This was to consist of three sections: *Genesis of Self-Consciousness, The Origins of Madness, The Essence of the Family* and a final chapter entitled *Perspectives*. As far as we know only Kojève worked on achieving this program, drafting fifteen introductory pages dedicated to a critical confrontation between the Cartesian *cogito* and Hegelian Self-Consciousness. According to E. Roudinesco, however, in this work we find three fundamental concepts that Lacan was to use as from 1938: the ego (*je*) as the subject of/to desire, the *désir*, as a revelation of the truth being, the ego (*moi*) as a place of delusion and source of error. All this proves Lacan's special focus on the Kojèvian meaning of desire. In fact the *dialectics* of desire occupy a central position in his reflections as a whole, becoming the object of a continuous reworking responding to a double need: a need internal to psychoanalytical debate on the

---

[3] Meant to appear in "Recherches philophiques", it seems that only Kojève's mentioned introduction was ever drawn up. However, Elisabeth Roudinesco (1986) refers to a singular fact that, if anything, brings across Lacan's esoteric taste for Kojève's thinking: a few days after the philosopher's death, Lacan broke into his house to get hold of his personal copy, with hand-written notes, of *The Phenomenology of Spirit*. Auffret (1990) suggests that in this circumstance Lacan also illegitimately tried to seize the Kojèvian manuscript entitled *Hegel et Freud, essai d'une confrontation interprétative*.

one hand, i.e. reconsidering the function of hypnosis (meant as the identificational fascination preceding the oedipal triangulation), and on the other a need circularly linked to this, i.e. recovering the deep-down sense of recognition theory. As early as in the essay *The Mirror Phase* (Lacan, 1938), written under the immediate influence of Kojève,[4] Lacan conceives the forming of the self as the effect of a rebounding, as the Hegelian moment of reflection where being-for-self mediates itself in being-for-another. Ego and subject, in the phase under examination, have not as yet been distinguished. They appear, instead, as the mere reflection of the specular *alter ego* where primary alienation outlines itself. The mirror then has the function that is occupied in Kojèvian anthropology by the presence of another desire; it breaks the intact immediacy of subjective certainty to reduplicate it in its own simulacrum. On the surface of the mirror is where the sign that intensively represents the subject, ascribing to it the imaginary unity that belongs to idealization processes, composes itself. Indeed, the reflected image breaks up the sense of the self in its own representation (*Vor-stellung*), but at the same time it allows consciousness to become such even with respect to itself.

It is necessary, however, to note the limit of such an elaboration of the issue of self-consciousness: the dialectics conceived to found conscience in intersubjectivity, in being-in-the-world, played in these terms, run the risk of reducing themselves to a narcissistic short-circuit, i.e. to the process of identification of the ego in the self that stifles the movement in a self-referential dynamics and consigns otherness to the rank of mere appearance. Implicitly, in his 1953 *Rome Speech*, Lacan acknowledges his having misinterpreted Kojève's

---

[4] So "immediate", to be honest, to encourage the sarcasm of J.P.Aron (1985): "It all begins a bit on the sly in the thirties with what André Green gracefully calls a 'dioptrics of alienation'. To his flock at the Hautes Etudes Kojève announces that conscience is born out of desire, which is nothing but desire of the other. Lacan immediately exploits this trend in the *Encyclopédie Larousse*. Before his image reflected in the mirror, the small in man has a reaction of jubilation. First dive into the imaginary. First identification the sequences of which Hegel marks. Distinction between the image and the reality of the self. Recognition of the self in the other".

theory,[5] which, played within the mirror model, produces precisely the opposite effect from the one it had been formulated for: to elude to the self-evidence of the *cogito*, it runs aground onto the rocks of reified consciousness. And in fact, if one has identification of conscience derive from its objectification, one may capture it in a sort of tautology. As in the Narcissus myth[6], through the cancellation of the distance from the image and the alienation of the ego in the *imago* of the double, the mirror represents a premature symbolic death. With Lacan's next revisitation of the specular double (1974), the need is felt to broaden its meaning to the subject-world relationship. At the first accentuation of the captive value of the relationship, the centrality of the function that carries out the turn from the specular ego to the social ego is substituted in such a way that the mirror now goes to cover the decisive moment that links, in a broken circularity, inner world and surroundings (*Innenwelt* and *Umwelt*). At the same time, in the new arrangement, the Kojèvian mediation of desire as desire for the other makes its stately appearance on the stage:

> This moment at which the mirror stage comes to an end inaugurates, through identification with imago of one's semblable and the drama of primordial jealousy ... the dialectic that will henceforth link the *I* to socially elaborated situations (Lacan, 1966, Eng. tr. 2006, p. 79).[7]

As from the "Rome speech" the place of the specular ego is taken by non-identification with the symbolic "great Other"; the presentification of the former is substituted by the irreducible absence of the latter.

---

[5] Breaking a long silence, the Lacanian school appears prepared today to recognize what is a mere matter of fact, i.e. the Kojèvian roots of Lacan's reflections on the subject of desire, and J.-A. Miller himself (1996) admits that "this key Lacan brings at the beginning, which is the recognition of desire, and according to which desire requires a recognition, is a philosophical legacy from Kojève's reading of Hegel".

[6] "The world characteristic of this phase – Lacan writes (1938)- is therefore a narcissistic world". And further down: "Whether this meaning [of the myth of Narcissus] indicates death... or the mirror reflection (the *imago* of the double that is central to it) or the illusion of the image, this (narcissistic) world, as we shall see, does not contain the 'other'".

[7] Ibid.

According to Lacan:

> In short, nowhere does it appear more clearly that man's desire finds its meaning in the other's desire, not so much because the other holds the keys to the desired object, as because his first object(ive) is to be recognized by the other.[8]

And furthermore:

> But this desire itself to be satisfied in man requires that it be recognized, through the accord of speech or the struggle for prestige, in the symbol or the imaginary... and our path is the intersubjective experience by which this desire gains recognition.[9]

The pages of *The Signification of the Phallus* devoted to the issue of desire seem to offer a systematic milestone in this sense. Lacan declines the original relation between self-consciences in the primary mother-child relationship, in the form of a constituent dependence. The difference between ego and subject now goes through this, in the sense that whereas the former can imagine itself as an independent *res* in the imaginary register, the former turns out to be structurally *subject to* a binding symbolical dependence. Following Kojève literally, Lacan ends up defining in this sense madness as the most radical manifestation of the ego: to be mad is thinking you're an ego, removing the other from the self, and thus the desire and subordination of the subject to the law of recognition. On the other hand,

> The phenomenology that emerges from analytic experience is certainly of a kind to demonstrate the paradoxical, deviant, erratic, eccentric, and even scandalous nature of desire that distinguishes it from need.[10]

With these words Lacan introduces the distinction between the registers of desire and need.[11] If the latter corresponds to the level of

---

[8] Lacan, 1966; Eng. tr. 2006, p. 222.
[9] Ibid, p. 231.
[10] Ibid, p. 579.

life, to self-preservation drives, to the unilateral denial of the object through a specific action, desire affirms itself as the denaturalization of the object intentioned by need and, correlationally, by the content of the satisfaction associated to it. The passage occurs when the particularity of need is subordinated to the universality of Demand (of recognition), in other words when the needs of the child reach the point of formulating themselves in the signifiers. In this sense Demand is a signifying shaping of need. But its condition of possibility resides in the Other, in the possibility for the pre-linguistic articulation of the child's scream to be received and returned in an act of translation that turns it into a request, inserting it in the dialectical register of desire. With the aim of pointing to the authentically dialectical value of this movement, Lacan employs the Hegelian concept of *Aufhebung*, implicitly adopting its triple meaning of negation, overcoming (or sublimation) and conservation. This pattern (which represents "the privilege of the Other") is in actual fact a movement that diverts Demand from presence (the vital satisfaction of need) to lack, insofar as the object demanded is indeed a non-presence, a desire invoked as a desire of love. Demand, Lacan writes,

> annuls (*aufhebt*) the particularity of everything that can be granted, by transmuting it into a proof of love, and the very satisfactions demand obtains for need are debased to the point of being no more than the crushing brought on by the demand of love.[12]

---

[11] Once again, the desire device works to release the subject from the logics of needs, eluding the delusion that there can be an objectual relation, or at least a dual one, that can cover for its "accidental" lack. As Benvenuto writes (1983, p.25): "Freudian 'lack' is actually one of theory, not of its object, and it consists of the fact that on the one hand the cause of desire is the other, but this other is such only insofar as desire 'recognizes' it... We may go as far as to say that in Freud the efficient cause, on the conceptual plain, is rather the *more*: Freudian desire is this 'more', a tension yearning for annihilation, and Eros is just this excess in being the aim of which is however death, i.e. the elimination of this excess, of this 'more', of the excrescence. In Lacan, conversely, the *manque*, the Freudian theoretical fault, is rationalistically ontologized: subjective dialectics, the sayable and the analyzable, become the effect of this *manque*, lack or deficit, that is in the end the *foundation* and cause of desire, and thus of the S.o.R [Subject of Recognition]".

[12] Lacan, 1966, Eng. tr. 2006, p. 580.

The peculiarity of need does not disappear as such, as need. Only the peculiar character of this peculiarity is abolished, the attachment to the positiveness of the "this", the condition determined by fulfillment. Through this canceling desire reappears as "an absolute condition": a symbolic surplus value that invests every relational object intentioned by Demand with self and at the same time exceeds it in the register of the signifier.

The inscription of the subject in the space of Demand has for Lacan the radical form of the gift, in the sense that the other is called upon to give what he does not have: neither this nor that, but the absolute condition or horizon of the love request that transcends every determined presence. It's worth noting, however, that not too differently from what the anthropology of Mauss (2000) has taught us, the nature of this gift too bears the sign of a profound ambiguity. First of all, language, which opens the space of conscience in the other, is a deadly gift: it announces the finite destination that inscribes the subject in being for death, since that there can be no experience of death if not in the field of the signifier. We shall return on this point further down. There is, in fact, another ambivalence to capture. Differently from need, desire aims to find what cannot by definition be found, fixing the subject to a constitutionally unsaturated condition, exposed to the insignificance of the object and the paradox of a recognition that, insofar as it is the object of desire, reveals itself as a source of frustration. Radicalizing the premises of Kojève's arguments, desire is for Lacan the desire for nothing, desire of the other caught with the mark of lack, i.e. insofar as the other is "cause" of desire.[13] It is here, however, that the Kojève-Lacan comparison enters its deepest and most problematic aspect. According to Kojève the anthropological premise cannot evade the political question, the

---

[13] According to Pierre Macherey (1991, p. 319) the barrier over-determining the absence of the subject as alienated and dependent on the place of the other's desire also has its philosophical roots in Kojève, and particularly in his interpretation of Heidegger: "It is from there [from *Being and Time*] that Kojève develops his theory of historical man as nullifying subject wielding his essential negativity through the combined forms of mourning and labor and at the same time defines himself as subject of desire, in the sense of a desire condemned, by its very nature, to remaining unsatisfied. One can see here a prefiguration of the Lacanian theory of *Spaltung*, of the barred subject etc." (My translation).

"thing in itself" of Hegelian philosophy: if the circle of self-consciousness is constitutionally anarchical, lacking *archè*, a foundation, how will it be possible to establish a *nomos*, a law, for it? How is it possible to think, in other words, that social organization can make up for the splitting (*Spaltung*) that crosses the subject, insofar as it is subject "to" and "of" desire? It should be remembered that, if history is the history of the servant, as Kojève kept tirelessly repeating, it is, even more deep-down, the history of the elaboration of a mourning: the impossibility to say "I" (*Je*) without the guarantee of the other's independence, through which I am allowed to be myself (*moi*).

For Kojève, at the end of history the absolutist State (the Communist State) then appears as the guardian of the nothingness we all are; it becomes the incarnation of the absolute Master or of death itself as the negation of any particularity. Thus Kojève's Final State guarantees the rational, homogeneous and universal apportionment of recognitions, coming to occupy the position of «absolute condition» evoked by Lacan. What makes individuals perfectly interchangeable is precisely the possibility of subtracting from them the "privilege of the other". Of course Kojève is well aware that the result of this subtraction is the negation of the subject as such (a negation linked to the theory of the death of man at the End of History). But it is also the condition for the history of self-consciousness to go beyond the statute of dependence and obtain the promise of satisfaction desire has been waiting from the very start.

The post-revolutionary event of the citizen regaining possession of the source of courtly jouissance in the mediation of praxis – in this way overcoming in himself his history of servitude – is precisely, as Derrida[14] found, the *end of the finished man*: the place where the surmounting of the constitutive aporia of the subject as desiring conscience takes place and, even more so, the place of death. The figure of the Hegelian Self thus coincides, according to Kojève, with the epiphany of the Thing, the real in itself, an epiphany where in a single act the satisfaction of the servant determines the abolition

[14] Derrida, 1982.

of man precisely in the sense of Being There (in Heidegger's terms). This is certainly not a material effect, but rather a canceling that strikes the symbolic register where what is human in man expresses itself: not only the dynamics of recognition and time as the phenomenal expression of difference, but strictly speaking, according to Kojève, the very possibility of language. That this conclusion sounds humorous to Lacan[15] – he goes as far as saying that he finds *Phenomenology of Spirit* incredibly witty – should neither be a surprise nor induce to a superficial underestimation of the problem. The humor lies in the fact that the promise of jouissance accompanying the dialectic telling of the history of the Servant from beginning to end, and that ultimately crowns truth on its throne, has a sense and a legitimacy only within the limits of the discourse on knowledge (or, more precisely, of structurally ideological university discourse) of which Hegel is the "sublime representative". On the other hand, the real and actual ideology – towards which both the communist and liberal utopias converge from different positions – consists in the pretence that the State is capable of producing a subject with no relation to the debt of Demand and immune to the signifying excess of the Master, to the unitary trait of being-for-death.

It then becomes necessary to point out the insurgence of a peculiar ambiguity: Lacan only accepts the aporetic elements of Kojèvian dialectics, whereas the Hegelian and Marxist aspects, where desire appears as the powerfulness of theological becoming and of the emancipation promoted by praxis, are eclipsed (or better still, rejected):

> The work, Hegel tells us, to which the slave submits in giving up jouissance out of fear of death, is precisely the path by which he achieves freedom. There can be no more obvious lure than this, politically or psychologically.[16]

As a true Kojèvian, something which he was throughout his life, Lacan knows by heart the epistemological squint linking, in his

[15] Lacan, 1982.
[16] Lacan, 1966, Eng. tr. 2006, p. 686.

master's thinking, the work of death to historical Prometheism. Bringing both aspects to the spotlight and stiffening them in an instrumental opposition, his reading comes to a crossroads: to subjectivity split in the interception of desire we find the contraposition of the "ideal solution", of "a subject finalized in his self-identity", "*Selbstbewußtsein*, the being of the conscious, wholly conscious self",[17] as if, from the same stock, could be born at once a radically anti-humanist instance and that conjunction between the symbolic and the real which would give rise once more, and more strongly than ever, to the Cartesian subject.

For Lacan this uncanny ambivalence by which Kojève's Hegelism is revealed to be at once assimilable and non-assimilable to psychoanalytic theory, both familiar and alien, had to cease. Overlapping dangerously with his hermeneutics, the Russian's epistemology runs the risk of dragging Freud on the ground he'd least have wanted to tread: under the enlightenment horizon of absolute knowledge, in the light of which the humanistic matrix of desire and the psychoanalytic subject glitters.

In 1955 Lacan decides it's time to cut the Gordian knot,[18] to free Freud from the bond he himself had tied him to, by staging a showdown, which would open up a vital and definitive gap: in the seminar *Freud, Hegel and the Machine*[19] the match comes to a theatrical close at the climax of an extremely delicate theoretical passage with a decision that replaces the two systems of thinking in mutual difference. Let us note that the seminar comes immediately after the "Rome speech" and is almost contemporary to the essay *Variants of the Typical Treatment* (written between 1953 and 1955, the year of its publication) and the article *Introduction to Jean Hyppolite's Commentary* (1954). It therefore belongs to a crucial stage when Lacan is rethinking the deep-down structure of subjectivity and the end of analysis on the basis of the anthropogenetic function of

---

[17] Ibid, p. 675.
[18] To define it with E. Roudinesco (1986, p.152): "...Lacan stands to Freud as Kojève stands to Hegel". An equation that risks turning into: Lacan stands to Kojève as Freud stands to Hegel (My translation).
[19] Lacan, 1978b.

desire, which evolves and amplifies the sense of the morphogenetic function, previously found in the phenomenon of mirror recognition. The psychoanalytical ego, Lacan reasserts in the aforementioned essay, has nothing to do with the transcendental unity general psychology derives from "synthetic functions". Indeed, the ego – in its genesis and essence – cannot be distinguished from the imaginary captures that constitute it "by an other and for an other";

> Stated differently, the dialectic that sustains our experience, being situated at the most enveloping level of the subject's efficacy, obliges us to understand the ego entirely in the movement of progressive alienation in which self-consciousness is constituted in Hegel's phenomenology.[20]

But what's the fundamental contribution of Kojève's circle of desire to psychoanalysis? Once again

> to return psychonalysis to a veridical path, it is worth recalling that analysis managed to go so far in the revelation of man's desires only by following, in the veins of neurosis and marginal subjectivity of the individual, the structure proper to a desire that thus proves to model it at an unexpected depth – namely, the desire to have his desire recognized. This desire, in which it is literally virified that man's desire is alienated in the other's desire, in effect structures the drives discovered in analysis.[21]

These reflections are echoed in the Seminar *The Ego in Freud's Theory and in Psychoanalytic Technique* (1954-1955), an authentic intellectual laboratory that begins with the enigmatic discussion entitled *Freud, Hegel and the Machine* (12 January 1955). In its passages we find the zenith of his confrontation with Kojève, disguised as one with Hegel. The threatening shadow of a third main player looms over the entire dialogue, Heidegger's *Letter on "Humanism"* (1987), the presence of which furtively dominates the convergence of the discourse's internal logic, causing the activation of a whole range of conditions. Lacan fears that Freud's psychoanalytical doctrine may find itself crushed between the Hegelian-Kojèvian themes he refounded it on and

[20] Lacan, 1966, Eng. tr. 2006, p. 312.
[21] Ibid, p. 285.

Heidegger's attack on humanistic anthropocentrism. Lacan fears, even more frankly, that, faced with the threat of Heidegger's "letter", his hermeneutics may meet the same fate as Sartre's existential analytics. This is where the emergence of the dialogue resides, in the overriding urgency of freeing Freud from the stranglehold he himself pushed him into, with an intellectual surgery to free him from Hegel-Kojève, from the primacy of self-consciousness, from the historical liberation of *humanitas*, fulfilling itself in the compact and purified figure of a disalienated subjectuality.

The question must then be put in these terms:

> what is there that's new, if we place them on the same register, in moving from Hegel to Freud?[22]

The answer is destined to remain in suspense because of the interpolation of a second premise with clear Kojèvian, and hence Battaillean and Derridean, origins: whatever one does, *even without thinking*, one does it, or rather, one is it, *within* "the progress of the phenomenology of spirit". However momentary, this is undoubtedly an admission: historical man is man's historical knowledge and his determination, whether affirmative or negative, is always prey to the limen marked by *phenomeno-logy*, by the language and logic put into action herein. In this sense, Freud's thought too is inscribed in Hegel's historicizing gesture and seems to belong to the horizon of absolute knowledge. After the admissions comes the attack: "The end of history – Lacan claims – that's absolute knowledge. You can't get out of that – if consciousness is knowledge, written as such in Hegel".[23] The decisive argument is encrypted. In just one page Lacan touches upon many key points of the concept of "end", focusing his analysis on the first note of the twelfth lesson of Kojève's 1938-1939 course. The object of this lesson, to which he returns to in the famous "note added to the second edition", is the definition of a notion often held to be exoteric: "the disappearance of Man at the end of history".

---

[22] Lacan, 1978b; Eng. tr. 1991, p. 68.
[23] Ibid, p. 71.

The interest aroused by this can thus be easily understood within the context of the problems Lacan is debating.

The decisive dissertation consists of three passages. First of all the discursive end of history is evoked, its accomplishment in the language element structured within the Hegelian absolute Discourse. According to Kojève, the content of absolute knowledge is the circular totality of Sense, depleting any possibility of signifying. Lacan evokes this event correctly pointing out the epochal moment of this taking place in «post-revolutionary phases» and adding, acutely, that then "there won't be any further need to speak".[24] Note that Lacan explicitly argues that the topical genesis and structure of the Meaning of Discourse within the grammar of dialectical knowledge, "the embodiment of absolute knowledge", "is more than a myth, it is the very meaning of the forward march of the symbol". In turn, the possession of this knowledge and this symbology is the exclusive privilege of the Wise Men, a term that Lacan loosely translates with «*savants*», the scientists. What is important at this point is that the lords of knowledge and of knowing oneself are a limited number of individuals, the Wise Men alone, while all others, deprived of their humanity by the effect of the end of history (the effect of the desiring dynamics at its foundation) will suffer the event of the end entirely unwittingly. Lacan, and this is his second move, stresses this rift:

> When the scientists – this is more than a myth, it is the very meaning of the forward march of the symbol – succeed in bringing human discourse to a close, they are in possession of it, and those who don't have it have nothing left but to turn to jazz, to dance, to entertain themselves, the good fellows, the nice guys, the libidinal thypes.[25]

The wisdom-Jazz opposition may sound extravagant, but it is actually an encrypted quote from a passage in which Kojève employs certain metaphors to indicate the field of post-historic existence, largely arranged with a covert reference to specific traits of characters

[24] Ivi.
[25] Lacan, 1978b; Eng. tr. 1991, p. 72.

from the novels of Queneau (characters in turn inspired to the theme of the end of history). The theory of the disappearance of man at the end of history does not imply a "cosmic catastrophe" nor any form of obscure soteriology. The end of history invests exclusively the historical dialectics of recognition. Kojève argues:

> But all the rest can be preserved indefinitely: art, love, play, etc.; in short, everything that makes Man *happy*.[26]

But, whereas the dead man, *insofar as he is a man*, falls into an eternal "Sunday of life", the *savant*, on the other hand, preserves the meaning of this death. Now, between the desire for knowledge and the libidinal economy of desire (what is "to be known"), is where for Lacan the schism in Hegelian anthropology opens up:

> Within the absolute knowledge, there remains one last separation, ontological if I may say, whitin man.

Thus, at the end of history too,

> In the end, there is a reciprocal alienation, and, I want to insist on this, it is irreducible, with no way out.[27]

With this acute foray in Kojèvian end of history, Lacan ends the game: the Hegelian absolute object is segregated in the archives of western philosophical myths, while absolute knowledge reveals itself as the recognition of an extreme limit determining the boundaries of both history and desire: "That is where, I think, in the last istance, Hegel leads us to". There's only one thing left for Lacan to do at this point, and that is to collect the fruits of his complex strategy that culminates in a peremptory verdict where, with the mask of humanism, the threshold of the end comes back onto the stage: "Hegel is the limit of anthropology. Freud got out of it".[28] The wheel has turned full circle. Or rather, it has been opened with a

---

[26] Kojève, 1947; Eng. tr. 1980, p. 158n.
[27] Lacan, 1978b; Eng. tr. 1991, p. 72.
[28] Ibid.

thin fissure where the game of inside and outside repeats itself, leaving the very nature of *limit* and *dam* unexplained. What remains to be explained is precisely how Freudian theory can place itself beyond metaphysics, safe from the banishment signed by Heidegger. It is therefore well worth remembering what Lacan writes at the beginning of the *Éncore* seminar (1971-1973, p.5):

> It is for this reason that the unconscious has been invented – in order to realize that man's desire is the desire of the Other.

Recognizing the inexorability of this Law, and raising it above the subject, above *cogito*, the Freudian unconscious frees us (and itself) from the metaphysical legacy that still distorts Hegelian philosophy in the humanistic sense.

> Hegel, even though he does not abandon the central function of consciousness... allows us to free ourselves from it.[29]

In this precise point the chiasmus that links the Kojèvian interpretation of Hegel to the Lacanian interpretation of Freud couldn't be more obvious. In Lacan's eyes, Hegel is undoubtedly the thinker of absolute knowledge, he who sees thorough to completion, with the theory of self-conscience, the subjectivistic declension that dominates modern philosophical tradition as a whole. But the hidden premises in his argument, those Kojève claimed to be his contribution to philosophy, don't let themselves be captured by the system. Essentially, proof enough of this for Lacan is the very theory of the end of history, ably staged by Kojève to unmask with lurking irony Hegelian reason, the absurdity of its "astuteness":

> Note the comicality... of this reason, which needs these interminable deceits to lead us to what? To what designates itself, with the end of history, as absolute knowledge. What comes to mind at this point? The mockery made of such a type of knowledge that Queneau's humor managed to forge, because he sat at the same school desks as me for Hegel, in other words the "Sunday of life", or the advent of the idler and the good

---

[29] Ibid, p. 73.

for nothing, who shows with absolute laziness the knowledge capable of satisfying the animal? Or only the wisdom authentified by the sardonic laughter of Kojève, who was a teacher to both? Let us keep to this contrast: the astuteness of reason would ultimately annihilate his game.[30]

Bibliography

Aron, J. P., *Les Modernes*, Paris: Gallimard, 1984

Auffret, D., *Alexandre Kojève*, Paris: Grasset, 1990

Benvenuto, S., *Del soggetto, ovvero il sogno di Lacan*, in AA.VV. *La psicoanalisi, un itinerario di frontiera*, Florence: Vallecchi, 1983

Derrida, J., *Margins of Philosophy*, Brighton: Harvester Press, 1982

Forrester, J., *The seductions of psychoanalysis: Freud, Lacan and Derrida*, Cambridge: Cambridge University Press, 1990

Heidegger, M., *Pathmarks*, Cambridge: Cambridge University Press, 1998

Kojève, A.:
- *Introduction à la lecture d'Hegel*, Paris: Gallimard, 1947; Engl. transl.: *Introduction to the Reading of Hegel*, Ithaca and London: Cornell University Press, 1980
- "Correspondances avec Tran-Duc-Thao", *Genèse*, 2, 1990

Lacan, J.:
- "Les complexes familiaux dans la formation de l'individu", *Encyclopédie Française*, VIII, part II, sect. A, 1938
- *Écrits*, Paris: Seuil, 1966; Engl. Transl.: London: W.W. Norton, 2006
- *Scilicet, I* , Paris: Seuil, 1968
- *Le Séminaire XX: Encore*, Paris: Seuil, 1972-1973
- *Le Séminaire II: Le moi dans la théorie de Freud et dans la technique de la psychanalyse*, Paris: Seuil, 1978b; Engl. Transl.: *The seminar of Jacques Lacan: The Ego in Freud's theory and the technique of psychoanalysis*, London: W.W. Norton, 1991
- *L'Envers de la psychanalyse*, Paris: Seuil, 1982

---

[30] Lacan, 1968, p. 33. My translation.

- *The seminar of Jacques Lacan: Freud's papers on technique 1953-54*, Cambridge: Cambridge University Press, 1988
- *Le Séminaire* VIII: *Le transfert*, Paris: Seuil, 2001

Macherey, P., "Lacan avec Kojève, philosophie et psychanalyse", in *Lacan avec les philosophes*, Paris: Albin Michel, 1991

Mauss, M., *A general theory of magic*, London: Routledge, 2001

Miller, J.-A., "Silet", *La psicoanalisi*, n.20, 1996

Queneau, R., *Journaux*, Paris: Gallimard, 1996

Roudinesco, E.:
- *La bataille des cent ans. Histoire de la psychanalyse en France*, Paris: Seuil, 1986
- "Vibrant hommage de Jacques Lacan à Martin Heidegger", in *Lacan avec les philosophes*, Paris: Albin Michel, 1991
- *Jacques Lacan*, Cambridge: Polity Press, 1997

Vegetti, M., *La fine della storia*, Milan: Jaca Book, 1999

Viderman, S., "Un psychanalyste hégélien", in *Lacan avec les philosophes*, Paris: Albin Michel, 1991

Development of Psychosomatics and the Therapeutic Relationship.
The Impact of the Budapest School of Psychoanalysis

Márta Csabai

Keywords: Psychosomatics – Therapeutic relationship – Budapest school – History of psychoanalysis

Summary: *Among the theorists connected to the Budapest school of psychoanalysis presumably Franz Alexander and Michael Balint received the widest scientific recognition. Nevertheless they enjoyed much success and reputation in medicine, the significance of their psychoanalytic theories has not been acknowledged adequately. On the other hand, in psychoanalytic theorizing, their names are primarily connected to certain concepts, and the more general medical relevance of their work is neglected. Further, the fact that George Engel, the founder of the biopsychosocial model, and Thomas Szasz, pioneer of the antipsychiatry movement, were both students of Alexander is almost unknown, and the significance of their "Budapest" inheritance has neither received enough attention. This paper attempts a common understanding of the fragmented evaluations of these theorists. It argues that not only the roots of Alexander's and Balint's concepts are common – both can be originated from the theories of Ferenczi – but they have other strong intellectual ties, too. They can be characterized equally by the emphasis on the relational/ emotional aspects, and a psychosomatic orientation.*

The Budapest school of psychoanalysis which lived its heydays between the two world wars, gave several outstanding thinkers to the psychoanalytic "world heritage". The most influential figure of the Budapest school was undoubtedly Sándor Ferenczi, whose life-work has received its worthily evaluation only in the last few decades, late after Ferenczi's death. However there were two representatives of the Hungarian school – Franz Alexander and Michael Balint – who gained outstanding international attention and fame during their career. Paradoxically, their reputation, which exceeded even the name of Ferenczi, was the highest *outside* of the psychoanalytic world (which does not mean necessarily that they, especially Balint, were not regarded as outstanding psychoanalysts in most of the psychoanalytic circles). Both of them became well-known mainly in the medical field, Alexander as the founder of the modern psychosomatic approach, Balint as a reformer of doctor-patient relationship. Nonetheless the psychoanalytic background of their work is hardly acknowledged in the medical sciences. This bias is manifested on the other side as well. We can find only sporadic evaluations of Alexander's analytic work in psychoanalytic theorizing. This is mainly the corrective emotional experience which is cited under his name as a psychoanalytic construct. Beside this, Alexander is categorized under the rubrique of psychosomatic medicine. The same can be said about Balint, whose name in psychoanalysis is mostly connected to the concept of therapeutic regression and the "new beginning", but the significance of these phenomena is generally neglected in the medical studies of doctor-patient relationship.

In this paper I would like to make an attempt to resolve the closures resulted from disciplinary boundaries and the differences of professional discourse, through the search of the connections between Balint and Alexander (and followers of the latter, George Engel and Thomas Szasz). Although my intention is to apply the so-called network-principle in contrast to hierarchical genealogy, I hope to be able to prove the common origin of their thoughts in the "Budapest spirit", and particularly in the work of Sándor Ferenczi.

I From Budapest to Chicago

Franz Alexander was born in Budapest in 1891. His father, Bernát Alexander was a famous professor of philosophy, and a Shakespeare scholar. After his studies in Budapest, Gottingen and Cambridge, Franz Alexander graduated as a medical doctor in 1912. Then he started his psychoanalytic training with Hans Sachs. In 1924 he became a lecturer in the Berlin Psychoanalytic Institute, where he gave lectures mostly to medical doctors (French, 1964). Freud invited him to become his assistant, but Alexander decided to move to Chicago where he received a professorship, and later, from 1932 to 1953, was director of the Chicago Psychoanalytic Institute. Nevertheless his relationship with Freud never broke. Alexander visited him every summer, and Freud in turn, requited for his loyalty by calling him as "his best American student" (Migone, 1993). Alexander did much for the American propagation of psychoanalysis. In his institute, whose mission was the training of psychiatrists, and psychoanalytic research, he held courses for social scientists and jurists, too. It was partly related to Alexander's former interest in criminology. His field of interest was exceptionally wide, but his research activity focused mostly on the problems of short analytic therapies and psychosomatics. Mainly his work on the latter field brought him international recognition and fame. He was the director of the Chicago Institute until 1953 when he moved to Los Angeles. It was the consequence of the strengthening of analytic orthodoxy in Chicago and the overshadowing of psycho-analytic psychosomatics by the new trends in medical sciences. Alexander was an upholder of integration and the holistic approaches in psychosomatics, and made efforts to reconcile the Freudian theory with the concepts of the "wild analyst", Georg Groddeck. Alexander was never an active member of the Budapest School, but his entire life-work can be characterized by two significant features of the Hungarian psychoanalytic tradition: a strong accent on therapeutic relationship and an interdisciplinary tendency. This is reflected also in his influential work *Psychoanalytic Therapy: Principles and Application* (Alexander et al, 1946). He wrote this book together with other colleagues, e.g. Theresa Benedek, also a Hungarian-born psychoanalyst. Alexander's chapters discussed the development of psychoanalytic therapy and the phenomenon of corrective emotional experience. Similarly to the other authers of the book, these papers followed the guiding principle of the Chicago school: in psycho-therapy the emphasis should be put on the emotional relationship.[1]

III From transference neurosis to corrective emotional experience

Alexander followed the evolution of the Freudian theory in developing his therapeutic approach. As it is well-known, after the cathartic and free association techniques Freud considered transference reactions (transference neurosis) and the dynamic restructuration of the pathogen past as basis of psychoanalytic therapy (Freud 1905). According to Alexander, psychoanalytic treatment was part of the patient's ego-development, and analytic sessions in turn were catalysts which might enable and speed up the formation of new relationships and experiences. Alexander called attention to the fact that the goal of psychoanalysis had been for a long time the exploration of memories, and this trend received undue attention. He argued that the real goal of therapy was that the patient in the transference situation could cope with the formerly unbearable feelings. At this point Alexander directly joined Ferenczi's approach. Ferenczi and Rank were the first to recognize that the success of psychotherapy did not assume the recollection of all memories (Ferenczi and Rank, 1924). This thought became the basic principle of the Chicago school, too, when they laid down that the recollection of memories and intellectual reconstruction had to give place to emotional experiences.

Alexander carried on these thoughts when pointed out that the patient had to come through an emotional experience which was suitable for the improvement of former traumatic effects. He emphasized that it was of secondary importance that this *corrective emotional experience* appeared in the therapeutic situation or in the everyday life of the patient. Alexander suggested that in the therapeutic process former conflict-solutions should be repeated until the patient would feel safe with the new solution (in order to this the similarity

[1] We can find the of roots Kohutian self-psychology also in this tradition. The mediator between the Chicago school and Kohut was the Hungarian-born John Gedo, who studied psychoanalytic work "beyond interpretation".

of old and new solutions should be emphasized.) He added that the creation of this safety was possible only through the experience of therapeutic relationship. Intellectual insight in itself was not enough, although it had specific significance. The concept of Alexander was significant also because it offered a fundamentally new solution for the elaboration of trauma instead of the Freudian repetition-compulsion theory where Freud suggested that driven by the death-inctinct, subjects often tend to repeat or re-enact their traumatic experiences (Freud [1920], 1961). In this way Alexander could emphasize the more creative forces of the subject. Alexander emphasized that the deeper the therapist understood the development of the conflict and the earliest feelings, the more s/he could help in the formation of new attitudes. He illustrated the dynamics of the process by the example of Victor Hugo's protagonist, Jean Valjean. Like Valjean's behaviour became more brutal after he had experienced goodness from the bishop whom he wanted to rob, the symptom or the neurotic attitude in the same way might become ruder when it is "assaulted" in psychotherapy. Transformation and improvement occurs only after this. Alexander considered this example as model (or probably better to say metaphor) of short-term psychotherapy. He argued that the patient should pass through new emotional experiences in order to get rid of neurotic feelings and behaviour. It was a very important recognition because it made clear that the experience of the former conflict (or the re-enactment as in the Freudian repetition-compulsion theory) was not enough in itself. In other words it suggested that the conflict should be approached in a new perspective. Alexander partly followed the Ferenczian liberal tradition, and partly he might inbuild the effect of the new American humanistic and existentialist therapeutic approaches of the era, when he declared that the technique by which the therapist could trigger the corrective emotional experience, was of secondary importance.[2] He argued that standard psychoanalysis was only one method among many, and moreover he went on saying that each technique which strengthens the integrative capacities of the self,

---

[2] See e.g. the therapeutic models of Carl Rogers, Erich Fromm or Rollo May.

should be called psychoanalysis even if it was only one or two sessions long.

No wonder that this concept which on the one hand wanted to integrate every therapeutic technique in psychoanalysis, and to deconstruct the classical image of psychoanalysis on the other, caused a strong outcry in the traditional analytic circles. The most serious and influential critique arrived from Kurt Eissler,[3] who discussed the "attack to psychoanalysis" from the Chicago society in a more than 50 pages long article (Eissler, 1950). The Alexander-Eissler debate well reflects the confrontations about psychoanalytic technique which started after the 2nd World War in the United States and became the cornerstones of all the similar polemics up to now.

Among others Eissler accused Alexander of inaccuracy in the definition of neurosis and that following the fashions of the era, Alexander declared happiness and success as goals of psychotherapy. According to Eissler he did not pay attention to the deeper structures in the background. Further Eissler called attention to the fact that Alexander's theory of transference and resistance was restricted to the description of the patient's avoidance behavior. Eissler emphasized that Alexander's patients became dependent because he did not apply the standard technique appropriately (that's why he was not able to close therapies in a regular way). He also pointed out that the corrective emotional experience was not a new technique, but the necessary connotation of the therapy of more serious cases (psychotics, addicts, serious neurotics). Eissler argued that the example of Jean Valjean was rather a proof of the drawbacks of corrective emotional experience, illustrating how someone could move from one extreme to the other. He wrote that in this way this concept did not describe the therapeutic process but its magic aspects. With this latter argument Eissler used the

---

[3] Kurt Eissler (1908-1999) was a Viennese psychoanalyst, who moved to Chicago in 1938. Beside his psychoanalytic practice he published 12 books. Eissler was the master of the illustrious-notorious psychoanalytic author, Jeffrey Masson, too. (Aron H. Esman, "Kurt Eissler 1909-1999", *The International Journal of Psychoanalysis*, 81, pp. 361-362, 2000; Janet Malcolm, "The Lives they Lived: Kurt Eissler, b. 1908, Keeper of Freud's Secrets", *The New York Times*, January 2, 2000.)

strongest weapon of the battles about psychotherapeutic techniques. It is well-known that in these debates the arguments that the given technique was "not scientific", or "not verifiable objectively" were real clinkers. The accusation of quackery is a frequently used weapon even now, because it is difficult to ward off, and in the public opinion it is stigmatizing. In this concrete case it may be suspected that Eissler protected rather the psychoanalytic institution than the theory itself. It was supported also by the fact that Alexander's main ambition was to institutionalize the scientifically established psychoanalytic research, which had been proved also by his psychosomatic activity.

ⅢⅢ The great epoch of psychoanalytic psychosomatics

Psychoanalytic research always struggled with its idiographic nature and case-centeredness. It was particularly disturbing after the 1930s when the new taxonomic models and statistically based methods started to appear in psychology (mostly in the United States, following the works of Gordon W. Allport and Raymond Cattell). Alexander's main endeavor was to start such research projects in the Chicago Institute whose basic criterion was the comparison of a great number of cases. A further aim was to provide basic scientific results for the new psychosomatic approach. Together with Flanders Dunbar, Alexander was a founder of this movement. The institutionalization of modern, holistic psychosomatics, which could integrate the psychoanalytic approach, was connected to his name. His etiological theory of psychosomatic diseases was one of the most influential – but without doubt the most popular – 20th century concept for the explanation of functional symptoms. Although he always wanted to pass psychosomatics as a general explanatory principle for medical practice, in his etiological concept he did not follow completely the holistic model of Georg Groddeck. (Groddeck's main argument was that all diseases were psychosomatic by nature. See e.g. Groddeck, 1977). After the Freudian symbolic conversion-concept and the "organ-neurosis" theory, propagated by Georg Groddeck and Felix Deutsch, Alexander chose a third way to integrate and probably to reconcile these models. The secret of his great success could be explained mostly by his endeavor to assimilate psychoanalysis and psychophysiology under the category of "vegetative neurosis". His model assumed a linear correlation between psychological and somatic suffering, and considered both as negative. The "choice" of illness also referred to the functioning of a given organ, which was connected to a specific vegetative pattern. The most well-known component of his theory is that he defined seven diseases as "psychosomatic". These were peptic ulcer, asthma, rheumatoid arthritis, colitis ulcerosa, essential hypertension, neurodermatitis, and thyreotexicosis (Alexander, 1950). The theory became very popular because Alexander explained the development of these illnesses by specific unconscious conflicts. In professional – and also in the lay – representations it often appears even today in such stereotypical explanations as e.g. asthma is caused by the fear of the loss of the mother, the cause of hypertension is repressed aggression, and skin problems in turn are connected to the refusal of physical contact. However Alexander's original concept was much more detailed and underpinned than these dreambook-like explanations in public opinion. His basic starting-point was that there could be found specific emotions in the background of somatic diseases (Alexander, 1934). He connected this to the vector-theory of personality which was actually an extension of the concept of oral, anal, and genital character types. For example he considered oral eroticism as a specific type of a receptive vector, which meant not only the drive of eating, but the desire of love and help, the acquisition of money and gift, moreover the need of appropriation, castration, or theft (Alexander, 1935). The vector was related not only to stomach acid (as it was often supposed in simplistic theories of gastric ulcer), but also to other incorporative functions, like the inhalation phase of respiration, or swallow. After these initial recognitions Alexander and his colleagues studied for more than 15 years the psychophysiological and psychosomatic correlations of a number of diseases. Alexander's exceptionally influential masterwork, *Psychosomatic Medicine* (1950) was a summary of these studies. This volume also contributed to the huge popularity of psychosomatics in the United States in the 1950s. Popular magazines, like *Reader's Digest*, or *Ladies' Home Journal* published psychosomatic articles, and psychosomatics appeared even as the theme of Broadway plays. However precise identity definition was always missing, and debates about the real content of psychosomatic therapy came to stay. This led to recurrent identity crises, and due also to other factors, psychoanalytic psychosomatics in a few years had become over-shadowed by other trends.

In 1962, two years before his death, Alexander summarized the development of psychosomatic medicine, and called attention to the problem that the well-known terminology for the description of the seven "psychosomatic" illnesses, "specificity hypothesis" had a misleading interpretation in public opinion (Alexander, 1962). He made it clear that these psychodynamic patterns could be found in other cases, too. He emphasized multicausality, saying that beside the emotional sensitivity, organic vulnerability and genetic causes should also be taken in consideration. With the connection of psychodynamics and psychophysiology Alexander seemingly opened the way between psychoanalysis and medicine, but at the same time closed it because he marked out, even if not intentionally, a very narrow path when he laid down his basic concept of the seven psycho-somatic illnesses, which gave place to several misunderstandings.

IV Disciples and new paradigms: the work of George Engel and Thomas Szasz

Although the heydays of psychoanalytic psychosomatics ceased after the death of Alexander, the emphasis on unconscious factors and emotional contact carried on and integrated in the paradigmatic biopsychosocial model of George Engel, outstanding member of the Chicago Institute of Psychoanalysis. Like certain hereditary factors are manifested more expressly in the grandchildren than in children, Engel's work reflects even more clearly the influence of the Budapest school, although he might have less direct connection with Ferenczi and his followers than Alexander. Engel has very high reputation in medicine due to his famous biopsychosocial concept, but the psychoanalytic roots of this theory are practically unknown. In psychoanalytic scholarship in turn, the evaluation of his life-work is almost missing.

George Engel (1913-1999), after his graduation in medicine got in very intensive relationship with psychoanalytic psychosomatics in 1940, right after the foundation of the approach. The most influential period for him was between 1950 and 1955, when he took part in training analysis with the Hungarian-born Sandor Feldman, and had strong working relationship with Theresa Benedek, also a Hungarian dissident. The most important increment of these connections was that in all of his further works Engel handled as basic principle the Ferenczian thought that doctor-patient relationship always had an impact on the development of symptoms and the progression of disease.

One of the most widespread commonplaces about medicine is that the treatment of diseases is the question of science, and the care of patients is an art. Engel declared that the latter field needs more scientific knowledge, and otherwise both activities can be considered as art (Engel, 1977a). He added that doctors should examine not only the patient but their own behaviour, and its influence on the patient. In these thoughts we may easily discover the impact of psychoanalytic theorizing about transference and counter-transference. These concepts were originally connected to the problems of doctor-patient relationship in the Budapest school of psychoanalysis. Engel's further significant psychoanalytic contribution to psychosomatics was the recognition of the importance of mother-child relationship in the etiology and progress of diseases (Engel, 1954). He extended the correlations between object loss and cardiovascular death even to the analysis of his own reactions. He developed a specific "anniversary-pathology" which suggested that people would react with health-problems on the anniversary of the death of a beloved person (Engel, 1975). It should be mentioned that Ferenczi also dealt with "anniversary neurosis" and its specific forms of "Sunday" and "vacation" neuroses (Ferenczi, 1960). This psychoanalytic antecedent of Engel's work is completely unknown in the medical literature, nevertheless physicians regularly have to struggle with the proliferation of patients after a weekend or holiday.

Although he brought a radically new approach, Engel did not contradict completely Franz Alexander, because he also considered intrapsychic conflicts as part of the multiple causes of diseases. However instead of the search of specific unconscious conflicts, Engel examined the interpersonal relationships of patients. His goal was not the exploration of causes by any means, but the formation of a rewarding dependency relationship in therapy, where the therapist replaced the lost – or never-found – object.

We can see how the "Budapest" problematic of attachment, dependency and relationship appeared in the different phases of Engel's life-work. However we cannot identify his approach only as the foundation of an interpersonal psychosomatics. It is much more the reflection of an epoch-making, new paradigm, where the basic principle was the relationship – or correlation – of phenomena. This principle led him to the foundation of the biopsychosocial approach, which emphasized – instead of linear causation, typical of classical psychoanalytic and medical thinking – he multiple factors contributing to the development of diseases (Engel, 1977b).

Among the students of Franz Alexander we should remember another paradigmatic thinker, Thomas Szasz, who played an outstanding role in the foundation of the antipsychiatric movement. His connections to the Budapest school cannot be described only by the mediating role of Alexander and the Chicago Institute, because Szasz was born in Budapest in 1920 and moved to the US in 1938. He worked in the Chicago Institute between 1947 and 1956 as the favorite student of Alexander (Pols, 2005). In this period he published several psychosomatic articles with the ambition to find psychoanalytic explanations for the new theories of Alexander. He summarized the conclusions of his psychophysiological-psychoanalytic studies in a common paper with Alexander (Szasz and Alexander, 1952). Here, like in the other works of the Chicago school, the emphasis was on the correlations of the functioning of the autonomous nervous system and psychodynamic processes. Szasz' attention in the mid 1950s turned to the psychological mechanisms of pain, and he published his first book about this subject (Szasz, 1957). This volume can be regarded as a psychoanalytic study of somatic feelings. Szasz considered pain as the most important feeling, and handled it as a psychological phenomenon. He rejected the organic/psychological distinction and declared that in the patient's illness experience it did not matter whether the disease was "somatic" or "mental". He added that this distinction was only important for the professionals, i.e. the different classifications served only their purposes. He summarized these thoughts later in his influential book, *The Myth of Mental Illness* (Szasz, 1974). The exploration of the potential correlations with the Ferenczian tradition and the antipsychiatric movement would extend the boundaries of this article. What can be said for sure however is that the psychoanalytic psychosomatics founded by Alexander reflects vigorously the relational-emotional traditions of the Budapest school, and this allowed to paradigmatic insights the two most prominent students of the Chicago Institute, George Engel and Thomas Szasz.

V From neutral observer to active participant. The role of Michael Balint in the transmission of the "relational approach"

The most important contribution of the Budapest school to the development of psychoanalytic theory and technique was the new understanding of transference phenomena. Mostly in his later works, but also in their common paper with Rank, Ferenczi suggested that the goal of psychoanalysis was the reproduction of the original – primarily Oedipal – scene, where the therapist should replace the parent (Ferenczi and Rank, 1924). This proposition generated a very deep and long debate in the history of the psychoanalytic movement (Haynal, 1988). Today many therpists regard the quality of relationship (transference and countertransference) as a natural factor, but the accent on "loving relationship" still remains ambiguous, even amongst the followers of Ferenczi. Although the Chicago school also focused on the questions of relationship, and in many respects drew on the Ferenczian heritage, it was Michael Balint, who faithfully and consequently carried on this line, and made doctor-patient relationship an acknowledged theme of research.[4]

As a student of Ferenczi, Balint met the simple principle which was described by Erich Fromm as the change of the position of a neutral observer to an active participant of the relationship, a "loving human being" (Fromm, 1958). Balint published his first paper about the therapeutic effect of transference at the Wiesbaden Psychoanalytic Congress, and delineated his thoughts in more details in a common article with his first wife, Alice Balint (Balint, 1933; Balint and Balint, 1939). In the latter paper they called attention to the fact that the therapist had to work in an emotional style the most suitable for herself. This thought was further developed in the concept, where Balint argued that psychoanalysis could not be regarded as a pure technique but the relationship of two persons (it might seem a new recognition at the time, although the same conclusion could be made even reading the first clinical cases of Freud). Probably the most felicitous description of this was when he called psychoanalysis a "two-body psychology" (Balint, 1965). Here he refers to the proposition of Ferenczi that transference in the analytic situation could be originated from the early relationship with the parents, even from the earliest dual union. Balint's work might have an important role in that contemporary intersubjectivity and bodily transference research "found its way back" to the Ferenczian roots (see e.g. Klugman, 2001).

Ferenczi put forward in several works that medical doctors should take part in psychoanalytic training in order to acquire the flexible, open way of thinking, necessary for medical practice (see e.g. Ferenczi, 1919). This thought became fully elaborated in Balint's work, but it is important to note that similarly to Balint, Franz Alexander started his Chicago career by giving psychoanalytic lectures to practicing medical doctors, and he defined psychoanalytic psychosomatics as the basic principle of healing. For Balint the most important starting point was the Ferenczian proposition that the doctor's personality might

---

[4] About the life and work of Michael Balint see the summary of Haynal (1988). Here I deal only with those elements of Balint's life-work which are related to the psychoanalytic background of his work in doctor-patient relationship, and psychosomatics.

have greater influence on the patient's state than the medicine he prescribed (Ferenczi, 1936). Evidently Balint used this as a starting point when he introduced the concept "the doctor is the drug" (Balint, 1956). According to this metaphor the personality and the behavior of the doctor have the same therapeutic effect as chemical drugs, but proper "dosage" should be ensured in the relationship by considering the "risks" and "side-effects" of the "drug". Balint recognized the advantages of the parallel application of medical treatment and psychotherapy even a few years after he completed his psychoanalytic training, when he started his first seminars for physicians in Budapest in 1926. Although it was not called like that, it was a real psychosomatic activity. The correlations between the relational and psychosomatic approaches become more clear if we take in consideration that later Balint defined the goal of his seminars which he organized in London – the famous Balint-groups, which made him world-famous after the 1950s –, the making of a specific "relational diagnosis" (Balint, 1956). His outstanding book, where he summarized the experiences of these seminars, *The Doctor, His Patient and the Illness,* has kept its extraordinary popularity in medicine since 1956. However its psychoanalytic background is hardly known. The reason is not only the disciplinary discrepancy but also that the psychoanalytic relevance of this book cannot be understood without Balint's whole psychoanalytic life-work. Although seemingly deal with a different theme, particularly his books about regression help to understand the outstanding importance of Balint's recognition that the doctor's feelings and emotions could be "symptoms" of the patient (Balint, 1959, 1968). In his book, *The Basic Fault* he declared that Ferenczi's experiment to follow his patients into regression was a mistaken endeavor. According to Balint, for the acceptance of regression the analyst needs to have a critical attitude but also s/he has to create an appropriate, empathetic therapeutic atmosphere. In the other book, *Thrills and Regressions* he delineated that the desire of clinging on the therapist was not the manifestation of primary love, as it had been proposed by Ferenczi, but a response to a trauma, and also the expression of the defense against neglect and loneliness.

Consequently he regarded this desire as a secondary phenomenon which had the goal to restore the original identity of subject and object (Balint, 1959). The theory goes back to the early approach of the Budapest School in the 1920s which did not accept the stage of "objectless narcissism". Instead, Hungarian psychoanalysts held that life begins with the *relationship* between the baby and the mother. In other words, the infant's primary instinctive needs were considered to be aiming at a contact with the mother. These thoughts may make clear also for the practicing physician that this is the anxiety and regression induced by the disease which lies behind the emotional and behavioral reactions of "difficult" patients. This anxiety and regression evokes the transference reactions which in many cases may seem strange and difficult to understand for a medical doctor. Balint also made it clear that this was the reason why the solution was not to assign the patient for psychotherapy (which would be a counter-transference reaction from the physician), but to choose the more effective solution of creating a safe relationship.

In a few years ago the prestigious *British Journal of General Practitioners* celebrated Balint as one of the most outstanding doctors of the 20th century, mentioning that he was also an excellent psychotherapist, teacher, and writer (Lakasing, 2005). As we could see above, Franz Alexander also received the highest appreciation in medicine. However it does not mean that their theories would have become general principles in everyday therapeutic practice. On the other hand, there is no doubt that the following thought of Ferenczi is accepted by most healing professionals:

> This is the primary practical interest of mankind that physicians should possess also those methods by which they can help not only somatic, but also mentally ill patients, but as a matter of fact somatic patients, too, because there is no such illness where the consideration of the mental status would not be of primary importance. (Ferenczi 1919, 120-121).

Nevertheless this is accepted as a general principle, in its realization there are serious deficiencies even today. The re-reading of Alexander's and Balint's psychoanalytic work and the recognition of their "kinship" may help also in the solution of these problems.

Bibliography

Alexander, F.:
- "The Influence of Psychologic Factors Upon Gastrointestinal Disturbances: A Symposium", *Psychoanalytic Quarterly*, pp. 181-207, 1934
- "The Logic of Emotions and Its Dynamic Background", *International Journal of Psycho-Analysis* 16, pp. 399-413, 1935
- *Psychosomatic Medicine: Its Principles and Applications*, New York: W.W. Norton & Co., 1950
- "The development of psychosomatic medicine", *Psychosomatic Medicine*, XXIV, No. 1, pp. 11-23, 1962
Alexander, F., French, T. M., et al., *Psychoanalytic Therapy: Principles and Application*, New York: Ronald Press, 1946
Balint A., Balint M., "On Transference and Counter Transference", *International Journal of Psychoanalysis*, XX, pp. 223-230, 1939
Balint, M.:
- *Primary Love and Psychoanalytic Technique*, London: Tavistock Publications, pp. 165-177, 1933-1965
- *Thrills and regressions*, London: The Hogarth Press and The Institute of Psycho-Analysis, 1959
- *The Basic Fault. Therapeutic Aspects of Regression*, London: Tavistock Publications, 1968
Eissler, K., "The Chicago Institute of Psychoanalysis and the sixth period of development of psychoanalytic technique", *Journal of General Psychology*, 42, pp. 103-157, 1950

Engel, G. L.:
- "Selection of clinical material in psychosomatic medicine. The need for a new physiology", *Psychosomatic Medicine*, 16, pp. 368-373, 1954
- "The death of a twin: mourning and anniversary reactions. Fragments of 10 years of self-analysis", *International Journal of Psychoanalysis*, 56, pp. 23-40, 1975
- "The care of the patient: art or science?", *Johns Hopkins Medical Journal*, 140, pp. 222-232, 1977a
- "The need of a new medical model: A challenge for biomedicine", *Science*, 196, pp. 129-136, 1977b

Ferenczi, S., "Az orvosképzés reformja" [The Reform of Medical Education, in Hungarian], *Gyógyászat*, 59, 8, pp. 120-121, 1919

Ferenczi, S., Rank, O., *Entvicklungsziele der Psychoanalyse*, Wien: Internationaler Psychoanalytischer Verlag, 1924

French, T. M., "In Memoriam Franz Alexander", *Psychosomatic Medicine*, Vol. XXVI, No. 3, pp. 203-206, 1964

Freud, S.:
- *Fragment of an analysis of a case of hysteria* (Dora) [1905], *GW*, 5; *SE*, 7, pp. 7-78
- *Beyond the Pleasure Principle* [1920], *GW* 13; *SE* 18, pp. 7-60

Fromm, E., "Psychoanalysis-Science or Party Line?", *The Saturday Review*, June 14, 1958

Groddeck, G., *The Meaning of Illness. Selected Psychoanalytic Writings*, Madison, CT: International Universities Press, 1977

Haynal, A., *The Technique at Issue. Controversies in Psychoanalysis from Freud and Ferenczi to Michael Balint*, London: Karnac Books, 1988

Klugman, D., "Empathy's Romantic Dialectic: Self Psychology, Intersubjectivity, and Imagination", *Psychoanalytic Psychology*, Vol. 18 (4), pp. 684-704, 2001

Lakasing, E., "Michael Balint: an outstanding medical life", *British Journal of General Practitioners*, 55 (518), pp. 724-725, 2005

Migone, P., "L'esperienza emozionale correttiva", *Psicoterapia e Scienze Umane*, XXVII, 2. pp. 85-101, 1993

Pols, J., *The Politics of Mental Illness: Myth and Power in the Work of Thomas S. Szasz*. e-book www.janpols.net, 2005 (accessed 15 May 2005)

Szasz, T.:
- *Pain and Pleasure. A Study of Bodily Feelings*, London: Basic Books, 1957
- *The Myth of Mental Illness. Foundations of a Theory of Personal Conduct*, New York: Harper and Row, 1974

Szasz, T., Alexander, F., "The Psychosomatic Approach in Medicine", in Alexander, F. and Ross, H. (eds), *Dynamic Psychiatry*, Chicago: University of Chicago Press, pp. 369-400, 1952

REVIEWS

Antonello Sciacchitano, *Wissenschaft als Hysterie*,
by **Luigi Gaffuri**

In Freud's Tracks

CONVERSATIONS FROM THE
JOURNAL OF EUROPEAN PSYCHOANALYSIS

edited by

Sergio Benvenuto
and Anthony Molino

Antonello Sciacchitano, *Wissenschaft als Hysterie*, Wien: Turia + Kant, 2002; Italian transl.: *Scienza come isteria*. *Il soggetto della scienza da Cartesio a Freud e la questione dell'infinito*, Pasian di Prato, UD: Campanotto Editore, 2005

Antonello Sciacchitano is a Milan-based psychiatrist and practicing psychoanalyst. Of Lacanian training, he has co-edited the psychoanalysis journal «Scibbolet», for a critical return to Freud. He has been a member of several psychoanalytic associations and, after founding some of his own, came to the hard decision of going ahead as a *free raider*, perceiving the idea of belonging to a "school" as a tight uniform no longer worth wearing, not even by stretching the buttons. He has translated into Italian various important volumes, including *Le Seminaire - Livre 1, Les écrits techniques de Freud* by Jacques Lacan, *Dementia Praecox;* or the *Group of Schizophrenias* by E. Bleuler and, more recently *Le plus sublime des hystériques - Hegel passe* by S. Žižek. He also writes on French, German, Spanish and Portuguese journals. Author of *Anoressia, sintomo e angoscia* (Milan: Guerini, 1994) and *Il terzo incluso. Saggio di logica epistemica* (Florence: Shakespeare and Company, 1995), he has also published in German the volume *Das Unendliche und das Subjekt. Zürcher Gespräche* (Zürich: Riss Verlag, 2004) and edited the proceedings of the conference on "the social bond of psychoanalysts", *Il legame sociale degli psicanalisti* (Pisa: ETS, 2003) together with Maria Vittoria Lodovichi. He currently publishes essays, articles and translations on *aut aut*, one of the most long-lived and authoritative Italian philosophical journals, founded by Enzo Paci and currently edited by Pier Aldo Rovatti.

It is well worth lingering over his *Wissenschaft als Hysterie* ("Science as Hysteria") to do justice to an intellectual enterprise consisting of a lifetime devotion to analytical research and "analytical practice" – despite the Italian public's lukewarm reception so far, which is contrasted, however, by the interest it has stirred in the English and German speaking scientific world. But to begin, let's stress something that should be obvious: this is an important book for the questions it asks rather than for the answers it supplies; in other words, its significance lies in the problems it raises, rather than the ways it tries to solve them. "How" some problems are dealt with is a question that concerns the author, while readers will reap greater rewards with a curiosity for the paths the author's reflection opens up and the questions it raises.

We should, in other words, finally persuade ourselves that no empirical or symbolical observation can be carried out problem free and that the types of answers supplied depend on the questions that are put and on their formulation. This is the concept that René Scheu's *Introduction* to the volume develops. This introduction does not give exegetical, supplemental or alternative rough outlines contrasting Sciacchitano's, but instead contributes to polishing the spirit or cultural meaning of this anomalous, unique work in the current publishing outlook. Its aim can basically be summed up with an expression reminiscent of the slogan from an old Italian TV ad: "get rid of the sediment with care", because it has only been removed clumsily and temporarily.

To avoid misunderstandings and get his point across more effectively, Antonello Sciacchitano brings to the forestage the binarity of classical logic, only to lash out against it if it presents itself too rigidly. He therefore lines up a range of opposing dyads, and the book is full of them, that not only incarnate the *tertium non datur*, but also generate a spectrum of terms and concepts that summarize the history of scientific and philosophical thinking. To the author these are not pure binary oppositions, albeit they are often perceived as such, but are rather the result of the dualistic approach he takes in facing dichotomies of this kind. Not to make this potentially endless list too long, we will present here a version which is partial and unorganized but that does, however, allow a certain supposed order transpire, and precisely a dualistic one: subject-object, science-knowledge, res cogitans-res extensa, unconscious-conscious, assertion-denial, infinite-finite, knowing-being, other-I, incompleteness-completeness, uncertainty-certainty, weak thought-strong thought, hysteria-obsession, epistemology-ontology, freedom-responsibility, real-reality, invention-discovery, impossible-possible, in-out, unknown-known, psychoanalysis-psychotherapy, new-old, creativity-adapting, doubt-dogma, knowing how to deal with the infinite-madness, active-passive, probability-necessity, truth-falsehood, fertility-sterility, becoming-being, will-intellect, constructivism-realism, a posteriori-a priori, archive-encyclopedia, truth-knowing, relative-absolute, proper classes-sets...

Now, these opposing dyads make up the first elements of a geography without boundaries that opens and accompanies the scientific adventure as a *tableau of dualisms*. The most precious results of this long process give rise to the sciences, which one always considers revocable and approximate (but which actually harbor different assumptions), to be made available by human beings to themselves and to the various communities through a codified transmission. Such a list could therefore be a synoptic table or chartography of the colors and expressions used in scientific research, the diverse senses of which one can master through the constant training scientific praxis demands. Concepts of this kind, presented dualistically, are the backdrop that makes the act that "explains" the meaning of the word science entirely non-ambiguous, leaving room for the indefiniteness typical of the contact between language and reality.

The book's theoretical and practical core is the result of several scientific-disciplinary crossings as the distillate of one or two weak beliefs, developed in the years, on which Sciacchitano makes the whole intellectual enterprise of this book stand. The first belief is that "psychoanalysis is a practical philosophy". It is the ethics for the subject of modernity, i.e. for the subject of science" (p. 104). The author thus reminds the reader of the centre of the book, even though it is a work without a center, or rather with several centers, in the same way as the infinites that could make up the authentic object of the volume are numerous and plural. But, for the sake of coherence, this authentic object should be one that is not there, or that does not exist too much. And in fact it seems ascribable to "the identity of the subject of science and of the unconscious" (p. 168), which, by innervating the second belief, is the book's main thesis, a basic principle, the heart of a position reached with weakening after weakening – basically the book's core, its *Hauptsatz*. The author believes that "the subject of science is the same that functions in the Freudian unconscious" (p. 157). Everything is then based on three pillars: *subject, unconscious, ethics,* supporting a pile-dwelling built by sticking the piles themselves in the marshes of contemporary psychoanalysis. The first pillar is not just any subject, but specifically the subject of science, which after long interrogations imprisons knowledge not so much for the crimes it has committed (as errors can be recognized and re-elaborated), but rather to avoid crimes yet to be committed. The second pillar, the unconscious, has to do with the infinite and its representation, while ethics has to do with uncertainty and action. Let's try and look at these epistemic nuclei one by one.

To avoid ambiguity, the author begins by listing what is not the focal subject of the book with three negations to circumscribe the field: it is not substance meant in the Aristotelian sense (the substratum), it is not the subject of logical analysis and it is not even the subject of the unconscious. Next, the target is better identified as "auto-reference of the enunciation", counterpointed by "etero-reference of the sentence". It is on this relational system that the discourse of and upon "the subject of science", synonym of "subject of modernity", moves. But how can you conjugate in psychoanalysis the declared need to rediscover the subject with today's technological drift of scientific thinking, which tends not to recognize its role and privileges the intersubjective dimension? According to the author it can be conjugated by playing with one's own subjective uncertainty, and that of others, about knowledge referred to oneself, within the scope of a psychoanalysis meant as theory and practice of the "subject of science".

This might seem an evasive answer, but it is not. First of all, if on the one hand uncertainty has become one of the distinctive traits of our era, on the other auto-referred uncertainty is also the driving force behind analytical practice. Secondly, overlooking the more general saying "without doubts there can be no science", consider how the pivot of scientific thinking has always been a subject that has gone ahead hesitantly, by trial and error (it's true that it is only during the twentieth century that this became a temporarily stable acquisition of contemporary epistemology, the important results of which, in every branch of knowledge, are before the eyes even of those who do their best to keep them shut). And the subject of science, in psychoanalytical practice, temporarily suspends its certainties, it travels between its prejudices and its fears and navigates in its nightmares, uttering only its many uncertainties on its being – ultimately, a subjective uncertainty over its ontological status, which can find encouragement only after re-elaborating the "ever new" that emerges in analysis as the result of an auto-referred knowledge continuously subject to review. Here, in this confrontation repeated countless times, is where the elusiveness of an object of desire, that is by definition and actually *not-bypassable*, lies.

In this passage from subject to object the infinite enters the stage, an entrance in turn connected to a finite unconscious. In fact, as well as a declared sympathy for Descartes, Sciacchitano has a "strong weakness" for the infinite. After warning the reader that dealing with the infinite is a risky praxis, the author explains that the infinite he refers to is not the oceanic feeling, with its religious connotations, nor the eternal repetition of the identical, of Freudian and Nietzschean memory; it is not something ineffable, however difficult it may be to define. More technically, the infinite is never defined *a priori* nor once and for all, because it is an *in fieri* notion, it is dynamic, based on a soft logic of intuitionistic derivation – an *a posteriori* logic of subjectivity *vs* an *a priori* logic of objectivity. Within this framework, according to the author, two infinites are the most adequate for psychoanalytical theory and practice: the defined infinite and the undefined infinite.

The former applies to the partial and temporary models of the object of desire, exemplified by the gaze, the breast, the voice, nothingness, feces, the analyst. Within this horizon "the object causing desire is an infinite that exists 'lightly', little more than the unconscious that hosts it" (p. 84). The latter concerns the symbolic world of the subject moving between truth, the law and knowledge: examples of undefined infinite are the unconscious, language, otherness, narcissistic similarity, the paternal, the feminine, play. Despite this definition the undefined infinite is in turn a notion that can be captured only partially and incompletely: its identification is arduous because as soon as it is detected by some quality or property, it falls into contradiction. In more mathematical terms, we could say that the undefined infinite is closely related to Von Neumann's "proper classes", i.e. classes that, not being elements of other classes, are not subjects of predicates. In more psychoanalytical terms, we can say instead that, though they preserve their drive properties, these type of infinites are the reflex and the instrument of a sublimation destined to "remain a creation from nothing of the subject of science" (p. 98).

The author, after admitting his weak spot for the infinite, goes on, however, to weaken Descartes' epistemological position, following a long laborious path between invoked clarity and badly concealed distinction. If psychoanalysis is ultimately a philosophy of the infinite, then the model of psychoanalysis put forward in the book is in some ways Cartesian, because it hinges on epistemology more than on ontology; in other words "it seeks the lever of being in knowledge. But it is also not Cartesian, because instead of aiming at the lowest irrefutable certainty – found in the *Cogito* – it aims at the highest analyzable uncertainty and calls it the unconscious" (p. 140). One anchor remains: the same structure of the "subject of science", which finds its paradigm in Descartes, presents itself, according to Sciacchitano with a different model, an isomorphous one, in psychoanalysis. Indeed, while Descartes' philosophizing ego achieves the certainty of its subjective existence *via* a suspension of the knowledge of the object, the subject in analysis achieves a lesser auto-referred uncertainty *via* a suspension of one's own known knowledge, which tends to conceal or disguise a primal object of desire, postponing its recognition indefinitely.

But why is the unconscious object of desire ultimately infinite? First of all, because the modes and word combinations to speak of it are potentially infinite – and this refers us back to the plasticity of language as well as to the "cadences of deceit" perpetrated by language and to the tricks it tries to play on our minds. Secondly, because to be equal to desire, in concrete everyday life, is a task that proves impossible in the long run, analogous to wanting to make the infinite fit into the finite. The reiterated attempts roughed out by the subject to impress it die down when faced with an elusive object that presents itself each time in different guises. The infinite thing is then the authentic "reason for that particular inadequacy of the subject, which we call desire" (p. 139) – an inadequacy that shows its most devastating effects when it comes to making operative decisions before existence, before the Other's saying and acting, which together implicate moral discourse. Indeed, often such steps are taken at the expense of pure reason, precisely because they are facts of practical reason.

When ethics enters the field, the shift is from uncertainty about the self-representation of the subject to self-referred uncertainty with respect to action. It is not a case of the latter substituting the former, nor is it an additive operation summing up two types of uncertainty; it is, rather, a matter of multiplication. This expands uncertainty in a geometrical progression observed, however, on the horizon of doing, on the ridge of an acting already blocked by the ontological uncertainty regarding one's being. Under these conditions the subject's operational scope becomes the infinite open sea of will: when the passage from the uncertain to the less uncertain does not take place, finite subjectivity breaks down, unable to draw an aprioristic moral conclusion on its concrete acting. For this reason practical will risks turning into an unlimited freedom to err, precisely because it concerns a finite subject that only has finite alternatives available. According to the author it is therefore necessary, when faced with a decision, to accept being able to say only *a posteriori*, i.e. once the choice has been made, "whether the action performed in that analysis, mine or others', is or is not analytic. Before the action I can say nothing, under penalty of reducing the analytical act to the appliance of a behavior code or deontology" (pp. 43-44). By tolerating the temporariness of moral choices, which always risk turning out to be wrong, on will be able to then correct them.

So, we are talking about a consequentialist ethics that tries in analysis to re-construct the object of desire as infinite, gradually substituting the reiterated fixation for the equal with an ever new attention for the different, for the unpredictable. In this way the subject is offered some interpretative chances, no matter how true they may be, with a practice that opens up the possibility of creating buried stories and places where a subjectivity has lost its way or hasn't been found again: spinning together real and imaginary, this is where the passage, always temporary and revocable, from absolute uncertainty to a less shaky uncertainty situates itself. Summing up extremely, we are faced with a *morale par provision* that generates an *analyse par révision*. The epistemic root of morals thus finds a slot to wedge itself into, precisely between *re-présentation* and action, dilating in a potentially infinite way this small space with the variable of time. What is being dealt with, however, is a time that one would like to consider epistemic, because the subject of science mainly dwells in the territory of duration. In this groove, what appears as old, in the sense of seeming to belong to the past, does not necessarily have a negative connotation: it is simply what the subject believes is well-known, the subject's public version. In the same way the new does not necessarily have a positive connotation: it is simply what one s trying to understand so as to be able to do. The same considerations go for the book being reviewed. As the author says himself, *Wissenschaft als Hysterie* is a book based on the old, in the sense of the Freudian and Lacanian psychoanalytical tradition meant as what has been so far published; but it also implies the new, i.e. what is being written now in an extensively conjectural way and that, for this reason, may also prove to be untrue. Only time will be able to say something less uncertain on the subject.

After recalling this list of points, is it possible to move on from a stratification of meanings to a syntax of sense? Hard to believe. In the mean time, as Sciacchitano has structured his book around the delicate passage from saying to doing, the author, though gratified, probably wouldn't be content with someone reading it and understanding it, but it is easy to predict that he wouldn't be disappointed if someone made good use of it – and we'll return to this point in a minute. If one wants to carry on trying to find a "sense" in the book, however, then this can perhaps be found in its ethics, however weak and *par provision* or *a posteriori*. An ethics that takes on subjective responsibility as the ability to correct an acting: an action the effectiveness which cannot, however, be predetermined in advance and that cannot be directed by "right" or widely accepted moral principles. Yet the true heart of the book doesn't lie, as the author suggests, in its *Hauptsatz*, but in something that is again hard to define, but that we can at least try and describe. We know that when a book is put into print, the ink battle is already over for its author, in other words the responsibility is transferred to the reader. After then, books are made mainly of silent reading, as well as of course any public presentations, intellectual debates, reviews and, in a more closed circle, friendly discussions or personal attacks. It is on this ridge between publication and reading that I think the heart of this book lies. The author privileges the clear and the distinct and is not too fond of ambiguity, though he includes it amongst the productive factors of effective communication based on word play, quips, puns, the serious irony the broken stories lying on the couch make room for. With these and other instruments *Wissenschaft als Hysterie* helps us know something we didn't know we knew. Indeed, if every research is a cure, then there can be no research without cure and vice versa. As we do not have a complete and categorical knowledge, because the subject who distills it is not complete and defined once and for all, we can only take ethical decisions. In this way morals, if we want them to be scientific, are always temporary, like any other scientific result. If knowledge is unconscious, all the more morals will be temporary, i.e. ratable only *a posteriori*, i.e. *par provision*. It is therefore necessary to always update one's judgments, to revise continuously, when we are up against subjective affairs, in the same way as one does with scientific theories. Morals are to be taken, therefore, as a scarcely deontological responsibility and one without too many virtues, i.e. as an ability to answer particular questions. In this sense the English language comes to our aid: it is a question of *respons-hability*. But responsibility for who and over what?

In fact, when psychoanalysis reaches its goals it does not cure the Other too much, because it actually cures itself, but it does try to make life bearable to various degrees: one can say that it somehow aims at an "impossible peacefulness" and never at happiness. That psychoanalysis does not pursue happiness, by definition momentary or temporary, is an open secret. Nonetheless its target is longer lasting because it uses time to acquire a sort of "know-how" with what is largely unknown to us but indelibly marks our existence. In other words, psychoanalysis is content with letting the subject reach a turbulent peace. It is not simple, but possible, not a state to reach in the long term, in the continuum of everyday life, but rather a primal state, one we are born into. A state the origin of which we cannot postulate, however, and the job of psychoanalysis is to remind the subject that it existed and, though its mechanism got jammed somewhere, with some hard work it can be partially repaired. It is not a stoical version of peacefulness as an exercise and a craving for desiring no longer, as the practice of a life void of passions or based on the control of passions that are impossible to organize. In the case critically examined here, centered on the book and its author, the case is vice versa of a passion for passions, of a desire to desire, of making it possible to desire again or to recognize our desires with ourselves and others.

Luigi Gaffuri

Contibutors

Fabiano Bassi, M.D., psychiatrist and psychotherapist, from 1991 to 2004 was Head of the Editorial Board of the Italian psychoanalytic journal *Psicoterapia e Scienze Umane*. He is analytic supervisor at the School of Psychiatry, University of Bologna. He teaches Psychopathology at the School of Ruolo Terapeutico in Genoa [fabianobassi@hotmail.com].

Sergio Benvenuto is a Researcher in psychology and philosophy at the National Research Council (CNR) in Rome, Italy. He is a psychoanalyst president of ISAP (Institute for Advanced Studies in Psychoanalysis). He is a contributor to cultural journals such as *Telos, Lettre Internationale*, (French, Spanish, Hungarian, Rumanian and Italian editions), *Texte* (Wien), *RISS* (Basel), *Journal for Lacanian Studies, L'évolution psychiatrique*. He translated into Italian Jacques Lacan's *Séminaire XX: Encore*. His books include *La strategia freudiana* (Naples: Liguori, 1984); *Dicerie e pettegolezzi* (Bologna: Il Mulino, 1999); *Un cannibale alla nostra mensa* (Bari: Dedalo, 2000); *Perversioni. Sessualità, etica, psicoanalisi* (Turin: Bollati Boringhieri, 2005); German ed. *Perversionen. Sexualität, Ethik und Psychoanalyse* (Wien: Turia + Kant, 2009); *Mechta Lacana*, in Russian (Sankt Peterburg: Aleteija, 2006); *Accidia. La passione dell'indifferenza* (Bologna: Il Mulino, 2008); with A. Molino, *On Freud's Tracks* (New York: Aronson, 2008) [benvenuto.jep@mclink.it].

Cristiana Cimino, M.D., psychiatrist, lives in Rome where she is a practising psychoanalyst. She is a member of the Italian Psychoanalytical Society (IPA) and of ISAP (Institute for Advanced Studies in Psychoanalysis). For several years she dealt with transcultural psychiatric studies, focusing particularly on traditional African cultures. She has taken part, as external consultant, in ethnopsychiatric and neurophysiological research projects funded by the Italian National Research Council (CNR), and for many years practised as a psychiatrist in a psychiatric institution dealing mainly with psychotic patients. Her published works include: "I fenomeni proiettivi nella psicopatologia delle culture africane", *Psichiatria e Psicoterapia*

Analitica, 12, 1988; "Melancholia: a defence Mechanism-Test Study", *Perceptual and Motor Skills,* 79, 1994, pp 487-498; "La psicosi e il continuo", *Rivista Italiana di Psicoanalisi,* 1, 2003; "Il vuoto necessario", *Rivista Italiana di Psicoanalisi,* 1, 2005; "Projective Identification and Consciousness Alteration: a bridge between psychoanalysis and neuroscience?", *International Journal of Psychoanalysis,* 89, 2005 [cristianacimino.jep@gmail.com].

Márta Csabai, psychologist, is associate professor at the Karoli Gaspar University in Budapest and senior researcher at the Institute for Psychology of the Hungarian Academy of Sciences. She also lectures in the Theoretical Psychoanalysis PhD Programme of the University of Pécs, Hungary. Her main research areas are the social representations of the body and health, and the relationship of psychoanalysis, psycho-somatics and self concepts [csabaim@mtapi.hu].

Heiko Feldner, senior lecturer in German History, is Co-Director of the Centre for Ideology Critique and Žižek Studies at Cardiff University, School of European Studies and general editor of Hadders's Writing History series on historiography and historical theory. His research links European intellectual history, political theory and theoretical psycho-analysis. Among his publications: *Das Erfahrnis der Ordnung* (Frankfurt on Main: Haag + Herchen, 1999); *Writing History: Theory and Practice* (London and New York: Hadder Arnold, 2003); *Žižek Beyond Foucault,* with Fabio Vighi (Basingstoke: Palgrave Macmillan, 2007); *Did somebody say Ideology? On Slavoj Žižek and Consequence,* edited with Fabio Vighi (Newcastle: Cambridge Scholars Publishing, 2007); *The Last Decade: The 1950s in European History, Society, Economy and Culture,* edited with Claire Gorrara and Kevin Passmore (Newcastle, Cambridge Scholar Publishing, forthcoming in December 2009); "Ideology Critique or Discourse Analysis? Žižek against Foucault", in *European Journal of Political Theory,* 6, 2007, no. 2, pp. 158-176 (with Fabio Vighi). "Pathological Attachments: Slavoj Žižek on anti-Capitalism and Liberal Democracy", with Fabio Vighi, in *Rethinking Marxism,* vol. 21 (2009), no. 2, pp. 290-297; "From Subject to Politics: the Žižekian Field Today", in *Subjectivity,* vol. 26 (2009), no. 3 forthcoming (with Fabio Vighi) [FeldnerHM@cardiff.ac.uk].

Bruce Fink is a practicing Lacanian psychoanalyst, analytic supervisor, and Professor of Psychology at Duquesne University in Pittsburgh, Pennsylvania. He trained as a psychoanalyst in France for seven years and is now a member of the psychoanalytic institute Lacan created shortly before his death, the *Ecole de la Cause Freudienne* in Paris. He is also an affiliated member of the Pittsburgh Psychoanalytic Society and Institute. He also trained at the University of Paris VIII (Saint-Denis). He is the author of four books on Lacan: *The Lacanian Subject: Between Language and Jouissance* (Princeton: Princeton University Press, 1995); *A Clinical Introduction to Lacanian Psychoanalysis: Theory and Technique* (Cambridge: Harvard University Press, 1997); *Lacan to the Letter: Reading* Ecrits *Closely* (Minneapolis: University of Minnesota Press, 2004); *Fundamentals of Psychoanalytic Technique: A Lacanian Approach for Practitioners* (New York: W.W. Norton & Co., 2007). He has co-edited three collections of papers on Lacan's work with SUNY press. His books have been translated into German, Spanish, Japanese, Korean, Portuguese, Polish and Greek. He is also a translator of Lacan's works into English. His translation of *Seminar XX, Encore: On Feminine Sexuality,* was published in 1998, and his translation of Lacan's magnus opus *Ecrits: The first Complete Edition in English* came out in 2006, both by W.W. Norton; the latter was awarded the 2007 nonfiction translation prize by the French-American Foundation and the Florence Gould Foundation [fink@duq.edu].

Luigi Gaffuri teaches Geography of Power, Human Geography and Geography of Africa at the Department of Arts, University of L'Aquila and University of Ferrara, Italy. He has been editor and author of the chronicle *Terra d'Africa* and has also been a member of its scientific board. His university research interests involved field studies in Tropical Africa (Niger, Ivory Coast, Senegal, Ethiopia, Eritrea, Cameroon, Gabon, South Africa, Mozambique, Guinea, Sudan, Kenya, Chad and Democratic Republic of Congo). He is part of the Science Committee for the release of a "Report on the Level of Territorial Assimilation of Immigrants in Italy" supported by the National Council for Economy and Labour. He is a member of the editorial board of the "Statistical Report on Immigration", published by Caritas and Migrantes (Rome, IDOS) and is part of the editorial staff of *Tutto da capo*, a periodical dedicated to culture, art, politics and technology [luisgaffuri@iol.it].

Gianpaolo Lai is a psychoanalyst and Full Member of the Swiss Psychoanalytical Society (IPA). He worked at the Psychiatric Clinic of the University of Lausanne, where he received a classical Freudian training. In his psychoanalytic research he has inserted the philosophy of language into the theory and practice of psychoanalysis (see *Le parole del primo colloquio*, 1976; *Un sogno di Freud*, 1977; *Due errori di Freud*, 1978, all published by Boringhieri, Turin). He has privileged the ethical over the cognitive aspect, substituting the search for happiness for the research of truth (see *La conversazione felice*, Milan: Il Saggiatore, 1985). He has studied the loss of identity and the dissolution of the psychological Ego (cf. *Disidentità*, Milan: Feltrinelli, 1988). He has elaborated a conceptual and practical design, "Conversationalism", which revolves around three key words: material conversation, immaterial conversation, adventures of the grammatical subject (see *Conversazionalismo*, 1993; *La conversazione immateriale*, 1995; both published by Bollati Boringhieri, Turin). He is a Professor in the School for Specialization in Psychotherapy at the State University of Milan, President of the research group "Accademia delle tecniche conversazionali", and editor of the journal *Tecniche conversazionali* [Via Camperio 9 - 20123 Milan, Italy; giampaolo.lai@fastwebnet.it].

Pierrette Lavanchy, M.D., was born in Aigle (Switzerland) and graduated in Medicine at the University of Lausanne. She is a Full Member of the Swiss Psychoanalytical Society and of the International Psychoanalytical Association (IPA). Her papers on methodology (*La Pietà fiorentina di Michelangelo tra iconografia e psicoanalisi* and *La confessione della strega*), presented at the "Colloqui sulla Interpretazione" organized by the University of Macerata, Italy, were published in the Proceedings respectively of the VIIth and XIIth Colloquio (Turin 1986 and Genoa 1988: Marietti). Her book *Il corpo in fame* (Milan: Rizzoli, 1994) dealt with anorexia and bulimia. She is Editor of the online Journal *Tecniche conversazionali*, www.tecnicheconversazionali.it [via Camperio, 9 – 20123 Milan, Italy; pierrette.lavanchy@fastwebnet.it].

Antonio Maiolino was born in Naples, where he works as a psychoanalyst. He is a member of the School of Psychoanalysis' Forum of the Lacanian Field and of the Institute for Advanced Studies in Psychoanalysis (ISAP). He worked in a therapeutic community for drug addicts at the "Frullone" Mental Hospital in Naples, and in 2000 he became a psychotherapeutic counselor at a Therapeutic Rehabilitation Community for psychotics in Formia, Italy. He has participated as a speaker in various psychoanalitic symposiums and taught as a professor in Dynamic Psychology at the Universiy of Cassino, Italy, in Child Psychoanalisis at the ICLeS (an institute for the formation of psychotherapists), and on relational approach via the CLAAIform (Institution of formation, promotion, study and research). Presently he is the head psychotherapist at a Medical-Social-Psycho-Pedagogic Rehabilitation Center in the county of Naples; and is a psychology professor on contract at the Faculty of Medicine and Surgery at the University of Naples [antonio_maiolino@fastwebnet.it].

René Major, M.D., President of the Institute for Advanced Psycho-analytic Studies, psychiatrist and psychoanalyst who has been a programme director at the International College of Philosophy, is the author of many books, among which: *Lacan avec Derrida* (Paris: Aubier, 1991; Paris: Champs Flammarion 2001); *Au commencement, la vie la mort* (Paris: Galilée, 1999); *La Démocratie en Cruauté* (Paris: Galilée, 2003); with Chantal Talagrand, *Freud* (Paris: Gallimard, 2006), *L'homme sans particularités* (Paris: Circé, 2008) [major.rene@wanadoo.fr].

Jean-Luc Nancy teaches Philosophy at the University of Strasburg and previously taught at the University of California San Diego. Among his works: with Philippe Lacoue-Labarthe, *Le titre de la lettre. Une lecture de Lacan* (Paris: Galilée, 1972) and *L'Absolu littéraire* (Paris: Le Seuil, 1978); *La communauté désoeuvrée* (Paris: 1986, 2001); *L'expérience de la liberté* (Paris: Galilée, 1988); *Etre singulier pluriel* (Paris: 1996); *Hegel, L'inquiétude du négatif* (Paris: 1997); *Le regard du portrait* (Paris: Galilée, 2000); *L'"il y a" du rapport sexuel* (Paris: Galilée, 2001) [Jean-Luc.Nancy@wanadoo.fr].

Matteo Vegetti (born in 1971) teaches Aesthetics at the Politecnico of Milan, and at the Academy of Architecture of Mendrisio (Switzerland). He is the author of several books such as *La fine della storia* (Milan: Jaca Book, 1999), *Hegel e i confini dell'Occidente* (Naples: Bibliopolis, 2005), ed., *Filosofie della metropoli* (Rome: Carocci, 2009) [matteovegetti@hotmail.it].

Fabio Vighi is Senior Lecturer at Cardiff University. His research areas include film, psychoanalytic theory, critical and political theory. He received his BA in Modern Languages and Literature in 1984 from the Università degli Studi di Bologna, Italy, and his Ph.D. in 1999 ("Pier Paolo Pasolini's Intellectual Formation") from Reading University, UK. Among his publications: *Sexual Difference in European Cinema: the Curse of Enjoyment* (Basingstoke: Palgrave-Macmillan, 2009); with Heiko Feldner *Žižek: Beyond Foucault* (Basingstoke: Palgrave-Macmillan, 2007); co-edited with Heiko Feldner, *Did Somebody Say Ideology? On Slavoj Žižek and Consequences* (Newcastle: Cambridge Scholar Publishing, 2007); *Traumatic Encounters in Italian Film: Locating and Cinematic Unconscious* (Bristol: Intellect, 2006); *Le ragioni dell'altro. La formazione intellettuale di Pasolini tra saggistica, letteratura e cinema* (Ravenna: Longo, 2001); "Il dolore della liberazione: il masochismo in Pasolini", in Emanuela Patti, ed., *L'eredità intelletuale di Pier Paolo Pasolini* (Novi Ligure: Joker, 2009); "Fractious companions: psychoanalysis, Italian cinema, and sexual difference" in *Thinking Italian Cinema* (Special issue of *Italian Studies, 2008)*, pp. 235-254; "Sexual difference in and out of European Cinema: Žižek as a reader of Truffaut" in Vighi F. and Feldner H., eds, *Did somebody say Ideology? On Slavoj Žižek and Consequences* (Newcastle: Cambridge Scholar Publishing, 2007), pp. 250-276; with Heiko Feldner, "Discourse Analysis and Ideology Critique: Exploring Žižek through Foucault", in *European Journal of Political Theory,* 6(2), 2007, pp. 141-159. [vighif@cardiff.ac.uk]

Slavoj Žižek, Marxist philosopher, is co-Director of the International Center for Humanities, Birkbeck College, University of London. Among his latest publications are *The Parallax View* (Cambridge, MA.: MIT Press, 2006) and *How to Read Lacan (How to Read)* (New York: W.W. Norton, 2007).

Information for Contributors

The *European Journal of Psychoanalysis* will consider unsolicited manuscripts. These papers will be received and blindly peer-reviewed with the understanding that they are being contributed solely to this journal; those accepted for publication may not be published elsewhere without written permission.

Authors are responsible for all statements in their manuscripts. Published articles do not necessarily reflect official views of the Editorial Board of the *European Journal of Psychoanalysis*. Each manuscript should include a brief summary of the essential contributions of the paper, five Keywords summarizing the content of the same paper, and the author's complete e-mail address and telephone number. All papers will be copyedited.

Manuscript Form

Only electronic submissions of manuscripts will be accepted. Manuscripts should be submitted to Cristiana Cimino (cristianacimino.jep@gmail.com). All the information concerning the manuscript form can be found on IPOC's website www.ipocpress.com

JEP European Journal of Psychoanalysis Editors

JEP European Journal of Psychoanalysis Editorial Board

ISAP Members

Eric Anders (eric@anders.net), Sergio Benvenuto (president), Antonietta Censi (antonietta.censi@uniroma1.it), Cristiana Cimino, Sergio Contardi (brennfr@tin.it), Antonello Correale, Giusy Cuomo (giusy.cuomo@tin.it), Marino de Crescente (marinodecrescente@fastwebnet.it), Marco Focchi (focchi@fastwebnet.it), Adalinda Gasparini, Edy Gatti Pertegato (egape@tiscalinet.it), Luca Iacovino, Valeria La Via (la.via@tin.it), Antonio Maiolino (antonio_maiolino@fastwebnet.it), René Major (major.rene@wanadoo.fr), Valeria Medda (vmedda@fastwebnet.it), Bruno Moroncini (bmoroncini@unisa.it), Diego Napolitani (dinapol@libero.it), Letizia Proietti (letiziap@infinito.it), Pierfrancesco Sammartino (p.sammartino@tiscalinet.it), Antonello Sciacchitano, Anna Shane (ashane@jps.net), SGAI Società Gruppo-Analitica Italiana (franca.beatrice@fastwebnet.it), Janet Thormann, Giuseppina Valenti (valpina@tiscalinet.it), Adriano Verdecchia (adriano.verdecchia@fastwebnet.it)

Translators and Copy Editors

Guillaume Collett (gcollett84@hotmail.com), Agnès Jacob (agnasj_trad@hotmail.com), Gianmaria Senia (JEP@fastwebnet.it), Alvise Sforza-Tarabochia (A.Sforza-Tarabochia@kent.ac.uk), Claudia Vaughn (pugwash@iol.it)

Lightning Source UK Ltd.
Milton Keynes UK
09 March 2010

151152UK00001B/21/P

9 788896 732014